The Asbury Theological Seminary Series in World Christian Revitalization Movements

This volume is published in collaboration with the Center for the Study of World Christian Revitalization Movements at Asbury Seminary. Building on the work of the previous Wesleyan/Holiness Studies Center at the Seminary, the Center provides a focus for research in the Wesleyan Holiness and other related Christian renewal movements, including Pietism and Pentecostal movements, which have had a world impact. The research seeks to develop analytical models of these movements, including their biblical and theological assessment. Using an interdisciplinary approach, the Center bridges relevant discourses in several areas in order to gain insights for effective Christian mission globally. It recognizes the need for conducting research that combines insights from the history of evangelical renewal and revival movements with anthropological and religious studies literature on revitalization movements. It also networks with similar or related research and study centers around the world, in addition to sponsoring a three-year research project (through 2011) under the funding of the Henry Luce Foundation.

This study by Ricardo Gomez examines mission practices, both Protestant and Catholic, in four selected Latin American nations in light of a Lukan model for integral mission By interfacing contextual field research with biblical/theological analysis, important insights are discerned for bringing into interaction spiritual and social justice missional components in Latin American culture, which have heretofore been only minimally joined. For this reason, Gomez' study demonstrates congruence with the mission of the Center and serves to advance its research objectives.

J. Steven O'Malley, Director
Center for the Study of World Christian Revitalization Movements
Asbury Theological Seminary

Sub-Series Foreword

Intercultural Studies

The behavioral science approach to the study of revitalization movements has a long history that has developed several models. Anthropologists, among others, observed that people responded to colonialism and the expansion of the West in various ways including armed resistance, selective acceptance, and passive resistance. The problems of the colonial frontier led to a memorandum on acculturation written by Robert Redfield, Ralph Linton and Melville Herskovits in 1936. Elsewhere in the world, anthropologists observed "nativistic" or "cultural renewal" movements as well: cargo cults in Melanesia, messianic movements in South Africa, and political revolutions in Latin America. Anthony F. C. Wallace brought some order to this area of study with his 1956 article where he named the stages and subsumed the movements under the name of "revitalization movements." Harold Turner contributed the notion of New Religious Movements to focus on the indigenous responses to mission work seen on every continent. This can be seen as part of a larger development, from the 1960s on, to develop Social Movement Theory where people are seen as agents intentionally acting to renew and reform society by organizing others to resist or dethrone the powers that be. Such movements develop a culture and social organization that give meaning and impetus to action on behalf of the movement's aims.

In this book, searches for the seeds of revival in the Catholic, Mainline Protestant and Pentecostal churches of Latin America. Historically, the church has been entangled with colonialism, and the people still suffer from neo-colonial and globalization woes. Gómez reviews the development of the churches, and asks about their theology and participation in society. Through the lens of Luke-Acts, Gómez asks how Scripture is accessed and deployed, conducting interviews with 4 priests or pastors from each tradition in 4 different countries. While he finds that the people still struggle with poverty, and the churches still struggle with a creation theology even in cities facing environmental problems, yet there are signs of renewal in all the churches, and particularly in the Catholic Church.

Michael A. Rynkiewich
Editor for the sub-series on Intercultural Studies

The Mission of God
In Latin America

Ricardo Gómez

Asbury Theological Seminary Series in
World Christian Revitalization Movements in Intercultural Studies, No. 4

EMETH PRESS
www.emethpress.com

The Mission of God in Latin America

Copyright © 2010 Ricardo Gómez
Printed in the United States of America on acid-free paper

All rights reserved. No part of this book may be reproduced, or stored in a retrieval system or transmitted in any form or by any means, electronic, mechanical, photocopying, recording, scanning or otherwise, except as permitted by the 1976 United States Copyright Act, or with the prior written permission of Emeth Press. Requests for permission should be addressed to: Emeth Press, P. O. Box 23961, Lexington, KY 40523-3961. http://www.emethpress.com.

Library of Congress Cataloging-in-Publication Data

Gómez, Ricardo, 1972-
 The mission of God in Latin America / by Ricardo Gomez.
    p. cm. -- (Asbury Theological Seminary series in world Christian revitalization movements in intercultural studies)
 Includes bibliographical references.
 ISBN 978-1-60947-003-6 (alk. paper)
 1. Mission of the church--Latin America. 2. Christian sociology--Latin America. 3. Latin America--Church history. I. Title.
 BR600.G65 2010
 262'.7098--dc22   2010017725

(Photograph of Latin America on front cover is public domain.
https://www.cia.gov/about-cia/site-policies/index.html#copy)

Contents

Figures..vii

Tables..ix

Foreword...xi

Acknowledgements..xiii

1. Has the Church Become the Problem Rather than the Solution?...................... 1

2. Historical Overview of Colonization and The Influence of the
   Church in Latin America...15

3. The Theology of Luke-Acts and Mission in the Latin
   American Context..47

4. Theology and Praxis of Mission Among Selected
   Roman Catholic Churches.. 79

5. Theology and Praxis of Mission Among Selected Mainline
   Protestant Churches... 107

6. Theology and Praxis of Mission Among Selected Pentecostal Protestant
   Churches..137

7. Redefining the Theology and Practice of the Church in Latin America..... 167

Appendices:

    Appendix A: Interview Schedule.. 195
    Appendix B: Theology and Praxis of Mission in Mexico..................... 197
    Appendix C: Theology and Praxis of Mission in Colombia................. 201
    Appendix D: Theology and Praxis of Mission in Peru 205
    Appendix E: Theology and Praxis of Mission in Argentina 209

Persons Interviewed.. 213

References Cited.. 217

Person Index... 227

Scripture Index 231

Subject Index 235

Figures

Figure 1. Demonstrates the Interrelatedness of the Topics being Studied.. 5
Figure 2. Cities Visited in Latin America.. 8
Figure 3. Showing the Synergy Between the Reading of Luke-Acts and the Analyses of the Latin American Church........................ 12
Figure 4. The Synergy between the Reading of Luke-Acts and the Analyses of the Latin American Church.............................. 77
Figure 5. The Synergy between the Reading of Luke-Acts and the Analyses of the Latin American Church.............................. 168
Figure 6. Roman Catholic Church in Latin America......................... 175
Figure 7. Model for Integral Mission.. 185
Figure 8. Demonstrates the interrelatedness of the Topics being Studied.. 188

Tables

Table 1. Population Distribution by Region, 2000, 2015, and 2030......	21
Table 2. Percentage of Latin American Population Living Below the National Poverty Lines in Urban and Rural Areas.............	23
Table 3. Unity and Relationship of Luke and Acts...........................	51
Table 4. Roman Catholic Priests/Parishes Interviewed in Mexico........	80
Table 5. Roman Catholic Priests/Parishes Interviewed in Colombia.....	86
Table 6. Roman Catholic Priests/Parishes Interviewed in Peru...........	94
Table 7. Roman Catholic Priests/Parishes Interviewed in Argentina....	98
Table 8. Mainline Protestant Pastors/Churches Interviewed in Mexico.	108
Table 9. Mainline Protestant Pastors/Churches Interviewed in Colombia...	114
Table 10. Mainline Protestant Pastors/Churches Interviewed in Peru...	121
Table 11. Mainline Protestant Pastors/Churches Interviewed in Argentina..	126
Table 12. Pentecostal Protestant Pastors/Churches Interviewed in Mexico..	138
Table 13. Pentecostal Protestant Pastors/Churches Interviewed in Colombia...	144
Table 14. Pentecostal Protestant Pastors/Churches Interviewed in Peru...	151
Table 15. Pentecostal Protestant Pastors/Churches Interviewed in Argentina..	158
Table 16. Theology and Praxis of Mission in Mexico.....................	197
Table 17. Theology and Praxis of Mission in Colombia...................	201
Table 18. Theology and Praxis of Mission in Peru.........................	205
Table 19. Theology and Praxis of Mission in Argentina...................	209

Foreword

Doctrine and life. Worship and mission. Education and evangelism. Forgiveness of sins and feeding the poor. What is the status of these paired words? For many Christians in the modern era, the one is unrelated to the other.

Unfortunately, these dualisms have masked the integral nature of the good news and have handicapped the church's understanding and practices of mission. This has been true of the church on both sides of the Atlantic in the northern hemisphere. Regrettably, these dualisms have taken root as well in Christian movements in the southern hemisphere, often as a result of western influence.

The good news is that we have the necessary resources for countering these dualisms — both to eradicate past and present intrusions of dualistic thinking and to vaccinate against their introduction in the future. As Ricardo Gómez recognizes and aptly illustrates, the good news itself, as this is articulated in the Gospel of Luke and the Acts of the Apostles, is astonishingly holistic in its understanding both of human need and of gospel response. Religion and economics, politics and spirituality, social status and geographical location — these are integral to one another. They cannot be segregated from one another as we attempt to diagnose the human situation or to grapple with the nature of God's good news. Those who are rich or poor, up or down, inside or outside — they are all challenged by the Spirit-empowered message of Jesus and his witnesses.

Churches in Latin America are resources too. On the one hand, they provide a fertile context within which to hear the announcement of the good news. We can hear the message of Luke's Gospel and Acts, Luke-Acts, differently, because we read them on Latin American soil. On the other hand, an analysis of the theology and missional practices of these churches puts on display the degree to which they have come to embody an integral gospel. As we might expect, Ricardo Gómez demonstrates that churches are capable of embodying the good news even when they did not set out to do so intentionally. Sometimes their practices are better than their theologies. This is simply the nature of the good news, which takes root and grows irrespective of our plans. Gómez also demonstrates that some churches exhibit the integral character of the gospel in Luke-Acts better than others. He shows that some churches need to be challenged to hear again and to put into practice Jesus' "good news to the poor." Accordingly, churches can learn not only from Luke-Acts but also from each other how best to engage in a mission that takes seriously Luke's missional gospel.

Ricardo Gómez' analysis centers on selected churches in Latin America. However, we would be mistaken if we were to imagine that his study is important only for what it tells us about the state of things in Mexico or Colombia, Peru or Argentina. Instead, he demonstrates the sort of hard-nosed investigation that we need in other contexts, too, if we are to understand how the challenge of the gospel has been domesticated by cultural forces intent on dulling its sharp edges. He demonstrates the hard-nosed investigation that we need if we are to develop sensibilities for how the gospel might take root and grow in other places in ways that are still good news. In this way, he demonstrates how we might engage in critical reflection on our church's theology and mission practices wherever we are. And he demonstrates how we might be challenged both by the Lukan message of good news to the poor and by exemplars of churches in other places that put that good news into practice.

Here, then, is a case study in integral theology. Those with ears to hear should pay attention!

Joel B. Green
Center for Advanced Theological Studies
Fuller Theological Seminary

Acknowledgements

I want to express my profound gratitude to many people who have contributed to make this project possible. First at all, I want to thank our Triune God who has inspired, empowered and provided the means necessary to bring me to this point.

I owe a debt of gratitude to several colleagues for their time, advice and encouragement on this project. Dr. Michael A. Rynkiewich has been a good friend and mentor, offering his wise direction and encouragement before and during the process of writing this investigation. Dr. Joel B. Green's scholarship and advice have truly enriched the outcome of this study. I am thankful for Dr. Hugo Magallanes' suggestions whose Latin American background and scholarship helped provide a contextual foundation for my investigation. I appreciate the assistance of Dr. Howard A. Snyder who helped get me started on the right track. I am also indebted to the E. Stanley Jones School of Mission and Evangelism, its faculty and staff for providing a solid community and the means necessary to accomplish my doctoral studies.

I thank my contacts in each country who facilitated the means for my field research, making this investigation possible: I thank Rev. Jorge Guarillo in Mexico City, Mexico; Rev. Cesar A. Garcia in Bogotá and Luis Alberto Vera in Bucaramanga, Colombia; Rev. José Luis López and Bertha Fiorella in Lima, Peru; Dr. C. René and Kathy Padilla in Buenos Aires, Argentina.

My beautiful, loving and virtuous wife, Beth, has been an inspiration, support and help for the last eight years. Thank you, for the hours of work, advice, patience, and wisdom that have given me with regard to this book. I thank God for our children, Juliana and Jonathan, who make our lives better and happier. I am grateful that you all slow me down and show me the priorities of life. You all are my inspiration that encourages me to persevere in achieving my life goals. Thanks.

I am also thankful to my extended family. I thank my parents, Alirio and Lilia Gómez, for their motivation and inspiration throughout my life.

Chapter 1

Has the Church Become the Problem Rather than the Solution?

Luis Alberto Vera Gómez calmly approached the police checkpoint on November 26, 2004. He was purchasing bus tickets for a holiday visit to his hometown of Bucaramanga, Colombia. Luis Alberto, age 24, had just completed his first year of study at the Biblical Seminary of Colombia in Medellín, where he had been elected class president and had been involved with the campus choral team. He and his wife Daisy decided to return with their 16-month-old son to Bucaramanga for a couple of weeks before going to the city of Saravena to complete an internship during the two-month semester break. Despite safety concerns in Saravena due to dangerous guerilla group activity, Luis Alberto and Daisy both believed that this was a good ministry opportunity for them. Luis Alberto's internship would involve assisting with the musical group at an 800-member Foursquare Church, the denomination in which he was an active member and a developing leader. As he retrieved his National ID card to show to the police, he noticed that the only other things in his bag were his Bible and notes from one of the classes he had just completed. He stood in line and mentally ticked off the things that still needed to be completed prior to their trip.

On the same day, November 26, 2004, my family and I were enjoying a nice Thanksgiving visit with my wife's sister and her family in Missouri. When the phone rang, it was for me; my family was calling from Colombia. Reading the concern on my face as I listened, my wife rushed to my side. Together we learned that my nephew, Luis Alberto Vera Gómez, had been arrested in Medellín. As the police checked the number on his national ID card they found an outstanding warrant for his arrest. Despite the fact that Luis Alberto showed them his Seminary ID and his Colombian Military Card, proving that he had been discharged in good standing after serving the mandatory term of service, his hands were cuffed behind his back and he was immediately taken to a criminal-processing center where he was allowed one phone call.

Daisy received his call and then jumped into action. Obviously their holiday plans had just changed. She contacted the family, and began looking for ways to secure an attorney. The criminal processing center did not provide beds or meals and so Daisy took a sleeping mat to her husband and began the arduous task of delivering three meals a day to the center. To add insult to injury, she was not allowed to see Luis Alberto and could only communicate with him through written messages.

It was almost one week after his arrest that Luis Alberto finally learned the charges against him: firearms trafficking and manufacture, and aggravated theft. According to the police, he allegedly was one of four men who participated in a 2002 mugging in Bucaramanga. As the lawyer looked further into the case, we learned that the victim had identified the gun-wielding thief in May 2004 to be between 25 and 30 years old with dark skin and dark eyes. He pointed to a photo of a man whom police identified as Luis Alberto Vera Gómez, but my nephew has honey-colored eyes and a light complexion. In addition, at the time that the crime took place he was only 22 years of age and was the music minister at one of the Foursquare churches in Bucaramanga.

Luis Alberto spent two weeks in the Medellín police-processing center before being transferred to the infamous Bellavista Prison, which was at one-time the deadliest prison in Colombia. Justice officials approved his release from the overcrowded prison in late December but placed him under house arrest on the seminary campus. Eventually, he was transferred to Bucaramanga and placed under house arrest at his mother's home until he was able to stand trial.

Through telephone conversations, Luis Alberto told me about how many times the Colombian justice system made mistakes. He said that upon his arrival at Bellavista on December 9, he was sent to a room where the prison director, the prison psychologist and other prison staff were waiting for him. Once there, he learned he had been sent to Bellavista to serve six years for rebellion. "They said I was a guerrilla," Luis Alberto told me. "The previous week they were accusing me of armed robbery, something I hadn't done, but then they weren't accusing me of being a guerrilla." Luis demanded that the information be corrected and discovered that the secretary had incorrectly transcribed his identification number on the forms causing this mistake. This mistake was corrected much more quickly than the original one; the one that placed an innocent man in prison and that placed the burden on him to prove his own innocence.

Unfortunately, my nephew's case is far from isolated. Colombians will testify that the Colombian judicial system has evolved from one where people had to be proven guilty into what it is today. In Colombia today, it seems that everyone is assumed guilty until proven innocent. Anti-terrorism laws have played a key role in presuming the guilt of those accused of crimes. Due to international pressure to "clean up" the country, authorities sometimes rush to imprison innocent people who actually may have been victims of identity theft or mistaken identity, as in the case of Luis Alberto.

After ten months of entanglement in Colombia's complicated and often sloppy judicial system, Luis Alberto Vera Gomez was released from house arrest and acquitted of all charges. "Glory to God!" Luis Alberto said. "My joy is great to be able to prove my case before the justice system." Luis Alberto's freedom came on September 6, 2005, after the victim, Wilson Silva Becerro, and his wife, who witnessed the 2002 crime, told the court that my nephew was not the man who attacked him. The prosecutor in this case was so convinced of Luis Alberto's innocence that she acted as if she were his lawyer, rather than the prosecution. In fact, at his final hearing the prosecutor asked Judge Gladys Mora to acquit him of all charges.

Over the months, Luis Alberto's legal defense bills mounted well beyond his or his family's ability to pay yet the Lord provided for these needs as well as the family's daily needs. While in prison, Luis Alberto met several prisoners in Bellavista who had been incarcerated for more than three years without any trial. In two cases, these innocent men were poor and unable to pay for a lawyer and had no assistance from the outside; therefore they have been marginalized and forgotten.

Before Luis Alberto and his family could carry on with their lives, Luis Alberto had to visit the places where he was jailed since his arrest and demand that his photo be removed from every file and destroyed. "Because they have this photo of me, I'll have more problems," Luis Alberto said. "Otherwise, any day of my life they could blame me for something else."

One Interpretation of the Problem

The Foursquare Church that Luis Alberto served at the time of the crime and incarceration in Bucaramanga was completely uninvolved while Luis Alberto and his family dealt with the injustice. They spoke to the pastor of the church asking his for support and were told that the only thing they could do as a church was pray because, "If you are suffering then perhaps it is God's will." This narrow view of the Christian life and ministry is characteristic of the view of many of the pastors, leaders and Christian churches in Latin America. They believe that the church's main goal is to care for the people's spiritual needs, avoiding any form of social, political, economic or environmental involvement.

When I learned about the church's lack of support in my nephew's situation, I called a friend who was also the president of the Foursquare Mission in Colombia. I requested the church's support of Rev. Edy Ester de Incinales for Luis Alberto and his family. I explained that Luis Alberto was alone in a very unfair situation and, as both a member and a church leader; I thought he needed the support of his congregation and the denomination. She responded, "What can we do?" and I had to offer some suggestions such as writing letters to the judge about the injustice, asking his pastor to be tangibly involved in supporting Luis Alberto, and to simply become a voice for Luis Alberto and others in his situation. Most of these suggestions she acted upon, but her action clearly was not an automatic response to this type of situation.

In contrast, Luis Alberto himself engaged prison as a ministry opportunity. He had the joy of leading 17 other incarcerated men to Christ and sharing the gospel with them in the police-processing center. Later, inside Bellavista Prison, he connected with many of the new converts and helped them join the jail's renowned prison fellowship ministry. He now wears the wristwatch that a converted guerilla gave him in appreciation for Luis Alberto's ministry to him.

When Luis Alberto returned to Medellín to resume his seminary studies in February 2006, he returned every Monday to Bellavista in order to provide one-on-one Bible studies with the prisoners there. He also directed worship during their chapel services.

The church is called to be God's agent of transformation, justice, mercy and truth in this world. This is a role that begins in the local church, but when the church loses its vitality, effectiveness, and saltiness the church can become an agent of oppression and injustice instead. In order for the church to be revitalized again, it needs to go back to its foundation (the gospel itself) and understand the gospel within the context where God has placed it. Knowing the core of the gospel and knowing the context should provide the elements for an integral[1], incarnational, and effective way of doing *missio Dei*. By understanding this, the church should not have to ask what to do, as in the case of my nephew, but be readily available to respond to human needs in an integral way, as Jesus modeled for us in Luke 4:18-19.

Unfortunately Luis Alberto's case reflects several realities facing the Latin American continent. On the one hand, it illustrates the socially, politically, economically and religiously oppressive structures that reign in much of Latin America. On the other hand, it reflects the negligence and ineffective role of many of the Christian churches (Roman Catholic and Protestant alike) that do not know how to act as an agent of justice and reconciliation. Although perhaps many North Americans assume that most non-Evangelical[2] Latin American theology is liberation theology, which cares primarily for the social, political, and economics needs of the people, this case demonstrates the fallacy of that assumption. The fact is that there are several expressions of Liberation Theology present in Latin America, some are based on a Marxist analysis but others are based on a genuine evangelical perspective. In many circles the theology that is lived out is nothing other than popular religiosity. Luis Alberto's story is but one small example of issues that face and plague Latin America.

What is the Problem?

Perhaps rather than serving as an agent of God's solution for the problems of the Latin American continent, the church is part of the problem. My hypothesis is that in large measure the church in Latin America, whether Catholic or Protestant, tends to have a dualistic view of the world, of salvation, and of the church's own part in the mission of God in the world. If it does, what has been the effect on theology, ecclesiology, and ultimately, missiology (see Figure 1)?

In order to accurately evaluate the Latin American situation, I have divided this book into three basic areas of study. They include: (1) the historical development of Latin America, specifically surveying the social, political, economic, environmental and religious factors that have contributed in some way to what Latin America is today. This provides a context for understanding the churches to be studied. (2) A thorough evaluation of Luke 4:16-30; 5:27-32; 19:1-10; Acts 2:42-47; and 4:32-37, which could provide a paradigm for integral mission in Latin America. (3) An investigation of the current practice and theology of some of the Protestant and Roman Catholic churches in four Latin American countries in order to understand the current theological views of the churches and their involvement in mission.

Figure 1. Demonstrates the Interrelatedness of the Topics being Studied.

My intent is to provide the church, pastors, leaders, mission organizations and missionaries with an awareness and better understanding of how the Latin American church operates; hopefully offering a broader and more relevant scope of Latin America's past and present history, combined with biblical and missiological strategies to produce an integral approach to ministry for future generations. I hope to provide a paradigm of doing mission based on a biblical view that will expand the Christian witness in all social, political, economic, environmental, and spiritual dimensions. Perhaps some of these findings may have larger, broader implications and applications for the global church in addition to the Latin American churches.

Finding an Answer and Building Local Theologies

The research within this book is structured to lay the groundwork for a theological perspective that encourages the church to deal with the social, political, economic, environmental, and spiritual needs that are affecting Latin America. This response is based on biblical foundations like, for example, that which is pointed out in Romans 12:1-2. It is a necessity that is described by C. René Padilla in his book *Mission Between the Times* when he writes, "The church either adapts itself to the world and betrays the gospel, or responds to the gospel and enters in conflict with the world. Conflict is inevitable when the church takes the gospel seriously" (1985:145).

Through balanced research, which combines theological analysis, historical analysis, and contemporary field research, I seek to enhance both the theory and praxis of mission by, in some ways, attempting to build a local theology of mission for Latin America through a process that can perhaps then be modified for other specific locations.

To this end, my goal is to answer the following questions:

1. Based on the history of the Roman Catholic and Protestant churches in Latin America, how do their present understandings of mission, their present structures for ministry, and their current practices of mission work? To answer this question I conducted a historical analysis of the presence of Roman Catholicism and Protestantism in Latin America and reviewed sociological, anthropological, and economic perspectives in order to provide a comprehensive understanding of the history of the continent for the last 500 years and its social, political, economic, environmental, and religious situation. I also focused specifically on the histories of the countries where I did my field research, in order to understand their Christian and colonial history. Finally, I reviewed the forces of urbanization and globalization that have been shaping Latin American in the last decades with the goal of providing the church, as well as missionaries and leaders, with a clear and comprehensive view of the complex situation the continent is facing as well as a better idea of how to minister to its needs.

2. What significant missiological insights could the Luke-Acts story, particularly Luke 4:16-30; 5:27-32; 19:1-10; Acts 2:42-47; and 4:32-37[3] provide about the local church's part in God's salvific mission in Latin America? Because these Lukan passages are used in some way by many of the churches in Latin America[4], a careful study of these passages may reveal a different view of the gospel than the ones they have been following. I will use these texts to explore the person, life and work of Jesus and the church in an effort to determine how this may provide a paradigm for integral, incarnational, and contextual ministry in our Latin American situation. The under girding idea is to be faithful to the Scriptures in the Latin American context.

3. What are some of the current biblical bases and missiological practices of the Roman Catholic and Protestant churches in Latin America and, specifically, how does their biblical understanding position them with respect to their cultural, social, and political context? I chose to answer this question through a contemporary field study of the church's theology and praxis of mission in Latin America through personal interviews[5] with 48 pastors and priests in four different Latin American countries. I tried to gain some diversity yet retain comparability by: (1) choosing pastors ministering in different socioeconomic backgrounds; (2) choosing pastors with different doctrinal affiliations; and (3) where possible, choosing pastors who belong to the same denomination in each one of the countries visited. My goal was to achieve a better representation of the actual reality that describes each city and country visited. Based upon interpretative notes of those interviews[6], I was able to look for meaningful and relevant answers to describe the theology of mission and praxis of the Christian churches in these countries.

4. Based upon the historical overview, a Lukan understanding of God's mission, and the field research, what kind of initiative can be developed in the Latin American context that would help to develop Roman Catholic and Protestant theologies of mission that could result in a healthier ecclesiology and that would prepare and energize the church for its integral missiological task? This research is significant to understanding Latin America for those who plan to minister there as well as for my own ministerial interest. Therefore, this book attempts to provide an overview and analysis of the philosophies that have prevailed in the continent and how these have affected people's worldview and their way of doing mission.

Research Design

My research strategies for this project began with grounded theory, an approach in which I let my initial hunch guide me until new understandings emerged. As previously indicated, I initiated the research by exploring through historical analysis both colonialism, neo-colonialism, and the role of Christianity (Roman Catholicism and Protestantism) in Latin America. Second, I conducted an exegetical and theological study of some Lukan passages, exploring a possible paradigm for integral mission in Latin America. Third, I used one-on-one semi-structured interviews to understand the theology and praxis of the church in Latin America. Finally, based on the data collected and the research, I attempted to provide a paradigm for integral mission in the Latin American context.

The following sections outline the structure that I used in order to generate the answers to the above research questions. Each section provides steps toward the completion of the investigation.

Data Collection

I used two primary methods to collect data for this investigation.

Library Research

Here, I focused specifically on writings of key leaders, historians, anthropologists and theologians, such as Catalina Romero, Arlene Tickner, Marta Palma, James and Teresa Palmer, Hugo Magallanes, Howard A. Snyder, Michael Rynkiewich, Mary Douglas, Louis Dumont, G. E. Lenski, Orlando Costas, Oscar Romero, Justo Gonzalez, Leonardo Boff, Miguez Bonino, Gustavo Gutierrez, John Sobrino, German Arciniegas, Miguez Nuñez, William Taylor, John A. Mackay, Eduardo Galeano, C. Rene Padilla, and Noam Chomsky. My purpose was to learn their view of the historical, sociological and spiritual journey of the Latin American region. I attempted to ascertain their understanding of the related problems of the area and what they have contributed to alleviate them. This contributes to understanding the background for the investigation.

In order to assess Luke-Acts I relied on commentaries and books by Joel B. Green, Justo González, Leslie J. Hoppe, Ben Witherington, Luke Timothy Johnson, Robert W. Wall, François Bovon, Scott Spencer, Larrimore C. Crockett, Beverly Roberts Gaventa, Joseph A. Fitzmayer, Darrell Bock, John Nolland, Howard Eilberg-Schawartz, and I. Howard Marshall to help me better understand the texts being studied and the social reality of the world of Luke-Acts.

Observation and Interview

The research conducted in Latin America attempts to evaluate the situation from several angles including geographic, denominational and socioeconomic. To this end, the field study was conducted in five main cities in four Latin American countries (see Latin American map in Figure 2): Buenos Aires, Argentina, Lima, Perú, Bucaramanga, Colombia, Bogotá, Colombia, and Mexico City, Mexico.

Figure 2. Cities Visited in Latin America

I chose these cities and countries for; (1) Their geographic locations: this provides a sample from the North (Mexico), to the middle (Colombia and Peru), to the South (Argentina); (2) Cultural and social diversity: I am including groups with more European influence such as Argentina and Colombia and with more indigenous influence such as Peru and Mexico.

I spent 10 days in each country and used local contacts in each country to help secure the interview appointments. On some occasions I went from one church to another asking for an interview.

As previously mention, in each country I selected four Roman Catholic Priests, four mainline Protestant pastors, and four Pentecostal Protestant pastors to interview[7] utilizing the interview model included in Apendix A. In an effort to provide a more complete picture of the Latin American situation, my goal was to interview the following:

1. Four Roman Catholic priests, at least one each from three different neighborhoods: upper class, middle class, and lower class (slums) neighborhoods. I chose four Roman Catholic churches in each country because the Roman Catholic Church is the dominant Christian Church in Latin America.

2. Four mainline Protestant pastors, at least one each from three different neighborhoods: upper class, middle class, and lower class (slum) neighborhoods. I tried to interview pastors from the Presbyterian, Methodist, Baptist, and Mennonite traditions, but this was not always possible. I chose these denominations because they are the most common mainline denominations in Latin America.

3. Four Pentecostal Protestant pastors, at least one each from three different neighborhoods: upper class, middle class, and lower class (slum) neighborhoods.

Using a grounded theory methodology, I observed, interviewed and collected data regarding the participants' experiences in dealing with issues through programs inside of the church, outreach, and general participation in issues of the community in areas such as social justice, feeding the poor, development, and environmental involvement. Through specific questions (see Appendix A) I wanted to determine what kind of theology, if any, motivates or leads them to do these things.

I used the qualitative inductive approach[8] as my research methodology, which "begins with specific observation and moves toward the development of general patterns that emerge from the cases under study" (Newton and Rudestam 2001:37). I made general observations of their services or social programs and I used an interview schedule (see Appendix A) to probe for their worldview, values and, specifically, the theological justification for their ministry and mission. The questions I used began with a very broad view to allow them freedom in their answers; then I used their answers to craft follow-up questions that were more specific and that led to my investigation goal.

Data Analysis and Interpretation

According to Creswell, "the process of data analysis involves making sense out of the text and image data. It involves preparing that data for analysis, conducting different analyses, moving deeper and deeper into understanding the data, representing the data, and making an interpretation of the larger meaning of the data" (2003:190). This is an ongoing process that involves continual reflection about the data, asking analytic questions, and writing memos throughout the study.

Taking Creswell's comments into consideration I employed the following steps in data analyses:

I reviewed the data repeatedly, to have an overall sense of it and to better understand what I was looking for, what was missing, and what might be new. I employed a coding system that helped me organize the material. The codes were developed according to the themes that arose from the data. Categories/themes emerged as patterns began to develop. In some cases the data and my interview questions went together and developed into the following categories: (1) church's programs; (2) social involvement; (3) environmental involvement; (4) biblical bases for the church's work; (5) theological issues; and (6) general statements. These categories help me understand the theology and praxis of the Christian church in Latin America. The interpretation of the meaning of the themes was analyzed based on the research flow, my own experience and existing literature. I made a comparative chart for each country visited (see Appendices C, D, E, and F). Based upon the charts and the information collected throughout the study I made some final conclusions in an attempt to answer the driving questions of this investigation and provide some practical suggestions for ministering effectively in the region. I concluded this investigation by pointing out some areas for future study.

The final presentation of the data was accomplished through a descriptive approach. The interpretation includes a call for action based on theological and missiological implications taken from the study of Lukan literature and that can be relevant to the Latin American context but the overall strategy can be applicable to other contexts as well.

Theoretical Lenses

Following are the theoretical lenses I employed to critically study the historical, political, economic, environmental, and spiritual realities in Latin America as well as the Luke-Acts narrative.

Historical Analysis

History is: "the stories we tell about our prior selves or that others tell about us" (Howell and Prevenir 2001:1). All cultures tell stories about themselves, it is these stories that help provide the meaning that makes sense of their own beliefs and worldviews. In order to understand Latin American history I explored what my predecessors and contemporaries have written about it. However, I do understand that "historians do not discover a past as much as they create it, they choose the events and people that they think constitute the past, and they decide what about them is important to know" (Howell and Prevenir 2001:1).

Therefore, realizing that the history I read was a subjective understanding of the happenings based on the historian's point of view, I took into consideration the following observations or techniques to analyze my sources.

1. I paid careful attention to how sources are chosen and interpreted. This means that I checked for authenticity, representative ness, and relevance (Howell and Prevenir 2001:1).

2. I attempted to comprehend, at the most basic level, language, handwriting, and vocabulary (Howell and Prevenir 2001:43).

3. I was mindful that every source must be carefully located in place and time (Howell and Prevenir 2001:43).

4. I did not rely on just one source to study an event or historical process, but on many, and in order to gain the best interpretation I should compare sources (Howell and Prevenir 2001:69).

In sum, making use of the historical methods facilitated the process and outcome of my investigation.

Hermeneutics: Understanding Luke-Acts

In order to understand the Lukan literature I made use of hermeneutical and interpretative analyses. A modern reading of Luke-Acts begins with the addresser, the context (message, medium) and the addressee. However, Green's graphic describes this process and exposes its inadequacy (1995a: 2).

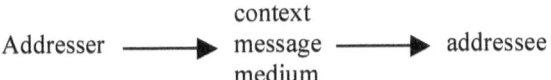

Because of my historical, social, cultural, and linguistic distance from the addresser, context, and addressee I followed some careful observations provided by Green in order to improve my reading of Luke-Acts. First, I learned that understanding is more than transferring information. The understanding received from reading the Lukan literature will make changes in the way one perceives, acts, and thinks and in some way it has practical and future behavioral implications.

> We may understand "hunger" differently, depending on whether we have actually experienced more than the odd missed meal. We may understand the causes or effects of world hunger along different lines or differ in our views of local responsibility for global affairs. Corresponding ambiguities reside in our attempts to "hear" the message of Paul as presented in 1 Corinthians. (Green 1995a: 2)

Second, we need to be aware of language problems: language is linear; language is selective; language is ambiguous; and language is culturally embedded (Green 1995a: 4-5).

Thus, making use of hermeneutical and interpretative techniques helped me do a more careful reading of Luke-Acts. The Lukan historiographical view enriches the outcome of this investigation. However, I focused on the final goal of exploring how the Lukan literature provides a paradigm for mission that can be applicable and relevant to the Latin American context and did not attempt to complete my job simply by understanding the Lukan literature.

The Lukan understanding supports my investigation in three ways: a). Luke-Acts provides an evaluation of the Latin American churches' theology of mission. b). Luke-Acts provides a model of mission for the Latin American churches. c). Luke-Acts questions and challenges the actual Latin American churches and the way they are doing mission.

A synergy developed between the reading of Luke-Acts and the analyses of the churches in Latin America. In one way, Luke-Acts evaluates how the church is doing mission and, in another way, the church in Latin America's method of doing mission provides a new lens through which to read Luke-Acts. The following graphic (Figure 3) illustrates this tension.

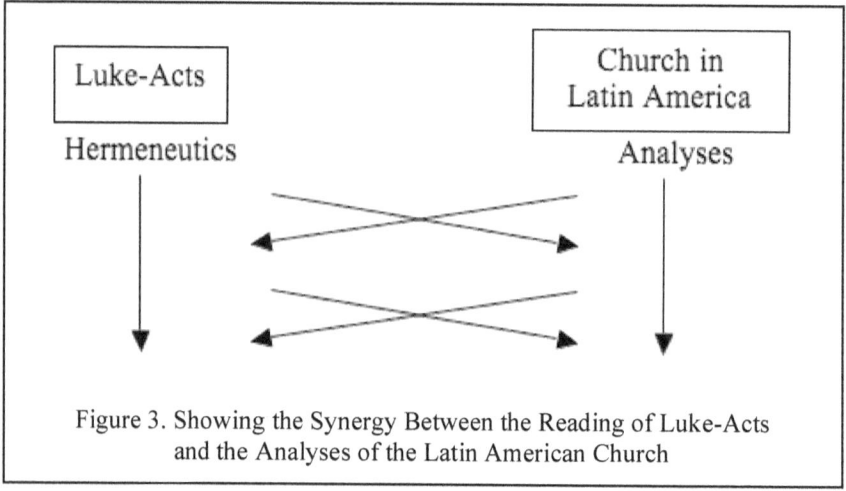

Figure 3. Showing the Synergy Between the Reading of Luke-Acts and the Analyses of the Latin American Church

Summary

This is a study of the socio-political, economic, environmental and spiritual reality of Latin America and the response of the Christian church. The call to the church comes from the heart of the gospel expressed in the fullness of God's revelation, the historical Jesus, who by the power of the Holy Spirit called and equipped the church to be agents of reconciliation, love, mercy and truth. The purpose of this investigation is to provide a paradigm for integral mission based on Luke-Acts that enables the Latin American church to embody the *missio Dei*.

In Chapter 2, I provide an overview of Latin America's history and, more specifically, I focus on the history of Mexico, Colombia, Peru, and Argentina. I highlight the role of the Christian church in these countries and also explore the impact that globalization and urbanization have had on this region of the world.

Notes

1. The terms Integral, Integral Ministry and Integral Mission are used throughout this book. "Integral mission" is a phrase that summarizes a distinctive way of perceiving the role of the church in the world as disciples of Christ. Integral mission stipulates the priesthood of all believers and emphasizes ministry to whole persons (emotional, intellectual, physical, and spiritual) and whole communities (social, political, economic, environmental, and spiritual). Thus, Integral mission reconciles orthodoxy and orthopraxy. The practice of integral mission assumes that the church and each of its members will give absolute priority to following Jesus in terms of missionary lifestyle.

2. In Latin America, the words "protestant" and "evangelical" (*evangelico*) are interchangeable. In this book I use Elizabeth Sendek's definition of evangelical. Evangelical is the segment of conservative Protestantism characterized by (1) strong adherence to the reliability and authority of the Bible, (2) the call to personal conversion, through faith in Jesus Christ, in order to attain salvation, (3) the urgent duty to proclaim this message to all creatures, and (4) the expectation of Christ's imminent return and the final judgment (1993:4).

3. In my study of Luke-Acts, I did not provide a word-by-word exegetical analysis or commentary but rather a theological investigation of the Lukan narrative, focusing instead upon the verses mentioned above.

4. I chose to study Luke 4:16-30 because this is one of the texts used by liberation theologians and is widely recognized as programmatic for Luke-Acts. I chose Luke 5:27-32 and 19:1-10 because they reflect explicitly on the character of Jesus' mission and because they deal with one of the main issues Latin America is facing, the problem of power, wealth and the segregation of the weak and poor. As Joel B. Green points out, "the rule of money, manifest in the drive for social praise and, so, in forms of life designed to keep those with power and privilege segregated from those of low status, the least, the lost, and the left-out" (1997:24). I chose Acts 2:42-47 because of its importance as a Lukan summary of the character of the church and because this is one of the texts widely use by the Pentecostal community in Latin America. I chose to study 4:32-37 in addition because it so closely parallels 2:24-47 and because this text provides a good example of the ecclesiological vitality of the church.

5. Due to a limitation of both time and financial resources, I did not study all of the countries in Latin America in my field research but focused only on five main cities located in four Latin American countries. Likewise, I did not interview all the Christian denominations present in the continent, focusing instead upon three main groups: Roman Catholic Churches, mainline Protestant churches, and Pentecostal Protestant churches. I interviewed four pastors and priests within each corresponding category in each country.

6. The initial interviews were audio- and hand- recorded in Spanish. However, rather than translating each interview word-for-word into English, I simply wrote interpretive notes in English.

7. The interviews with each priest or pastor were face-to-face and semi-structured. Their responses were recorded using a digital recorder, when possible, and notes were taken. The questions were open-ended and yet derived from the research questions. I

provided a safe environment where the participants felt free to share their experiences and insights. Because the interviews were conducted in Spanish, I wrote interpretive notes in English.

8. Some of the chief characteristics of the qualitative approach that I took into consideration when doing my research included the following (Creswell 2003:181-183):
- Qualitative research is intended to understand phenomena in their natural settings.
- Qualitative research seeks to present broad, panoramic views rather than microanalyses as it studies its subjects holistically. In other words, the holistic approach stresses that the whole is different from the sum of its parts.
- It involves in-depth methods that are interactive and social. It primarily uses observation, interviews, questionnaires, and document collection as chief instruments of data collection.
- It is emergent (meaning that it can change my view of the issue and the way I approach it) and hence the data collection and interpretation may continue to change as the researcher deeply explores the chosen area of study.
- The researcher's role is critical as this approach is fundamentally interpretive and the researcher interprets the data collected. Hence it is extremely important for the interpreter to be aware of his/her situated-ness and biases.
- The emergent data are generally descriptive, word pictures rather than numbers. High emphasis is placed on interpersonal dynamics and social construction of meaning.

Chapter 2

Historical Overview of Colonization and the Influence of the Church in Latin America

Latin America is widely considered to be a Christian region. According to the World Christian Database, Roman Catholicism is the predominant religion on the continent with approximately 483,032,645 Latin American Catholic adherents in 2005. This means that roughly 87 percent of the Latin American population professes to be Roman Catholic. A further 10 percent of the population professes to be Protestant (World Christian Database 2006).

From the religious standpoint, the Roman Catholic Church has dominated Latin America for more than five centuries. As Marta Palma states, "Between the Spanish conquest in the sixteenth century and the end of the nineteenth century, the Roman Catholic Church was predominant, and there was no counter-balance in the religious field in Latin America" (2004:223).

Although Protestantism has experienced considerable recent growth, some question whether this is necessarily good news for the sake of the gospel. Based upon his own experience of living thirty years in Latin America, William D. Taylor points out, "Many [Protestant] churches and denominations are large, but that does not necessarily mean they are healthy churches. Too many of them suffer from doctrinal deadness, insufficient biblical teaching, or from emotional overdoses" (Nuñez and Taylor 1989:132).

So, the spiritual health of Latin America is in question. Perhaps there are Christ-centered, apostolic and missional Catholic and Protestant churches, but many are not fulfilling the mandate of Christ and thus are not meeting the challenges of the times. How has the church come to this point and what challenges does the church face?

This chapter provides an overview of the history of Christianity in Latin America starting with colonization and ending with the present time. It focuses more specifically on the Christian history of four Latin American countries that are the primary context of this research: Mexico, Colombia, Peru and Argentina.

In addition, this chapter surveys the forces of urbanization and globalization in Latin America and outlines some of the challenges and opportunities that Latin America and Christianity in the region have faced in the past and continue to face today.

The History of Latin America: The Spanish and Portuguese Conquest

When the Spaniards and Portuguese colonized Latin America, they did not go there primarily looking for a new land in which they could live; they went there to extract its riches and return them to Spain or Portugal. Since the beginning of modern Latin American history there has been a big difference between the conquest and colonization of Latin America, on the one hand, and of Anglo-Saxon America, on the other hand. As John A. Crow points out,

> the Europeans mostly came to North America seeking religious and political liberty, and as settlers willing to till the soil. A desire for personal liberty, a willingness to endure hard labor, and the absence of gold or Indian slaves molded them quickly into an aggressive and forward-moving nation. From the very beginning they came with their wives and maintained the race. The Spaniards, and later the Portuguese, came to Latin America without women, in a crusade of conversion, and in search of gold and slaves. They found all that they were seeking and so for more than three centuries perpetuated and intensified the economy of exploitation, which is the economy of oppression, scarcity, poverty, and improvidence. (1992:224)

The conquerors came to Latin America holding in one hand the sword and, in the other, the image of the cross reflecting the civil power of Spain and Portugal and the religious power of the Roman Catholic Church, by which Spaniards and Portuguese came to rule. Both of these powers remain evident in the architecture of the main plazas even today. A cathedral and a government palace are the center of most Latin American towns and cities.

The conquistadores not only brought to Latin America their own culture and language but also their own viruses and bacteria. Jared Diamond points out that

> Diseases [were] transmitted to peoples lacking immunity by invading peoples with considerable immunity. Smallpox, measles, influenza, typhus, bubonic plague, and other infectious diseases endemic in Europe played a decisive role in European conquests, by decimating many people on other continents . . . Throughout the Americas, diseases introduced with Europeans spread from tribe to tribe far in advance of the Europeans themselves, killing an estimated 95 percent of the pre-Columbian Native American population. (1998:77-78)

During the first century of conquest the Indians died like flies; their organs had no defense against these new diseases (a point also made by Eduardo Galeano in *Open Veins of Latin America: Five Centuries of the Pillage of a*

Continent). The sword killed those who did not die from these new diseases. Thus, the sword, the cross, and the germ marched together in the conquest and plunder of Latin America (Galeano 1973:28).

John A. Mackay argued in his book *The Other Spanish Christ* that Spanish popular religion was and still is draped in a sense of tragedy and passion for immortality. "The sword and the cross formed an offensive alliance for the purpose of taking Christianity, or at least that which was considered to be such, to foreign lands" (Mackay 2001:27). Even though the Roman Catholics brought educational, economic and social development to Latin America, they also brought a deformed Christology based on Spanish tradition. This religion, often tyrannical and cruel in its expression, showed that its power was based more on the sword than on love.

Christology, of course, is never divorced from cultural context. Jose Miguez Bonino points out, "Each generation must come face to face with the mystery of Jesus, and in the attempt to define itself each generation will give him its new names of honor and glory and will thereby insert itself into the Christological process that began at the time of the apostles" (1984:13). During the time of colonization there was no opportunity for the indigenous people of Latin American to define the person and work of Christ in their own cultural understanding. Rather than enjoying such freedom of expression, the new converts were obliged to worship a distorted image of Christ; the Conquest Christ, as Mackay pointed out,

> However much overshadowed by His Mother, Christ too came to America. Journeying from Bethlehem and Calvary, He passed through Africa and Spain on His long westward journey to the pampas and cordilleras. And yet, was it really He who came, or another religious figure with His name and some of His works? Methinks the Christ, as He sojourned westward, went to prison in Spain, while another who took His name embarked with the Spanish crusaders for the New World, a Christ who was not born in Bethlehem but in North Africa. This Christ became naturalized in the Iberian colonies of Africa, while Mary's Son and Lord has been little else than a stranger and sojourner in these lands from Columbus's day to this. (2001:95)

A contemporary description of the Latin American situation made by Orlando E. Costas also affirms that in Latin America the Christ that has been propagated by the oppressive powers of this world is not the true Christ. Christ's image has been distorted beyond recognition. Referring to Latin America Costas points out,

> There are over one hundred and thirteen million people who live in a state of destitution. The majority of our nations are subjected to brutal military dictatorship and thousands upon thousands are suffering torture, imprisonments, harassment and exile. Latin Americans live in a perpetual state of terror, justified by a fanatic insistence that at stake is the defense of a so-called Christian civilization from godless forces that want to destroy it. So, in the name of Christ the dictators of Latin America have set out to oppress rather than liberate, to

murder rather than protect lives, to separate human beings from their loved ones rather than to reconcile them. (1979:28)

Rene C. Padilla also affirms that the gospel that is preached today in many countries of the world bears the marks of the nations that bring it. For instance, in today's case this is the "the American Way of Life."

> The Gospel thus becomes a type of merchandise the acquisition of which guarantees to the consumer the highest values—success in life and personal happiness now and forever. The act of "accepting Christ" is the means to reach the ideal of "good life" at no cost. The Cross has lost its offense, since it simply points to the sacrifice of Jesus Christ for us but does not present a call to discipleship. (Padilla 1985:16)

The Continuing Conquest: The Western Exploitation

During the last two centuries, Latin America has faced a new colonial power that has produced poverty and injustice in most of the Latin American countries. Part of the curse in Latin America is that its resources are often surrendered to imperialism due to the lack of natural resources of powerful nations. Latin America continues exporting its labor and property: the raw materials that the world market needs, and on whose sale the regional economy depends. Describing the economic situation most of Latin America is facing today, Padilla points out,

> A few years ago it was often said that, by selling their raw materials to the wealthy, the poor countries were mortgaging their future. Under the present capitalist global system their predicament has worsened to the point that there is no exaggeration in saying that no longer do the poor have a future to mortgage, for their future has been sold to the wealthy together with their present. (2004:60)

Today inequitable exchange functions as never before: poverty-level wages in Latin America help finance high salaries in the United States and Europe. This socio-economic reality in Latin America is not new. According to Eduardo Galeano, "Latin America is the region of open veins. Everything, from the discovery until our times, has always been transmuted into European—or later United States—capital, and as such has accumulated in distant centers of power" (1973:12).

For example, Brazil, despite its industrialization, continues to be substantially dependent on coffee and soybean exports, and Colombia on coffee. Bananas are primary exports from Central America and Argentina depends on the sale of meat. These crops do not satisfy the hunger of the natives and the wages earned are not sufficient, in many cases, for daily sustenance. Galeano points out, "underdevelopment in Latin America is a consequence of development elsewhere." He goes on to contend that because the Latin

American soil is rich, its inhabitants are poor. He says, "places privileged by nature have been cursed by history" (1973:289).

Galeano's point is supported by an economic historian Andre Gunder Frank in his article: *Sociology of Development and Underdevelopment of Sociology* when he writes, "development of the world capitalist metropolis in Europe and North America is hindered by the drag of its undeveloped hinterland in Asia, Africa, and Latin America. . . . Where [did] the capital for the development of the already developed countries [come] from? . . . it came from the consequently now underdeveloped countries" (1969:76-77).

Thus, in Latin America, the system produces much less than the necessary monetary demand and inflation results from this structural impotence. One needs only look at the effect of the North American Free Trade Agreement (NAFTA) on Mexico's economy to fully realize the harsh reality. According to the Mexican Chamber of Commerce, more than half of Mexican businesses have suffered since its passage (Chomsky 1999:98).

In March 2006 Latin American leaders were wrestling with the decision whether to sign the *Tratado de Libre Comercio* (TLC), a Free Trade Agreement with the United States; a treaty that Venezuela's President, Hugo Chavez, called an "imposition." Colombian President Alvaro Uribe supported the agreement and wanted an appointment to work as a moderator between the USA and other Latin American nations. If the agreement was ratified, the USA, which is the number one soybean producer in the world, would grant Colombia an annual coupon for 900,000 tons of soybeans in exchange for open access to Colombia's textile market. At the time, Colombia purchased 500,000 tons of soybeans at a cost of $165 million a year from Bolivia, so passage of the TLC would have directly or indirectly had an immediate, negative effect upon the 120,000 Bolivian businesses currently involved in the production of soybeans. This is but one example of how the TLC would likely continue the trends of exploitation and economic subjugation that have been seen throughout history. This is why Latin Americans, and more specifically Native Americans in some countries, were protesting and pressuring their leaders not to sign the agreement (*El Tiempo* 2006).

Free Trade Agreements are part of the neopluralistic democracy that is vigorously promoted in Latin American countries. The Global Report of Human Settlement produced by the United Nations points out that

> Neopluralism revolves around the belief that the best balance of interest and values within a given polity is produced by competition among individuals in the rational pursuit of their self-interest. Ultimate political authority is decided on through a free market of votes. But once elected, officials have few checks on their power and frequently bypass representative democratic institutions. (2001:65)

There are three aspects of Latin America's neoliberal democracy that highlight the nature of democratic challenge: (1) economic insecurity, (2) crime rates and the dominant responses to them, and (3) fragmentation of civil society (United Nations Center for Human Settlements 2001:65).

Latin America has been subordinated to the Western imperial powers and their violence ever since its colonization. The oppression continues in the foreign debt crisis, in the threats of inventions, in the highly distorted forms of development, and in the frequently extreme social backwardness of many areas that have great cultural wealth. According to the World Bank, Latin American debt by the 1970s was about $60 billion. By 1980 it had reached $200 billion, in 1990 the debt had increased to about $433 billion and by the year 2004 the debt was $1,545 billion (The World Bank 2006). "It's clear that the debt will never be paid. It's impossible to pay. It's getting bigger and bigger, it's more and more of a capital drain from the poor to the rich, and that will continue and escalate without any change" (Chomsky 2000:98).

Native Americans continue to be at the bottom of the racial prejudice scale and, in fact, they are considered virtually nonexistent. According to Noam Chomsky what happened 500 years ago is still happening today. The indigenous population was overwhelmingly eliminated and right now, "Latin America is being subjugated. The social and economic structural adjustment is only a modern phase of the massacre of indigenous people" (Chomsky 1999:16).

The On-going Conquest: The Forces of Urbanization and Globalization in Latin America

Like the rest of the world, Latin America is facing the consequences of the urbanization phenomena that has been taking place since the last century. Alan Gilbert and Josef Gugler contend that

> The twentieth century may come to be seen as the age of urbanization. Urban settlements were first established more than 500 years ago, but as recently as 1900 only one in eight people lived in urban areas. Before the end of this century half of the world's populations will be urbanites, and of these three billion people two-thirds will live in the Third World. (1992: V)

Data obtained from the United Nations argues that while Gilbert and Gugler's prediction of 50 percent world urbanization may not have been the reality in the year 2000, by 2010 the world had crossed that threshold. The following table (Table 1) illustrates the population distribution by region and how population growth is expected to take place in the coming years. As the world's urban population increases, it is following trends already established in Latin America. While, the World Urbanization Prospects of the United Nations predicted in 2007 that 51 percent of the world's population would be urbanized in 2010 Latin America crossed the 50 percent urbanization threshold in the 1960s and by 2010, the UN projected that 79 percent of the Latin American population would be already living in cities (United Nations 2008). This reality brings with it social, spiritual and structural opportunities as well as environmental, social, economic, and spiritual challenges.

Table 1. Population Distribution by Region, 2000, 2015, and 2030

Region	Population (in Millions)						% Urban		
	2000		2015		2030		2000	2015	2030
	Urban	Rural	Urban	Rural	Urban	Rural			
Africa	295	526	484	665	759	759	36	42	50
Asia	1373	2332	1987	2402	2669	2612	37	45	54
Europe	520	208	535	192	550	157	71	74	78
Latin America & Caribbean	394	128	508	120	603	109	75	81	85
North America	250	66	304	60	351	54	79	83	87
Oceania*	22	9	27	11	31	12	70	71	73
World	2854	3270	3845	3450	4965	3353	47	53	60

*Oceania includes Australia, New Zealand, Melanesia, Micronesia and Polynesia.

One consequence of increased urbanization is increased poverty. Bill Green contends that, "urban poverty in all the world shares the common problems of lack of adequate housing, access to health treatment, access to work, family breakdown and loss of traditional cultural or social identity. Another effect of urbanization that virtually no culture has resisted is individualism" (Green 2000). This has produced serious consequences in the moral values and structural formation of the society in urban Latin America; for example, the family has suffered in the city, and we see a marked increase in divorces, separations and a general lack of solidarity. Thus, many cultures that once had healthy, solid family structures, have succumbed to the devastating forces of the city.

In Latin America, the children of many very religious parents today live with virtually no religion. Millions of people live trapped in the web of consumerism; worshiping money as their god. Many feel that powerful forces manage these economies, but there is a fatalistic sense of powerlessness to change things.

Likewise, globalization has profoundly affected many cultures, bringing with it alien values that have, in turn, created new cultural forms by mixing the old and the new. Howard A. Snyder, in his book *EarthCurrents,* refers to this new global dimension when he writes, "Throughout Latin America, much of Asia, and elsewhere, economic pragmatism is replacing ideologies. Or becoming the new ideology. Thus economics is not just about money, goods, and services. It also touches worldview questions" (1995:48). These changes bring with them a series of important challenges for the Church.

Latin America has not escaped the winds of globalization. Some of the consequences of globalization affecting Latin America are well addressed by Catalina Romero in her article called "Globalization, Civil and Religion from a Latin American Standpoint." According to Romero many of the new urban dwellers are now comfortable using equipment such as computers, video cameras and tape recorders thanks to the technological revolution that has taken place in the last twenty years. This has opened their eyes to a new dimension of values and expectations (Romero 2001:483). Advances in communication systems and the mass media have brought people from distant regions of the world in touch with each other and now, for example, if cities in Latin America do not offer what the young people are seeking, they are prepared to continue their journeys and migrate to other cities in the world. This has produced changes and is challenged by both internal and external migration. According to Herbert Blumer, massive migrations are a specific form of spatial movement, formed by individuals making decisions on their own (as part of the growing evidence of increasing levels of individualism) yet sharing similar goals (1995:83).

Romero continues, saying that the cities in Latin America have been inundated by individuals who are motivated to challenge existing social arrangements and laws, to build and settle on previously unused lands, and to create a new world for themselves in a new place (Romero 2001:483). Because sufficient infrastructures are not in place to support this, poverty continues to be a major social problem but today it is mainly urban rather than rural poverty.

The following table (Table 2) demonstrates the percentage of the population who are living under the poverty line in urban and rural areas in some of the Latin America. These people are not only economically poor but they also are excluded by the social standards of the continent; they are politically, economically, and socially segregated. Most of the time, these people do not have a voice, neither a place to live, nor access to education, jobs, and food. Generally, these people are the most vulnerable to any kind of emotional and physical exploitation. The statistics in Table 2, although dated, reflect the alarming situation most Latin Americans are living under, especially when considering that the numbers are higher today (The World Bank 2008).

Table 2. Percentage of Latin American Population Living Below the National Poverty Lines in Rural and Urban Areas

Country	Survey Year	Urban %	Rural %
Argentina	2002	53	
Bolivia	2002	54	82
Brazil	2002-03	18	41
Colombia	1999	55	79
Costa Rica	2004	21	28
Dominican Republic	2004	35	56
Ecuador	1998	30	69
El Salvador	2002	29	50
Guatemala	2000	27	75
Honduras	2004	30	70
Mexico	2004	11	28
Nicaragua	2001	29	64
Paraguay	1990	20	29
Peru	2001	42	77

Fortunately, in some areas, the poor in cities do have the opportunity to improve their living conditions and to become more educated and more modern as they move from the local and encounter the global. As a result, urban Latin

America is quite different from rural Latin America. However, once in the cities, the poor are also exposed to many kinds of human rights violations, especially among women and children.

Globalization has brought some good news to minorities. Gender awareness has transformed the role of women in the family and in society and continues to offer women opportunities for education and political participation (Romero, 2001:483). Yet is this really good? Such transformations have perhaps hurt the family. Increasingly all parents within a home, whether it be a dual or single parent homes, are working and leaving the children to raise themselves or be raised by institutions who will teach the standards of the globalized world rather than the standards of a Christian family or the church.

Clearly urbanization and globalization have caused profound and permanent changes in many societies. These changes bring with them a series of important challenges for the Latin American church and the way it does mission. Latin America, as other non-western societies, is facing a very complex problem that demands integral and coordinated answers. The interrelated character of our economies and cultures today facilitate and require a global focus.

The Role of the Church in Latin America's History

Latin America's attempt to discover Christ in its people and its world is an ongoing quest; the conclusion of which has perhaps been skewed by the very forces that introduced Christianity to the region, the Roman Catholic and Protestant churches.

Roman Catholicism in Latin America

Since the beginning of colonization, the Roman Catholic Church "was closely linked to the state and Spanish rule and was a church identified with the structures of power, which determined the extremely conservative role it played during the achievement of independence in Latin America," notes Palma (2004:223). In this sense the Roman Catholic Church was identified with the upper and ruling social class that exercised the role of oppressor to the enormous, primarily poor, landless, excluded, and marginalized from and by the society, majority of people on the continent.

The person of Jesus Christ introduced by the Spaniards was not the Christ of the Gospels, the Son of the living God. Instead he was a lonely victim who was worthy of sorrow and compassion, not hope. As Nuñez and Taylor write, "Hispano-America has not only wept *with* Christ; it has also—and to greater degree—wept *for* him" (1989:218). Catholics in Latin America often portray Mary as the symbol of salvation, redemption and hope. Jesus came as the Lord of death and of the life that is to be; the Virgin Mary came as sovereign leader of the life of the present time. Mackay continues by evaluating this Christ as

> a Christ known in life as an infant and in death as a corpse, over whose helpless childhood and tragic fate the Virgin Mother presides; a Christ who became man in the interests of eschatology, whose permanent reality resides in a magic wafer bestowing immortality; a Virgin Mother who by not tasting death, became the Queen of Life—that is the Christ and that the Virgin who came to America! He came as Lord of Death and of the life that is to be; she came as Sovereign Lady of the life that now is. (2001:102)

In contrast to this deteriorated Christology, the picture of Mary is represented as a queen who is an affectionate and loving mother who not only cares for her son but also sustains humankind. Mary represents not only the mother of Jesus but also the symbol of redemption. The worship of Mary[1] represents one of the biggest religious celebrations in Latin America. For instance, in Mexico celebration of the Virgin of Guadalupe represents one of the main religious celebrations of the country; in Argentina the Virgin of Ducan is the maximal figure of the popular religiosity of the country. Many cities and buildings throughout Latin America are dedicated to the protection of Mary; for example, Lima Peru is dedicated to the Virgin of Santa Rosa. Throughout the Latin American region owning a figure of Mary is a symbol of protection and good luck.

Catholicism also opened the door to a number of rituals and cult practices, which were adapted, often from non-Christian sources, as part of the popular religion. This became a strategy used in order to

> captivate a population, which could not raise itself suddenly to a spiritual religion. The Indians were baptized in masses. Their ancient fetishes were given Christians names: Incan gods were substituted by the effigies of Catholic saints, while Catholic ritual made possible the emotional experiences of the old faith which were now injected into the new observances. (Mackay 2001:39)

Thus, the Catholic religion was superimposed upon indigenous rites without essentially transforming their content. "Such a policy had obviously great psychological value where the whole aim of evangelization was no more than that converts should learn certain religious formulas correctly and go through the mechanism of the established rites of Catholicism" (Mackay 2001:39).

Not all was bad regarding the presence of Roman Catholicism in the continent. The Jesuits, Franciscans, and Dominicans established mission settlements throughout the continent, providing in this way centers for protection of the Indians, education and development. Justo González points out, "Franciscans, Dominicans, or Jesuits lived among the people, and knew their plight. The vows of poverty of these missionaries, and the simplicity of their lifestyle, made it possible for them to live among the Indians, and to see the disastrous results of colonial policies" (1984:381). Thus, these settlements were centers of Indians rights, protection and learning from which universities eventually arose.

In the last seven decades there have been gatherings in which the Roman Catholic Church leadership has analyzed the evangelistic role of the church and its commitment to the Latin America continent. The General Assemblies of the

Bishops of Latin America in Rio de Janeiro (1955), Medellín (1968), Puebla (1979) and Santo Domingo (1992) were moments when the Pastors of the Church in Latin America were able to reflect together as brothers on the most urgent pastoral questions affecting that part of the continent. There have also been periodic pan-American meetings of Bishops, in which the participants could address issues affecting the entire continent, and exchange views on the common problems and challenges facing the Church in the countries of America.

Vatican Council II (1962-1965) was a main turning point in the way the Roman Catholic Church does mission. "Pope John XXIII's encyclicals *Mater et Magistra* and especially *Pacem in Terris* called for an end to ghetto Catholicism and cooperation with men of diverse persuasions in meeting the crises of the modern world" (Schmitt 1971:22). The 1968 Congress of Medellín also offered renewal to the Roman Catholic Church and is where Peruvian, Roman Catholic theologian Gustavo Gutiérrez introduced Liberation Theology thereby providing a new paradigm for missional enterprise in Latin America. This theology renewed the focus, purpose and means for mission among the poor, excluded, needy and oppressed (the majority in Latin America). Gutierrez illustrated the offerings of these two important gatherings in the following words

> At Medellín, the Latin American Church . . . began to be aware of its own coming of age and to take the reins of its own destiny. Vatican II speaks of the underdevelopment of peoples, of the developed countries and what they can and should do about this underdevelopment; Medellín tries to deal with the problem from the standpoint of the poor countries, characterizing them as subjected to a new kind of colonialism. Vatican II talks about a Church in the world and describes the relationship in a way, which tends to neutralize the conflicts; Medellín demonstrates that the world in which the Latin American Church ought to be present is in full revolution. Vatican II sketches a general outline for Church renewal; Medellín provides guidelines for a transformation of the Church in terms of its presence on a continent of misery and injustice. (1986:134)

Today the hierarchy of the Roman Catholic Church is not united in theology or mission. Nevertheless, the church is moving aggressively into the spheres of social, economic, and spiritual involvement in an effort to respond in a more integral way to the struggles that the Latin American people are facing. This movement has not been without cost or controversy. In 1980 archbishop of El Salvador Oscar Romero was assassinated for his support of the poor and out-right opposition of the government. In defense of his beliefs, ministry and continued opposition to the oppressive power, and despite repeated attacks on his life and ministry, he once said, "I cannot change, except to seek to follow the gospel more closely" (Collins and Price 1999:212).

Even though Liberation Theology provided a renewal to the missional focus of the Roman Catholic Church, there were some isolated extremist and revolutionary groups who assumed a non-biblical attitude of the mission. This new social-political participation of the church was based on a new image of Christ; this was the guerrilla Christ who took shape during the 1960s and 1970s.

This image portrays Jesus as only a political activist who denounced the establishment and collided with it, dying as a revolutionary martyr.

Second General Conference of Latin American Bishops (CELAM II) in Medellin, Colombia was the contextualization of official Catholic social doctrine in Latin America that opens the door of the so-called base ecclesial community groups. The base community[2] groups provide an ecclesiological renewal to the church starting in Brazil and moving throughout Latin America. João Batista Libânio defines the word base at three interrelated levels. The *psychological* (culture) meaning has the sense of "cellular," "nuclear," or "fundamental." *Sociologically* "base" refers to the "popular classes"—that is, to the poor. *Theologically* it has to do with the "elemental Christian fabric," the *koinonia* of lay persons (1979:5).

Thus, the base ecclesial community takes as a principle the biblical concept of the priesthood of all believers providing to those who are in more need of a safe and welcome environment where they can participate and develop their spiritual gifts. The base community groups open a new evangelistic and renewal dimension in the Roman Catholic Church that has provided fundamental results in the Latin American community.

Protestantism in Latin America

When the Protestants arrived in Latin America in the last two centuries, they introduced a different Christ than the one presented by their Roman Catholic predecessors. The Protestant (Anglo-Saxon) Christ was one with whom a relationship was possible. This was a Savior Christ, a Christ who lived, died, and suffered for the people and came to redeem their lives. Sadly, although the roots of the Protestant evangelism were biblical, there were some defective models within the Protestant teaching that distorted the image and work of Christ.

One defective Christological image is the *Santa Claus Christ* in which the emphasis is on the free gift of the gospel and salvation without any responsibility for those who receive it. In this image Jesus appears as "the rich father" who gives, gives, and gives because he has a lot of capital. Christ becomes a commodity, and the highest bidder gets him. It is basically a lottery for those who want to have good luck (Bonino 1984:40-41).

The *Santa Claus Christ* is also introduced as a *magic-potion Christ*. This Christ is great at solving the people's problems. He comes to spread peace, love, and happiness, the automatic solution to any problem. Once you accept Jesus as a personal savior all the problems will cease and he will provide riches, enabling you to become physically and spiritually wealthy (Bonino 1984:40).

Clearly Christ is introduced as the generous one who is always available to those who call for his service. Many sermons are concluded with questions like, "Who wants to receive Christ as their personal savior so that they do not have to go to hell? Who wishes to be healed this evening? Let's see the hands of those in need of accepting this gift of a healing Christ, come to him today." This is a message that is introduced time after time in Latin American settings.

Another image of Christ that is often proclaimed from Protestant pulpits is the image of a *Passport Christ*. This is the Christ that will give you a pass directly to heaven as an escape from physical and spiritual problems. This is the Christ who is not able to deal with the people's daily needs therefore the only solution is to escape from the cruel reality that people are facing. Regarding to this point Bonino states

> Heaven appears as an escape from earth, an evasion of life. Heaven-centered preaching is an implicit contradiction of the Word who left heaven and took flesh in order to live on earth. Christ is only incidental to this kind of preaching in any case. It makes use of a *decontextualized Christ*, a heavenly Christ who is soon to come and "kidnap" his church. You meet this "heavenly," over spiritualized Christ in the clouds, not on earth or in history. He is foreign to every human reality—removed from the world of our needs. (1984:42)

It is not uncommon for him to be introduced as a *Cosmic Christ* as well. The *Cosmic Christ* is a Christ of faith and glory but deprived of any connection with the historical Jesus. In this concept we find truth but also falsehood, it is biblical and at the same time unbiblical. "The cosmic Christ, the glorified Christ, is cosmic and glorified thanks to his historicity, his incarnation, his human nature as a real person of flesh and bone. It is thanks to his death and saving sacrifice that he has been elevated to the cosmic Christ" (Bonino 1984:42). It is because of this cosmic understanding of Christ that he is not accessible to the people's lives. He appears faraway from reality and daily life, indifferent and unreachable to any sense of relationship.

Finally, another image of Christ introduced in Protestant circles is the image of the *Beggar Christ*. Expressions like, "Don't cause Christ to suffer any more . . . he's waiting for you with open arms . . . don't make him wait. Surrender your hearts to him!" are often repeated. According to Bonino, this "is a Christ of Convention—that is, persons accept him if it suits them, if he offers them something they want. Otherwise he can just keep standing there, or go next door" (1984:41).

As with the Roman Catholic portrayals of Christ, these Protestant images of Christ represent only part of the gospel. In many cases, these images portray a Christ who is more interested in individual souls than the overall needs of the people. These images of Christ seem to be patterned after the idea of the missionaries—who as a guest in a foreign country do not get involved in its politics or social affairs—a guest in a world that is not their own. Because of this dualistic understanding, the Protestant church has been less effective in dealing with the needs of the suffering, the excluded and the powerless on the continent who sadly make up the majority of the population.

A Closer Look at Specific Latin American Countries

The fact is that Latin America is a continent that has been suffering from a variety of spiritual, social, cultural, political and economic illnesses; maladies that have created a lamentable tragedy of violence, marginality, civil war, narcotics, dysfunctional families, sorrows and hopelessness. Although there are areas in which the Roman Catholic and Protestant churches are doing integral mission, has the Christian Church, as a whole been effective in providing an integral and biblical Christian witness to a continent that suffers? Perhaps the inefficacy of the Christian church in the continent is because of the separation and, for a period of time, animosity between the Roman Catholic and Protestant circles. These divisions, instead of sustaining a complete Christian witness to the Latin American situation, added more struggles to already difficult social and spiritual situations. Or, perhaps the Christian church is unaware of the social, economic, political, and spiritual situation the continent is facing?

The following sections will provide a closer look at four Latin American countries (Mexico, Colombia, Peru, and Argentina) that in some ways describe a few of the complex situations the continent is facing.

Mexico, Christianity and Facts

At the beginning of its colonization Mexico was called the New Spain. When Hernán Cortés (1487-1547) captured the Aztec capital in 1521 the christianization of Mexico began. The first churches were built on the pyramids and the country's beginnings relied upon a close relationship between the church and the state. From the colonial period until after Mexico's independence from Spain, Roman Catholicism was the only permitted religion. Finally, religious liberty was introduced with the law of December 4, 1860 (Fahlbusch 2003:515).

Today the urban population of Mexico has reached enormous levels posing spiritual, social, economic, political and environmental challenges for both the Roman Catholics and Protestants present in the nation. Mexico is the second largest and second most populated country in Latin America and Mexico's capital city, Mexico City, is one of the most striking examples of rapid urbanization. From 1960 to 2000, the population of the metropolitan area grew from less than 5 million to over 20 million, with migrations from rural to urban making up almost half of the increase. The population is expected to continue to climb and it is estimated that 30 million people will call Mexico City home by the year 2020 (Ember and Ember 2002:184).

Only 60 percent of Mexico City's current population was born in the city, the remaining 40 percent have migrated there. The flow of immigrants continues at a rate of more than 15,000 new residents each month or an average of 500,000 new residents a year. Two thirds of this is internal growth, the excess of births over deaths. The city workers average $1,200 a year, but unemployment at any given moment is close to 40 percent (Crow 1992: 739). All of these people need food and water, shelter, and employment or schooling.

Because mountains surround the Mexico City metropolitan area, the whole valley where Mexico City is located is what is called a closed system. This means that the whole valley is exposed to air pollution, lack of potable water, and contamination by the sewage system that has to be pumped up over the mountains, making the task almost impossible (Palmer 1995).

Between 1940 and 1985, downtown Mexico City, built on the ruins of the ancient city of Tenochtitlan, sank by more than 7 meters. This phenomenon was due in large part to the excessive pumping of water from the hundreds of wells located just below the surface of the city. In fact, the amount of groundwater was reduced by 32 meters during the forty-five year period. Eighty percent of the water used in Mexico City is supplied from groundwater and in the year 2000 the increase in population pushed water use to a rate of 100,000 liters per second in Mexico City, aggravating an already grave situation (Ember and Ember 2002:189).

Not only has this phenomenon caused incredible concern about the future of the water supply, it has caused some of the greatest concerns of any city in the world. This alarming rate at which groundwater is being pumped has caused urban planners to question the survival of the city itself (Palmer 1995).

The *Gran Canal de Desague* was the sewage canal for the city, but as the city sank, so did the Canal. Since the 1970's the city sank so much that the water authorities could no longer count on gravity to carry the sewage away, forcing Mexico City to expand the sewage treatment and water recycling facilities. Today it takes 11 pumping stations, which run 24 hours a day, year-round to keep the sewage flowing and keep the summer rains from washing it back to the city (Palmer 1995). Yet this is still ineffective at handling the demand.

Air pollution is another serious crisis that is affecting Mexico City. There are 35,000 industrial establishments, and over four million automobiles that excrete 5.5 millions tons of contaminants into the air every year (Crow 1992:748). According to Country Analysis Briefs, "The Mexican Health Secretary says that more than a third of Mexico's disease burden is the result of environmental factors, the most serious of which is air pollution" (Country Analysis Briefs 2004). The same study reveals that Mexico City has the worst air pollution in the country of Mexico and is one of the most polluted cities of the world.

Diseases related with air contamination are increasing everyday. The main cause of air pollution, according Country Analysis Brief, is

> exhaust fumes from Mexico City's estimated 4 million motor vehicles, many of which are old and especially environmentally damaging... The city's air problem is aggravated by its unique geography. Mexico City resides in a basin more than 7,400 feet above sea level and is surrounded on three sides by mountains. These isolate the city from regional weather disturbances and trap pollution. (2004)

One needs only to look at the air or the water to see the effects that overpopulation has had on Mexico City. As the population continues to grow the problems will only become more amplified, endangering both the health of its residents and its environment. Clearly one cannot effectively introduce the gospel in this city without facing the economic, social, health and environmental issues it faces.

The social, political and environmental situation of Mexico City reflects the critical situation of Mexico as a whole. Crow points out that

> There is widespread malnutrition, hunger, and disease in the country. The death rate among the children is astronomical. Water is polluted almost everywhere. Women wash their clothes, themselves, and their children in filthy ponds, rivers, and streams. Contaminated drinking water is the scourge of millions, and the visiting tourist has come to dread it as the main source of the *turista*. (1992:743)

Corruption is another reality that is deeply rooted in Mexico. According to Crow, this corruption is present in all spheres; "every Mexican president sticks his hand in the till and retires from office a wealthy man. Corruption in business is closely linked with corruption in government" (1992:746). The social, political, economic, and environmental situation that Mexico is facing also has spiritual dimensions that have become a challenge for the Christian Church and her missional task.

Roman Catholicism in Mexico

The Franciscans were the first missionaries who arrived to New Spain. Later came other missionary groups: the Dominicans (1526), the Augustinians (1533), the Mercedarians (1537), and the Jesuits (1585) joined them (Fahlbusch 2003:515). A colonial church that was under the control of Spanish rule arose from the work of these Christian orders. As a result, churches and monasteries were built, schools and hospitals were created and philanthropic work began (Fahlbusch 2003:515).

The veneration to the Virgin of Guadalupe has become one of the most important folk celebrations and devotions for Mexicans. It all began after she appeared four times in 1531 to the Indian Juan Diego. This veneration peaked in 1895 when the Virgin of Guadalupe was solemnly crowned (Fahlbusch 2003:515).

As part of the political and religious power within Mexico, the Roman Catholic leadership opposed the fight for independence. Despite that, reformation laws that were passed between 1856 and 1860 separated the church and state and the power of the church was weakened. After the losses at independence, the number of clergy remained fairly constant throughout the nineteenth century. There were 3,463 in 1826, 3,232 in 1851, 3,576 in 1895, 4,015 in 1900, and 4,533 in1910 (Lynch 1986:533). Today, however, the Roman Catholic Church is still a force of intellectual and cultural influence.

Influenced by the encyclical *Rerum novarum* of Leo XIII (1878-1903), the Roman Catholic Church of Mexico began social work among the working classes and the rural population (Lynch 1986:589). The liberation theology that began in the 1960's reaffirmed this desire to work among the poor and oppressed.

Protestantism in Mexico

United States and Canadian efforts introduced Protestantism to Mexico and began ministry there in 1869. The missionary societies of the Mainline United States and Canadian denominations set up Methodist, Baptist, Presbyterian, and Episcopal churches (Fahlbusch 2003:515). The main strategy these groups implemented was to recruit members of different social groups. The church offered them educational programs for the children and also created schools and theological seminaries (Fahlbusch 2003:515).

The historical Protestant church grew in significant proportions to the point that by 1910 there were approximately 100,000 members and sympathizers in Mexico. Several missions began work in Mexico between 1920 and 1930 as missions to the native Mexicans. The most noted groups were the Mission Agency in the district of Huasteca and the Summer Institute of Linguistics that worked in conjunction with Wycliffe Bible Translators who came by 1935. By the 1960s a new faith society arose, especially for work among students (the Mexican branch of the U.S.-based Campus Crusade for Christ). Some characteristics of these mission groups were their strong fundamentalist and anti-Communist tendencies (Fahlbusch 2003:516).

By 1910 the Pentecostals churches arrived in Mexico with agricultural workers returning from the southern United States. This Pentecostal movement was the result of two main events that took place in the United States, the Topeka Revival[3] (Topeka, Kansas, 1901) and the Azusa Street Revival (Los Angeles, 1906) (Nuñez and Taylor 1989:152). By 2003 approximately 80 percent of the Mexican Protestants belonged to Pentecostal churches. According to the Encyclopedia of Christianity

> Their success may be traced to (1) their use of the healing rites and of glossolalia, which resemble traditional shamanistic practices, and (2) their millenarianism and the opposing of the traditional village caciques. . . . A further factor has been the destruction of the political, economic, and ideological monopoly anchored in the system of popular Roman Catholic festivals. (Fahlbusch 2003:516)

Protestantism in Mexico is growing rapidly, from a mere 0.38 percent of the population in 1900, to almost double that by 1930 (0.79 percent), to 1.66 percent by 1960. In the next three decades this number tripled until the Protestant population of Mexico was 4.92 percent of the population by 1990 (Klaiber 1998:245).

Conclusion

Understanding the history of Mexico and its social, political, economical, environmental, and spiritual dimensions is important for my investigation because it provides a framework through which to understand the present situation of the country and perhaps the continent as a whole. This section also illustrates the historical role of the Christian church in Mexico. Is the story similar in others parts of the continent, and indeed throughout all of Latin

America? The next section will attempt to start answering this question as the focus turns to Colombia.

Colombia, Christianity and Facts

Like Mexico, Colombia as a nation is predominantly Roman Catholic with a growing Protestant population. Like Mexico, Colombia is a country that has suffered social, political, economic, and religious crises that have resulted in thousands of deaths, and left many orphans, and widows. According to Crow, by 1992 Colombia still had "about 500,000 families without land, and this number is increasing at the rate of 10 percent a year" (Crow 1992:802). At the same time, he claims, the drug business is becoming stronger and stronger, bringing with it false economic improvement in the country but also leaving behind a path of death, crisis, and sorrow. One example of this took place during the twelve months prior the inauguration of President Cesar Gaviria in the early 1990s. In the city of Medellín alone the drug cartel had assassinated at least 3,000 people, among them 155 policemen (Crow 1992:806).

Paramilitary and guerrilla groups (started five decades ago) are today the principal producer and cultivator of drugs in the country. In 1999 the Colombian government proposed a strategy to the Clinton administration of the United States to help fight the drug war and the so called "Plan Colombia" was born. Colombia received millions of dollars plus US military support for two years under the plan. According to Chomsky this strategy sadly led to more deaths and violations of human rights that ever before (Chomsky 2000:62, 65).

The violence in the countryside and strong pressure on individual farmers to cooperate with the cultivation of narcotic crops has resulted in rapid urban migration. Of course, this migration has led to a population explosion in the countries large cities resulting in severe social challenges. "Card-board" *barrios* have sprung up in all of the main cities. These are neighborhoods that lack proper sanitation and health care; food, water, education and employment are scarce. Sadly hunger and deprivity breed among other things segregation, homelessness, prostitution, and ultimately more violence.

The social, economic and political situation in Colombia became worse in the 1990s as a result of the neoliberal reforms created in the 1991 constitution. These reforms, according to Arlene Tickner,[4] "reduced still further 'the effective participation of civil society' in policy formation by reforms intended to enhance executive power and reduce the autonomy of the judicial and legislative branches, and by concentrating macroeconomic planning in the hands of a smaller circle of technocrats" (1998:6). According to Chomsky, these neoliberal reforms have produced "alarming levels of poverty and inequality, by the year 2000 approximately 55 percent of Colombia's population lived below the poverty level" and "this situation has been aggravated by an acute crisis in agriculture, itself a result of the neoliberal programs" (2000:62, 65).

Roman Catholicism in Colombia

According to year 2000 statistics, Colombia is a country with a population of 42,321,000 people (Barrett, Kurian and Johnson 2000:2001). Roman Catholicism is the predominant religion in the country with 94 percent of the population professing to be Catholic.

Roman Catholicism began in Colombia in 1510 AD in Santa Maria de la Antigua del Darien, New Granada. The city of Bogotá (founded in 1538 and named a diocese in 1564) quickly became the center of colonization and evangelization. Evangelization took place with the Spanish exploration and occupation of the country. The church grew fastest where settlers were richest and most numerous. The areas that were well developed and had better social structures were converted more rapidly. The settlements high in the Andes and in the South particularly favored the establishment of a society that paid tribute to both the Spaniards and the church of the Spaniards (Fahlbusch 1999:604-605).

In 1819 Simon Bolivar challenged the government that the Spaniards had established. After ten years of conflict, he succeeded in defeating this government and established a new nation, Great Colombia, consisting of the newly independent regions of Northern South America.

The main problem for Colombian development in the 19th century was determining the role of the various institutions within this new nation, including the church. During the struggle for independence (1807-24) there was division among the Catholic clergy. The Colombian born Spanish descendants (called *Criollos*) and the lower clergy supported the revolution, but the higher Spanish clergy remained loyal to the Crown, to which they were tied by a system of patronage. Rome was reluctant to turn over the patronage, resulting in deep-seated difficulties within the church and state relationship. Thus, Colombian clergy took a liberal attitude toward independence. However, Bolivar, the Liberator, turned more and more to the Roman Catholic Church as a stabilizing institution and sought to facilitate an increase in the number of its clergy in this new nation. The tie between church and state that had already been established by the Spaniards was therefore strengthened during this time period (Latourette 1943:79). Eventually, "The New Granada" was the first Spanish American land to be recognized by the Holy See as independent (1835) (Latourette 1943:79).

Between 1835 and 1840, foreign clergymen entered Colombia and formed the basis of support for the Conservative Party, defending the church against the increasing Liberal radicalism. Liberals achieved the separation of church and state in 1853 and introduced civil marriage and divorce. The conflict between state and church led to constant civil strife.

Due to the structure of the national economy for the international market, Conservatives and Liberals united in 1880 and developed a new model of Christianity, one in which the church would be the "watchdog" of the social order and the ideological overseer. In 1886, the Catholic Church was officially named the "state church" (Fahlbusch 1999: 606).

Catholicism continued to spread throughout Colombia. By 1948, Colombia had 1,074 parishes, 2,263 churches and chapels, and 1,642 priests. In 1966, 4,214 priests were active, of whom 2,632 were diocesan and 1,852 religious; there were 2,221 brothers and 15,086 sisters. In 1971, Vatican statistics counted 56 ecclesiastical jurisdictions and 1,851 parishes (Jedin 1981:712).

One of the principal focuses of the Roman Catholic Church in Colombia was and is social action. Since 1944, Catholic Social Action has been established in urban and rural professional associations. Among those associations created by the Catholics is the *Unión de Trabajadores Colombianos (Colombian Workers Union)* (UTS), which all of the urban and rural associations gradually joined. Today UTS consists of more than 300 unions and over 150,000 members. It was out of this Roman Catholic organization that the groundwork for the appropriately named 'liberation theology' was laid.

Another important focus of the Roman Catholic Church at this time was education. High schools and universities were opening in the major cities throughout the country. Then, just as today, public high schools in Colombia were generally Catholic run institutions. The approach in these schools was to provide students with both an academic and technical education in order to better equip them for future employment. Of course, religion was and is also part of the curriculum, with school-wide devotions and religion and philosophy classes taught by priests.

To attend a public school, students must pass a very competitive exam. So, although the school fees are minimal due to governmental support, the academic level is very high. Private schools, on the other hand, are very expensive and focus only on academics. Therefore, the level of education at a private school is generally thought to be lower than that of the public, Catholic school.

In addition to Catholic-run public high schools, Colombia has two Papal universities: the Pontificia Universidad Javeriana at Bogotá, established July 31, 1939 with studies of theology, canon law, philosophy, literature, education, law, economics and social science, medicine and dentistry, and engineering and architecture; and the Pontificia Universidad Católica Bolivariana (Medellín), established on August 10, 1945 with studies of law, political and social sciences, economics and business, philosophy and education, literature, engineering, electricity and chemistry, architecture, city-planning and fine arts (Jedin 1981:713).

In addition to developing good educational institutions, the Roman Catholic Church supports 107 social welfare institutions at its own expense. These institutions include three leper stations (Aguas de Dios, Caño de Loro, and the Society of Saint Vincent de Paul). Some of these are cared for by Salesians (Jedin 1981:714).

Protestantism in Colombia

In 1819 the British delegation exercised its influence on some Colombian citizens favorable to the Liberal Party and advocated the founding of a protestant Church in Colombia. In 1825 James Thompson, founder of the British and

Foreign Bible Society supported by Roman Catholics, founded a national Bible society in Colombia. It was the first to publish the New Testament in South America (Fahlbusch 1999:606).

In the middle of the 19th century, the Presbyterians began working in Colombia and for a long time were the only Protestants in the country. They were famous for their schools and medical centers but otherwise made few advances. By 1910 they had founded only two congregations, one in Bogotá and one in Barranquilla; each was a church with only one hundred members. Between 1910 and 1930, another congregation was formed, facing little opposition from the Conservative government (Barrett, Kurian and Johnson 2000:202).

In 1906 the mission of the Evangelical Alliance that had begun in Venezuela moved to Colombia. In 1908 the Gospel Mission Association that came from Ecuador founded a printing press and began monthly publications. The Cumberland Presbyterians arrived in 1925 followed by the Salvation Army in 1929. The Christian Missionary Alliance and the Scandinavian Missionary Alliance were also working in Colombia by 1930 (Fahlbusch 1999:606).

In the beginning, some Protestant services were held secretly because of government opposition, but during the years of the Liberal government (from 1930 to 1946), Protestant churches were founded and met openly, some even enjoyed some government support. This openness provided the opportunity for other denominations to come to the country, such as the Evangelical Crusade and Plymouth Brethren (which arrived in 1933), the South America Native Mission (in 1934), and the Evangelical Lutheran Church (in 1936). Churches from the United States also entered Colombia at this time including, the United Pentecostal Church (in 1936), Baptists and the Methodist Wesleyan Church (in 1937), the Foursquare Gospel Church and the Evangelical Mission of South America (in 1940), in addition to many more small and independent groups (Fahlbusch 1999:606).

Due to the close ties of the Roman Catholic Church with the civil power Protestants were targeted during the civil war that started in 1948, where thousands of Protestant Christians were killed, 270 schools were closed, and 60 churches were destroyed (Crow 1992:800). However, the Protestant Churches grew comparatively strong, increasing from 2,000 members in 1900 to 324,927 in 1970, to 740,000 in 1990 (Barrett 1982:241).

After the war the Pentecostal Churches enjoyed spectacular growth. The Christian Pentecostal Church came to Colombia in 1964, the Pentecostal Church of Christ and Evangelical National Church of Colombia in 1965, and the United Pentecostal Church in 1970 (Fahlbusch 1999:606).

By the year 2000 the total number of Protestant denominations was approximately 175 with the number of affiliated adults near 1,100,000. The biggest denomination was the United Pentecostal Church of Colombia, which had 1,006 congregations and 230,000 members (Barrett, Kurian and Johnson 2000:202).

The new article (Number 19) of the Constitution of 1991 entitled "The Fundamental Rights," guaranteed freedom of religion for everybody in

Colombia. It says, "Everyone has the right to profess his or her own religion and share it in an individual or collective way (translation)" (1991:15).

Protestants in Colombia can be classified in two ways: on one side are the progressives and on the other side are the conservatives or fundamentalists. Fundamentalists oppose attempts to build social awareness. They emphasize personal conversion but tend to forget or ignore collective structures and needs, seeming to believe that only divine miracles will solve the social problems in Colombia. The interest of this group focuses on lifestyles that could be called either fraternal or sectarian, and social conflicts are overlooked. These people tend to be pacifists and less conscious of social injustice. The Pentecostals are the largest group that fit into this fundamental view.

The progressives, on the other hand, aim at social conversion. Their focus is more on liberating the poor. They tend to look at individuals as part of a group and attempt to deal with the larger social issues such as poverty and injustice. Usually they work in opposition to the current status quo as they look for social standards that help spread the wealth from the few to the many. The progressives are more socially aware than the fundamentalists and are therefore more aggressive in attempting to bring about change. Mainline Protestants tend to support this progressive view (Fahlbusch 1999:607), which is similar to those ideas that formed the creation of the communistic guerilla groups that are now in conflict with the government of Colombia.

There are positive and negative aspects to the arrival of Protestantism in Colombia. The free acceptance of the Bible was one of the biggest contributions Protestants brought not only to Colombia but also to South America, in that way, satisfying one of the most important needs of the people. With the arrival of Protestantism, many people started to read the Bible and to attend Bible study groups. As a result individuals increased their understanding of main theological concepts like salvation, redemption, and grace. However, true discipleship was not a focus of this Bible study and so today this is a topic that still needs to be considered. Protestants also introduced improvements in agriculture and later founded many missionary schools and hospitals (Fahlbusch 1999:607).

At the beginning of the Protestant movement, preachers went from place-to-place bringing with them the Word of God and also their own living testimony of the Word of God. The traveling preachers shared the word in ways that were valuable to the community, expressing their Christian faith in a tangible way. The main emphasis of the sermons was personal repentance and conversion (Barrett, Kurian and Johnson 2000:202).

Sadly, some preacher's sermons were extremely controversial and anti-Catholic. Although, at the beginning, it caused enthusiasm and brought many new people to the church, it eventually caused an anti-religion reaction within the same group of people (Barrett, Kurian and Johnson 2000:202).

Conclusion

The Colombian social, political, economic, environmental and spiritual situation is no better than Mexico's. The gap between the rich and the poor is bigger everyday. The army conflicts with the guerrilla and drug cartels have produced a history of deaths, widows, orphans and an increase in rural-urban migration. The population explosion of the major cities of the country is raising economic, social, environmental, and spiritual challenges to the government but also to the Christian community. Knowing these factors are important to help understand the situation in Colombia and Latin America. The next section will explore the political and religious history of Peru, a more southern Latin American country, to see if, indeed these same trends are seen throughout Latin America.

Peru, Christianity and Facts

The conquest of Peru began in 1532 when Francisco Pizarro (1475-1541) and his 166 men entered the Peruvian coast. "The gruesome conquest, which began in 1532 under Pizarro, lasted until 1572, when the last Inca place of residence, Vilcambamba, was seized by the Spaniards and the Inca ruler, Tupac Amarú, was executed" (Fahlbusch 2005:166). Because the Incan empire was just recovering from civil wars at the time of the conquest, the conquest was easier (Ellis 1975:65). Pizarro was amazed at the roads and other evidence of a highly civilized people. In fact, Peru was and is the land of the one of the most important and oldest American cultures, the Incas. The Incan language, Quechua, is still spoken by more than one-third of the Peruvian people (Crow 1992:95-96).

Since the time of colonization the Roman Catholic Church was more than a religious institution involved in proselytizing among the Indians, it was a political and police institution supporting a state whose field of jurisdiction touched the moral and spiritual realm. This political inquisition was brought to Peru in 1570 (Ellis 1975:95).

From the time of the colonization until the present time, Peru has been facing struggles with polarization of power, inequality, poverty, violations of human rights, injustice and more. It was estimated that, by the year 2003, 54 percent of the population would be living below the poverty level (Fahlbusch 2005:166).

This economic crisis is the result of bad political management. For instance, under the neoliberal president Belaunde Terry (1980-85) and Alan Garcia Perez (1985-90), foreign debt increased to over $20 billion, and hyperinflation (3,000 percent in 1990) accompanied the increase. It was during this time that a guerrilla group, *Sendero Luminoso*, "Shinning Path," became active. "In response, presidents Terry and Garcia consistently took control of the army. Massive human rights violations occurred at the hands of both the guerrilla and the army" (Fahlbusch 2005:166).

According to the *CIA World FactBook,* the election of the president Alberto Fujimori in 1990 ushered in a decade that saw a dramatic turnaround in the economy and significant progress in curtailing guerrilla activity. Nevertheless, the president's increasing reliance on authoritarian measures and an economic slump in the late 1990s generated mounting dissatisfaction with his regime. Fujimori won reelection to a third term in the spring of 2000, but international pressure and corruption scandals led to his dismissal by Congress in November of that year. A caretaker government oversaw new elections in the spring of 2001, which ushered in Alejandro Toledo as the new head of government. Toledo's presidency has been hampered by allegations of corruption (World FactBook 2006).

Land disproportion is another factor that makes the social problems of Peru very serious. After World War II, most precisely between 1950 and 1980, the population of Peruvian cities increased more than 100 percent due to migration. The land problem exists because Peru's "forty families" still own most of the good arable land (Crow 1992:811).

Some of the current environmental issues that Peru is facing is deforestation (some as the result of illegal logging); overgrazing of the slopes of the Costa and Sierra leading to soil erosion; desertification; air pollution in Lima; and pollution of rivers and coastal waters from municipal and mining wastes (World FactBook 2006).

Roman Catholicism in Peru

As in the other Latin American countries studied, Catholicism came to Peru as the religion of the conquerors. According to John Lynch, "The Peruvian Indians traditionally suffered from many exploiters, including clerics, whose extortionate behavior frequently went far beyond the just collection of fees for church services" (1986:539). Peru played a key role during the colonial period because it was there that Spain had a viceroy and was the administrative headquarters for their rule on the west coast of South America. After Peru achieved independence, the constitution of 1828 made Roman Catholicism the state religion, with corresponding protection for the church, a status enjoyed until it was finally eliminated by the constitution of 1979. The Peruvian constitution did recognize religious liberty in 1915, and individual freedom of religion was granted in 1933, but the Roman Catholic Church clung to its privilege of giving religious instruction in the public schools (Fahlbusch 2005:167).

Since the colonial period the Roman Catholic Church has being identified with the aristocratic and ruling class. For many centuries the church was distanced from the social struggles the Peruvians were facing and in many cases the church spiritualized these struggles. One example of this occurred in 1937 when the archbishop of Lima, Pedro Pascual Farfán, stated without opposition "poverty is the surest way to eternal felicity. Only the state that convinces the poor of the spiritual riches of poverty can solve social problems" (Fahlbusch 2005:167).

Vatican II provided a new evangelistic dimension in Peru. Since this event the Roman Catholic Church has repeatedly taken a critical public position regarding political, social, and economic development. One example of this participation took place on December 2, 1990; when one of the national Peruvian newspapers, *La República*, published an article composed by a group of theologians associated with Gustavo Gutierrez. This article publicly expressed the Roman Catholic Church's indignation of the oppression and marginalization of the majority of the Peruvian population. Emphasizing the concentration of power, wealth, tax evasion, money laundering, and access to luxury goods for the wealthy and ruling class, the article then pointed out that, "12 million Peruvians live in direct poverty, with minimum wage covering only 25 percent of the cost of supporting a family" (Fahlbusch 2005:168).

Vatican II brought more religious freedom, to the point that the separation of church and state was a reality in the 1979 constitution. Despite this separation, the Roman Catholic Church still maintained some position of influence in the society and political spheres as was recorded in article 50 of the constitution of 1993. "The government recognizes the Catholic Church as an important element in the historical, cultural, and moral formation of Peru and lends it its cooperation" (Political Constitution of Peru 1993).

Protestantism in Peru

During the time of Peruvian independence, there was a short period of religious tolerance that allowed the British and Foreign Bible Society to enter the country. In 1782 General San Martin, Peruvian liberator, sent James Thomson (1788-1854) to initiate public schools. During the time he was in Peru, he began to use the Bible as a textbook in the school. The Anglican work began in Peru in 1849, but it was limited to the English colony and to seamen (Fahlbusch 2005:168).

Missionary work among Peruvians started in 1888 when the Italian Francisco G. Penzotti came to Callao with his family and the Bible colporteur, J. B. Arancet, of Uruguay. The Methodist Church began its work in Peru in 1890 under Thomas Bond whose main strategy was educational work. By the year 2000 they had 24,000 affiliates. In 1896 independent Brethren missionary began work in Lima and the Christian Missionary Alliance began in 1933 under the Peruvian name of the Evangelical Church in Peru. By the year 2000 the Evangelical Church was the second largest Protestant church in the country with an affiliation of around 300,000 members (Fox 2003:268-269).

The Presbyterian Churches began by the work of the Free Church of Scotland and the help of Mackay. In 1917 they founded the Anglo-Peruvian College, the most prestigious Protestant school in Peru (Fahlbusch 2005:168).

The Pentecostals were led by the strongest and the fastest-growing church of Peru, the Assemblies of God with 238,000 members in the year 2000. Since 1921 the South American Indian Mission has been at work among the Indians of the interior. The Wycliffe Bible Translators also focused on this field after World War II; in the 1970s they had 236 workers among the 40 tribes (Barrett 1982:559).

Conclusion

Peru provides a good example of the relationship of church and state as they marched together. Because of its strategic location, Peru has played an important role in the colonization of the remainder of Latin America. Yet, Peruvians have been victims of presidential corruption that has led to a legacy of inequality, landless, and all kinds of social, economic, environmental struggles. Contributing to the calamities of the Peruvians for sadly more than four centuries, the Roman Catholic Church has been identified with the aristocratic and ruling power.

Now we are starting to see a more complete picture of Latin America allowing us to understand the social and economic realities, the political involvement, the environmental situation, and the spiritual condition of the continent. However, it is time now to go further south and look at the southern cone of Latin America, to get a more complete picture of the region as a whole. Argentina has enjoyed a more European presence than the other countries and perhaps has experienced a much different reality. It will be interesting to find out if this is indeed true as the study continues.

Argentina, Christianity and Facts

Argentina is a republic with 22 provinces and the eastern half of the territory of the *Tierra del Fuego*. Argentina is the second largest country in Latin America but has a slow rate of population growth (Ember and Ember 2002:447).

A first attempt by a Spanish expedition to establish a fort at Buenos Aires in 1536 was abandoned after five years, largely because of conflicts with Indians when Pedro de Mendoza led this first so-called Spanish gold-seeking expedition. Because of attacks by indigenous peoples in 1539 the settlers were forced to move to Asunción (now the capital of Paraguay). The original settlement was burned in 1541. A second, and this time permanent, settlement began in 1580 with 300 people under the leadership of Juan de Garay from Asunción. Although Spain long neglected Buenos Aires in favor of the riches of Mexico and Peru, the settlement's growth was enhanced by the development of trade, much of it contraband (Ember and Ember 2002:447).

In 1617 the province of Buenos Aires, or Río de la Plata, was separated from the administration of Asunción and was given its own governor. A bishopric was established there in 1620. During the 17th century indigenous peoples no longer threatened the city; instead French, Portuguese, and Danish raids were frequent (The Columbia Electronic Encyclopedia 2005).

Prosperity and demographic growth in Buenos Aires were stimulated by an increasing trade in hides and the removal of trade restrictions that originally had to go through Lima, Peru. In 1776 it became the capital of a newly created viceroyalty of the Río de la Plata, including much of present-day Argentina, Uruguay, Paraguay, and Bolivia and was no longer subjugated to the Spanish viceroy of Peru (The Columbia Electronic Encyclopedia 2005).

When Charles III of Spain opened the port at Buenos Aires it only made the locals more desirous of separation from the Spanish Empire. In 1806, British troops invaded Buenos Aires and were expelled by the colonial militia without Spanish help. This victory along with a second one over the British the following year further stimulated the drive for independence from Spain. On

May 25, 1810 (now celebrated as a national holiday), armed citizens of the *cabildo*, or "town council," successfully demanded the resignation of the Spanish viceroy and established a provisional representative government. This was the first of many Latin American revolts against Spanish rule (The Columbia Electronic Encyclopedia 2005).

Six years later, on July 9, Argentina officially gained its independence. This independence was not void of internal conflicts, particularly between the province and the city of Buenos Aires due to different desires for the governmental structure. However, "National political unity was finally achieved when Bartolomé Mitre became Argentina's president in 1862 and made Buenos Aires his capital" (The Columbia Electronic Encyclopedia 2005). This is not to say that tension did not continue to exist, at least for another couple of decades.

After 1853 and the establishment of an Argentinean constitution there was a period of confusion and conflicts. This was also a time of great immigration from Europe primarily from Italy, Spain, Poland, Ireland, and Germany, and also from the Near East and the Far East (Fahlbusch 1999:118).

Democracy emerged in the first decades of the twentieth-century, but the worldwide depression in 1930 initiated a time of political unrest and the struggle for a just economic and social order under the first presidency of Juan Peron (1946-55). A military coup forced Peron into exile in 1955 and further military takeovers occurred in 1962, 1966, and 1976. "Since the overthrow of Peron, Argentina has vacillated between military dictatorship and civilian rule, without being fully able to reestablish a democratic republic with a duly elected government and a duly observed constitution" (Crow 1992:845).

There was also a time of guerrilla movement especially after 1969. A "dirty war" (1976-83) against them cost tens of thousands of lives. Assassinations, imprisonments, and torture were everyday occurrences and between 15,000 and 30,000 Argentineans "disappeared" during this period (Fahlbusch 1999:118).

Economic crises continued to the point that by 1989 the inflation rate was over 6,000 percent. The Argentine economy had slipped into recession in late 1999, and Argentina was forced in to seek help from the International Monetary Fund (IMF) and private banks to reduce its debt. In December 2000, an aid package of nearly $40 billion was arranged, and the government announced a $20 billion public works program that was designed to help revive the economy (Infoplease 2006).

The economy remained in recession, however, aggravating the problems posed by the debt and by the restrictions that the IMF imposed in return for aid. Unemployment rose to around 20% at the end of 2001 and although the economy grew strongly in 2003 and 2004, reducing the unemployment rate to about 13 percent, the effects of the 2001–2002 economic collapse continued to hurt many Argentines (Infoplease 2006).

This reality is seen in Buenos Aires with approximately 15 million inhabitants. Slums dot the city landscape, homelessness, prostitution, and delinquency are serious problems resulting from increasing poverty. The effects of this massive population are drastically affecting the environment. Rivers and channels within the city have become public and corporate waste dumps and because much of the city lacks a proper sewage system, the stench can be unbearable not to mention the affect this has on the availability of potable water. The name Buenos Aires means "Good Air," and it is thanks to the geographic location of the city that the air pollution is not as evident as it is in closed systems like Mexico City but it is a growing problem.

Also because of the availability of land and the financial possibilities the economic slump provided to international investors, multinational companies have transformed cattle ranches into soybean farms. These soybeans are exported or used for fuel, not to feed the Argentinean people so. Not only then is this land not used to feed the native people but, according to experts, the aggressive soybean farming techniques used will render the land virtually useless in only a few years.

Roman Catholicism in Argentina

Like Peru, the Argentinean constitution guarantees religious freedom, yet it grants the Roman Catholic Church a special position as the religion supported by the state. From the beginning of the 20th century the Roman Catholic Church came to be increasingly recognized and effective as a social and intellectual power. In 1992 there were 13 archbishops and 49 dioceses in Argentina; there were churches and chapels in 2,459 parishes, 1,384 primary schools, 964 high schools, and 10 universities. In its service were 5,923 priests, 11,612 sisters, 1,079 brothers, and 2,126 seminarians. There were 589,000 Catholic baptisms in 1992 (Fahlbusch 1999:119).

Liturgical renewal, pastoral work oriented to actual problems, and concern for social rights were the influences Vatican II and the Conference of Medellín made to the Argentinean Roman Catholic Church. These also helped the Church deal with both spiritual and social conflicts in a unified and healing way. "During the military dictatorship of 1976-83, the national bishop's conference and individual bishops came out publicly with criticisms of the political and economic situation" (Fahlbusch 1999:119).

Protestantism in Argentina

Protestantism in Argentina was brought by both immigration and missionary work. Some of these churches are the Anglican Church, which has been in the country since 1825 (their main work was done among the Indians in the North), and the Scottish Presbyterian Church that dates from 1829. The Evangelical Church of El Rio de la Plata was called the German Evangelical La Plata Synod prior to 1956. This church originated from the German population and was established in Buenos Aires in 1843. New waves of immigrants came after 1918, 1933, and 1945. Those groups brought new churches that at the beginning had services in their own native languages moving later into the Spanish language (Barrett 1982:148).

In 1859 the Evangelical Waldensian Church came to Argentina and joined forces with the congregations that had been in Uruguay since 1857. The

Argentina Reformed Church, a derivation from the Dutch Reformed Church, came in 1889. The Argentinean Evangelical Lutheran Church came from the Missouri Synod in 1905 and consists mostly of German immigrants. The Evangelical Methodist Church came in 1836 to Argentina and was strongest in the cities. This congregation was very active in social criticism and leads in ecumenical cooperation. The Baptist churches have worked since 1878 in many parts of Argentina and in the year 1998 had about 700 congregations and an important seminary (Seminario Internacional Bautista) (Fahlbusch 1999:120).

The Evangelical Church Disciples of Christ resulted from the missionary work of the Disciples of Christ. In 1908 the United Evangelical Lutheran Church came to Argentina as a fruit of the missionary work of the North American Lutherans.

Since the late 1980s, there are many independent evangelical and Pentecostal churches and growing numbers of charismatic and neopentecostal movements in Argentina. By 1998 the classic Pentecostals included the Union of the Assemblies of God with approximately 3,000 congregations; the Christian Assemblies, with 750; the Assemblies of God, with 554; and the Church of God, with 495. In the last centuries neopentecostal churches in Argentina have been coming from Brazil, as do churches of the Kingdom of God and the Universal Church of Jesus Christ (Barrett 1982:148). The last two churches are the fastest growing churches in the country that preach a gospel of prosperity to a country facing severe economic crises.

In the early 1990s there were some 170 Protestant denominations. The largest was the National Union of Assemblies of God with 415,000 adherents and the indigenous Assemblies of God with 211,000 followers. Following in numbers were the *Visión del Futuro*, "the Future Vision," the Christian Brethren, the Christian Assemblies, and the Seventh-day Adventist. The historical churches came with the immigrants or missionary work (Fahlbusch 1999:119).

Conclusion

Although Argentina has a large population of European immigrants and for a while enjoyed economic stability, it has been the protagonist of economic, social, political, environmental, and spiritual turmoil. Violations of human rights, assassinations, imprisonments, torture, and for a while the worst inflation of Latin America plus an impotent and at times indifferent Christian church are some of the characteristics that describe Argentina. Despite its more diverse population, sadly Argentina's social, political, economic, environmental and religious reality is no better than Mexico's, Colombia's, and Peru's. This more complete picture of the Latin American situation demonstrates that it is a suffering region.

On the Other Hand

There are other positions that provide a quite different justification of the situation that Latin America is facing. One of these positions is called the "The Culture of Poverty," a social theory explaining the cycle of poverty. This social theory was introduced by Oscar Lewis in his book *Five Families* (1959), describing the daily lives of five Mexico City households. The concept appears again in his book entitled *Children of Sanchez* (1961), and later in its fully developed form in the introduction to *La Vida: A Puerto Rican Family in the Culture of Poverty* (1966), and in an article in *Scientific American* in 1966. Based on this concept, the poor have a unique value system and the "Culture of Poverty" theory suggests that the poor remain in poverty because of their adaptations to the burdens of poverty. I will revisit this understanding in Chapter 7.

Summary

This chapter provided a brief introduction into the history of the colonization and neo-colonization of Latin America and the factors that have made the region what it is today. We have started to answer the questions, how has the church come to this present point and what challenges does the church face? We studied the role of the church, forces of urbanization, globalization and the political, economic, social, environmental and spiritual reality of four main Latin America countries (Mexico, Colombia, Peru, and Argentina) in an attempt to illuminate the complex situation that the whole region is facing.

The Latin American history of colonization has been marked by massacre, exploitation, segregation, and the imposition of a cold and descontextualized Hispanic and Portuguese religion where the sword and the cross marched side by side. Together with sword and cross, the new American inhabitants also brought germs that produced several diseases, killing thousands of Native Americans. The lack of contextualization of the gospel allowed for the growth of a syncretistic religion that is present in the whole continent today.

Latin America has faced a new colonial power that has produced poverty, inequality and injustice in most of the Latin American countries. This neopluralistic democratic system has produced economic insecurity, increased crime rates and the dominant responses to them, and fragmentation of civil society. We learned how the forces of urbanization and globalization are challenging the political, economic, sociological, environmental, and spiritual spheres of the continent.

This chapter looked at the role of the Roman Catholic Church in the continent; first as the dominant power, where the church was closely linked to the civil power; and second as the restricted power, where the church, influenced by the General Assemblies of the Bishops of Latin America in Rio de Janeiro, Medellin, Puebla, Santo Domingo and the Vatican Council II, takes the side of the poor and needy.

The Protestant mission and church in Latin America were also covered. Although Protestants brought a new image of the person and work of Christ, they also brought a legalistic and individualistic view of Christianity that in one way or another bears the marks of the nations that brought it. Today in many of the Protestant circles there are resemblances of this poor theology in a deteriorated Christology, soteriology and missiology.

Although it would be simplistic to say that the core of the issues with which the continent is dealing have been addressed, a close look to the social, economic, political, environmental and spiritual situation of Mexico, Colombia, Peru and Argentina, does provide a big picture, describing part of the problems of Latin America.

This chapter presents challenges to local governments; to private, public and international organizations; to the general Latin America society; and more specifically to the Christian church. For instance, one of the challenges raised is: what should be the response to the exploding urban environment? What is the Latin American's response to the social complexities that result from modernization, migration, overpopulation and the influence of globalization? What should be the church's response regarding social issues such as: the violation of human rights, economic and social inequality, poverty and segregation and so on? Regarding a deteriorated Christology, what should be the ecclesiological, missiological and theological understanding of Christ that may be relevant to the Latin American people and culture?

This chapter begins to answer one of the driving questions of this investigation: Based on the history of the Roman Catholic and Protestant churches in Latin America how do their present understandings of mission, their present structures for ministry, and their current practices of mission work?

The next chapter (Chapter 3) will focus on the Lukan Literature in an attempt to continue finding answers to the main questions of this investigation. More specifically, what significant missiological implications could Luke 4:16-30; 5:27-32; 19:1-10; Acts 2:42-47; and 4:32-37 provide about the local church's role in God's salvific mission in Latin America?

Notes

1. Catholic theology distinguishes between "veneration" [e.g., of Mary, saints] and "worship" [due God alone] however this distinction is often lost in the popular mind.

2. For more information about the impact of the Base Community groups in Brazil see Guillermo Cook's PhD dissertation thesis *The Expectation of the Poor: A Protestant Missiological Study of the Catholic "Comunidades de Base" in Brazil*, 1982.

3. The Topeka Revival is considered by Pentecostal circles to be the first Pentecostal revival of the twentieth 1900 century that began on January 1, 1901. It is thought that this revival would give rise to the most dynamic force for evangelism and missions in modern times. According to Gary B. McGee, the revival came after 40 students of the Bethel Bible School led by the 27-year-old Charles F. Parham, convinced that God had commissioned them as missionaries in the "last days," gathered to pray for the promised

"latter rain" outpouring of the Holy Spirit (Joel 2:23,28,29), to acquire the same spiritual power that marked the expansion of the Early Church (2006).

4. Arlene Tickner is the general coordinator of the Center for International Studies at the University of the Andes, Bogotá.

Chapter 3

The Theology of Luke-Acts and Mission in the Latin American Context

In Chapter 2 we explored some historical factors that led to the social, political, economic, environmental and spiritual situation that characterizes Latin America today. We studied the role of the church and asked whether, instead of serving as an agent of God's solution for the problems of the Latin American continent, the Roman Catholic and Protestant Churches might be part of the problem.

Roman Catholicism and Protestantism, both being European in origin, tend to have a dualistic view of the world, of salvation, and of the church's own part in the mission of God in the world.[1] Perhaps this dualistic view of the gospel is the seed of a weak and distorted theology that has led to a broken ecclesiology producing a decontextualized and ineffective missiological presence in the continent.[2] This dichotomy however is not an issue that the Lukan account of Jesus' ministry would support.

Analyzing the Latin American situation and what has been the role of the church during the last five hundred years, we can infer that something is wrong. Why is it that current churches are not vital, evangelistic, or committed to social services? It could be related to the way Christ was introduced (along with the sword); or the way "the faith" was taught (with a weak Christology and thus soteriology); or the way it spread with a replacement theology of culture instead of a transformational theology of culture. All of this points to a poor theology and practice of mission, evangelism, discipleship and ecclesiology. So, what would a biblical theology of mission and church look like?

I chose to study the Lukan literature because it provides an integral view of salvation that involves spiritual and social action and that includes the whole community of believers and which, in one way or another, challenges the Latin American context. I chose the Lukan literature also, ironically, because the churches of Latin America draw heavily on this literature as their charter for existence. Green describes Luke's view of salvation using these words,

Salvation is neither ethereal nor merely future, but embraces life in the present, restoring the integrity of human life, revitalizing human communities, setting the cosmos in order, and commissioning the community of God's people to put God's grace into practice among themselves and toward ever-widening circles of others. The Third Evangelist knows nothing of such dichotomies as those sometimes drawn between social and spiritual or individual and communal. Salvation embraces the totality of embodied life, including its social, economic, and political concerns. (1997:24-25)

Luke 4:16-30:

And he came to Nazareth, where he had been brought up; and he went to the synagogue, as his custom was, on the Sabbath day. And he stood up to read; [17] and there was given to him the book of the prophet Isaiah. He opened the book and found the place where it was written, [18] "The Spirit of the Lord is upon me, because he has anointed me to preach good news to the poor. He has sent me to proclaim release to the captives and recovering of sight to the blind, to set at liberty those who are oppressed, [19] to proclaim the acceptable year of the Lord." [20] And he closed the book, and gave it back to the attendant, and sat down; and the eyes of all in the synagogue were fixed on him. [21] And he began to say to them, "Today this scripture has been fulfilled in your hearing." [22] And all spoke well of him, and wondered at the gracious words, which proceeded out of his mouth; and they said, "Is not this Joseph's son?" [23] And he said to them, "Doubtless you will quote to me this proverb, 'Physician, heal yourself; what we have heard you did at Capernaum, do here also in your own country.'" [24] And he said, "Truly, I say to you, no prophet is acceptable in his own country. [25] But in truth, I tell you, there were many widows in Israel in the days of Elijah, when the heaven was shut up three years and six months, when there came a great famine over all the land; [26] and Elijah was sent to none of them but only to Zarephath, in the land of Sidon, to a woman who was a widow. [27] And there were many lepers in Israel in the time of the prophet Elisha; and none of them was cleansed, but only Naaman the Syrian." [28] When they heard this, all in the synagogue were filled with wrath. [29] And they rose up and put him out of the city, and led him to the brow of the hill on which their city was built, that they might throw him down headlong. [30] But passing through the midst of them he went away.

Luke 5:27-32:

After this he went out, and saw a tax collector, named Levi, sitting at the tax office; and he said to him, "Follow me." [28] And he left everything, and rose and followed him. [29] And Levi made him a great feast in his house; and there was a large company of tax collectors and others sitting at table with them. [30] And the Pharisees and their scribes murmured against his disciples, saying, "Why do you eat and drink with tax collectors and sinners?" [31] And Jesus answered them, "Those who are well have no need of a physician, but those who are sick; [32] I have not come to call the righteous, but sinners to repentance."

Luke 19:1-10:

> He entered Jericho and was passing through. ² And there was a man named Zacchaeus; he was a chief tax collector, and rich. ³ And he sought to see who Jesus was, but could not, on account of the crowd, because he was small of stature. ⁴ So he ran on ahead and climbed up into a sycamore tree to see him, for he was to pass that way. ⁵ And when Jesus came to the place, he looked up and said to him, "Zacchaeus, make haste and come down; for I must stay at your house today." ⁶ So he made haste and came down, and received him joyfully. ⁷ And when they saw it they all murmured, "He has gone in to be the guest of a man who is a sinner." ⁸ And Zacchaeus stood and said to the Lord, "Behold, Lord, the half of my goods I give to the poor; and if I have defrauded any one of anything, I restore it fourfold." ⁹ And Jesus said to him, "Today salvation has come to this house, since he also is a son of Abraham. ¹⁰ For the Son of man came to seek and to save the lost."

Acts 2:42-47:

> And they devoted themselves to the apostles' teaching and fellowship, to the breaking of bread and the prayers. ⁴³ And fear came upon every soul; and many wonders and signs were done through the apostles. ⁴⁴ And all who believed were together and had all things in common; ⁴⁵ and they sold their possessions and goods and distributed them to all, as any had need. ⁴⁶ And day-by-day, attending the temple together and breaking bread in their homes, they partook of food with glad and generous hearts, ⁴⁷ praising God and having favor with all the people. And the Lord added to their number day by day those who were being saved.

Acts 4:32-37:

> Now the company of those who believed were of one heart and soul, and no one said that any of the things which he possessed was his own, but they had everything in common. ³³ And with great power the apostles gave their testimony to the resurrection of the Lord Jesus, and great grace was upon them all. ³⁴ There was not a needy person among them, for as many as were possessors of lands or houses sold them, and brought the proceeds of what was sold ³⁵ and laid it at the apostles' feet; and distribution was made to each as any had need. ³⁶ Thus Joseph who was surnamed by the apostles Barnabas (which means, Son of encouragement), a Levite, a native of Cyprus, ³⁷ sold a field which belonged to him, and brought the money and laid it at the apostles' feet.

Understanding the Lukan Narrative

This study regards Luke-Acts as a single unit, theologically and missiologically speaking. This study also adopts the position of Green: "[T]he Gospel of Luke creates needs related to God's purpose that go unfulfilled in Luke, but are addressed directly in Acts" (1995:48).

The Unity and Purpose of Luke-Acts

The vocabulary, grammar, style, and theological concerns of Luke and Acts demonstrate their common authorship (O'Toole 1983:2). Most scholars recognize authorial unity (the two works have the same author) and virtually everyone accepts the lack of canonical unity (that is, the two works are separated in modern Bibles). Robert F. O'Toole believes Luke-Acts must be read together in order to understand Luke's theology; to consider one book without the other would only truncate Lukan thought (1984:9). However, Stephen Wilson believes Acts was written many years after the Gospel and addresses an entirely different set of concerns (1983:50).

For our purposes, it is important to note several parallels between the Gospel of Luke and the book of Acts. These provide evidence of their unity and shared theological concerns. I. Howard Marshall believes that the book of Acts flows naturally from the book of Luke as it continues the narrative of Jesus' earthly ministry to that of the his continuing mission through the early church (1983:291-94). Likewise, Green claims that "Luke has consciously developed parallels between Jesus in the Gospel of Luke and his disciples in the Acts of the Apostles" (1997:8). Mark Alan Powell contends that the book of Acts seeks to demonstrate that early Christians remained faithful to the Jewish law (1991:7) and in a later book provides the following table (Table 3) to demonstrate the close unity and relationship that encourages us to read Luke-Acts as a single unit (1998:88).

Charles H. Talbert observes similar parallels between Luke and Acts in his book *Literary Patterns, Theological Themes, and the Genre of Luke-Acts*. Talbert believes that these parallels help the readers understand not only the unity of the books but also Luke's essential purpose and the unity between the mission of Christ and the mission of the church (1974:20).

Green, in *The Theology of the Gospel of Luke,* argues that "Luke's agenda is not to write the story of Jesus, followed by the story of the early church . . . rather, his design is to write the story of the continuation and fulfillment of God's project—a story that embraces both the work of Jesus and of the followers of Jesus after his ascension" (1995:47). The Gospel of Luke and the Acts of the Apostles narrate a continuous story that at the same time is the extension of the story of God's plan of salvation to the whole world. Robert C. Tannehill, in his book *The Narrative Unity of Luke-Acts,* agrees that Luke and Acts are intended to be read together. Acts does not tell a related but independent story; it completes the story begun in the gospel. Without Acts, the Gospel of Luke would be incomplete and without the Gospel, Acts would be misunderstood (1990:36).

Scholars also disagree whether Luke had a single purpose for writing Luke-Acts. Perhaps he had not a single purpose but many purposes in mind. Powell notes that scholars offer six main theories with regard to the purposes of Luke-Acts: irenic, polemical, apologetic, evangelistic, pastoral, and theological (Powell 1991:13). Most scholars agree that Luke's primary audience is not pagans but Christians. I. Howard Marshall affirms that the purpose of Luke was not only evangelistic (to educated Romans as the intended audience), but also to prepare the church for evangelism (1970:159). Marshall's point reaffirms the notion that the books are especially directed to believers within the church.

Table 3. Unity and Relationship of Luke and Acts

The Gospel of Luke	Acts of the Apostles
- Preface to Theophilus (1:1-4)	- Preface to Theophilus (1:1-5)
- Spirit descends on Jesus as he prays (3:21-22)	- Spirit comes to apostles as they pray (2:1-13)
- Sermon declares prophecy fulfilled (4:16-30)	- Sermon declares prophecy fulfilled (2:14-40)
- Jesus heals a lame man (5:17-26)	- Peter heals a lame man (3:1-10)
- Religious leaders attack Jesus (5:29-6:11)	- Religious leaders attack apostles (4:1-8:3)
- Centurion invites Jesus to his house (7:1-10)	- Centurion invites Peter to his house (10:1-23)
- Jesus raises window's son from death (7:11-17)	- Peter raises widow from death (9:36-43)
- Missionary journey to Gentiles (10:1-12)	- Missionary journey to Gentiles (13:1-19:20)
- Jesus travels to Jerusalem (9:51-19:28)	- Paul travels to Jerusalem (19:21-21:17)
- Jesus is received favorably (19:37)	- Paul is received favorably (21:17-20)
- Jesus is devoted on the temple (19:45-48)	- Paul is devoted on the temple (21:26)
- Sadducees opposed Jesus, but scribes supported him (20:27-29)	- Sadducees opposed Paul, but scribes supported him (23:6-9)
- Jesus breaks bread and gives thanks (22:19)	- Paul breaks bread and gives thanks (27:35)
- Jesus is seized by an angry mob (22:54)	- Paul is seized by an angry mob (21:30)
- Jesus is slapped by high priest's aides (22:63-64)	- Paul is slapped at high priest's commands (23:2)
- Jesus is tried four times and declared innocent three times (22:66-23:13)	- Paul is tried four times and declared innocent three times (23:1-26:32)
- Jesus is rejected by the Jews (23:18)	- Paul is rejected by the Jews (21:36)
- Jesus regarded favorably by centurion (23:47)	- Paul regarded favorably by centurion (27:43)
- Final confirmation that Scriptures have been fulfilled (24:45-47)	- Final confirmation that Scriptures have been fulfilled (28:23-28)

Assuming that Luke-Acts has specific purposes for the church, the following sections explore some ecclesiological and missiological factors present in the Lukan narrative.

Missiology and Ecclesiology in Luke-Acts

Scholars generally agree that Luke's ecclesiology is determined by his sense of mission, and that he thinks of mission as both universal (inclusive of Gentiles) and Spirit-driven (Powell 1991:108).

In the Lukan literature we find that the promise of a Messiah figure (the Christ), expected by Israel, is now available and present in Jesus to all Jews as well as Gentiles.[3] Jesus Christ is not only the object of salvation; he also portrays the model of life for those who enjoy that salvation, Jew and Gentile alike. The gospel is the good news that God has put himself within human reach.

In other words, Jesus came not only to be Savior but also Lord. Thus, Luke not only provides the message about the redemptive work of Jesus, he also describes the way this message came alive through the power of the Holy Spirit in and through Jesus and later the church. "Jesus himself prepares the way for this universal mission, not by engaging much with non-Jews, but by repeatedly calling into question those barriers that divide ethnic groups, men and women, adults and children, rich and poor, righteous and sinner, and so on" (Green 1995:47-48). In the Acts narrative we see the fulfillment of God's purpose, particularly in Acts 2-15.

The words "savior" and "salvation" are linked with Jesus and later with the church's missionary task. Powell notes that "salvation for Luke can mean the bestowal of any divine gift. Healing, exorcisms, and miracles are all saving acts. The primary benefit that Jesus offers, however, is the forgiveness of sins, which assures the individual [sic] of a renewed relationship with God" (1991:47).

The words "savior" and "salvation" are not used at all in Matthew or in Mark but are found eight times in the Gospel of Luke and nine times in the book of Acts. This emphasis in the Lukan narrative leads scholars like Marshall to insist that salvation is the principal theme of both Luke and Acts (1970:116). Acts presents Jesus as providing salvation, not primarily by virtue of his suffering and death, but by virtue of his resurrection, exaltation and continuing lordship (1970:169). Salvation has not only ethical but also missiological implications for those who are recipients and participants of it (cf. Acts 1:8). For instance, repentance in Acts signifies turning toward God, an inward change of heart that finds expression in outward actions (Acts 26:20).

The Lukan narrative illustrates the person and work of Jesus Christ and the role of the church as an agent of the continuation of God's plan to the world. As, Green writes,

> Salvation [in Luke-Acts] is neither ethereal nor merely future, but embraces life in the present, restoring the integrity of human life, revitalizing human communities, setting the cosmos in order, and commissioning the community of God's people to put God's grace into practice themselves and toward ever-widening circles of others. The Third Evangelist knows nothing of such dichotomies as those sometimes drawn between social and spiritual or individual and communal. Salvation embraces the totality of embodied life, including its social, economic, and political concerns. For Luke, the God of Israel is the Great Benefactor whose redemptive purpose is manifest in the career of Jesus, whose message is that this benefaction enables and inspires new ways for living in the world. (1997:24-25)

There are several examples in Luke-Acts that show an integral dimension of salvation. For instance, for the woman in Luke 7:36-50 considered sinful by the Pharisees, salvation meant forgiveness of sin and acceptance as part of God's people; for the sick women in Luke 8:40-47 and 13:10-17 salvation meant healing from their twelve and eighteen years of sickness. On the other hand, for Zacchaeus (Luke 19:1-10), salvation meant acceptance and restoration into the Jewish society. In the book of Acts there is a continuation of the integral understanding of salvation; for example, for a crippled man in Acts 3:1-10 salvation meant healing; for those tormented by evil spirits in Acts 5:12-16 salvation meant liberation; for Saul in Acts 9:1-19 salvation meant a turning point in his life and ministry; for Cornelius in Acts 10 salvation meant cleanliness, being welcomed into God's family without crossing cultural borders, receiving the fullness of the Spirit, and baptism by water.

The Lukan narrative of salvation thus has integral dimensions that are very relevant in today's world, and especially for Two-Thirds world countries. The gospel introduced by Luke is the good news of salvation for Latin America today. Luke gives particular emphasis to "the poor," the outsider and oppressed and criticizes those who produce segregation.[4] Usually when we think about the words "poor" or "poverty" we think of economic factors. However, when we think about the reality of Latin America and most of the Two-Third world countries, the "poor" are not only those who are economically marginalized but also those who are facing many kinds of social, political, physical, and emotional oppression or marginality.

Before studying the Lukan understanding of "the poor," I will briefly explain how the concept of "the poor" has been used and its implications from a Latin America point-of-view. Is the message of "the good news" in Luke's Gospel also good news to the majority of Latin Americans who are living in a state of economic, social, political, emotional and spiritual discrimination and segregation? If so, what are the implications for the church in this suffering region of the world and what will be the implications for the church's theology, ecclesiology, and missiology?

Defining *Pobre* from a Latin American Perspective

The expressions "poor" in English or "*pobre*" in Spanish are not perhaps the best words to describe the reality most of the Latin American people are dealing with. Despite this, Luke uses the word "poor" or "*pobre*" ten times in his gospel. The terminology remains the same throughout nine translations of the Bible; the word "poor" is used in the King James Version (1611/1769), the English Standard Version (2001), the New International Version (1984), the Revised Standard Version (1952), and the New Living Translation (1996), and the word "*pobre*" is used in *La Biblia de las Americas* (1986), the Spanish *Reina-Valera* Revised (1960), the Spanish *Reina – Valera* Update (1995), and the *Reina-Valera Actualizada* (1989). These last four versions represent the Bibles most frequently used by Latin American Protestants. Only *The Message*[5] (2002) uses words other than "poor" in four of the ten passages. In Luke 6:20 it use the terminology, "lost it all," "wretched of the earth" in 7:22, "misfits from the wrong side of the tracks" in 14:13, and "who look like they need a square meal" in 14:21.

English dictionaries (e.g., the *Cambridge Dictionary*, *Western Dictionary*, *Encarta Dictionary*, and *Oxford Dictionary*) typically define "poor" as "having little money and/or few possessions." If we use this definition to explore the reality of Latin America, we might assume that the lack of money and/or possessions is the main problem of the region and therefore that the solution is monetary and/or material. However, close analysis of the Latin American reality reveals that the lack of money and/or possessions is not the only factor affecting the region today and, in fact, there are many other issues. While the recently published *Message* acknowledges that "poor" deals with much more than economic hardship, there is no Spanish equivalent of this version that is used widely throughout Latin America and therefore this narrow view of *pobre* as only an economic factor continues to be propagated.

Taking into account both the gospel as narrated in Luke-Acts and a comprehensive view of the contemporary Latin America reality, this research understands "the poor" and "poverty" as referring to the people who are experiencing social, spatial, political, economic, and religious marginality.

Pobre as the Socially and Spatially Marginalized

Social and spatial marginality need to be considered together because, in some ways, one is the result of the other. For instance, when people are displaced (i.e., spatially marginalized)--as we have seen happen throughout Latin America in instances of rural to urban migration, which has occurred in many cases due to war, or lack of opportunity, or for health needs--they also face social crises.

Chapter 2 pointed out that Latin America is the most urbanized continent in the world and noted that this was not necessarily good news for the continent. Most of the urbanites are suffering from hunger and/or malnutrition. The lack of facilities and basic resources such as water, electricity, food, or sewage systems have produced many kinds of diseases and dysfunctions within the society. Therefore, when one thinks especially about the *pobre* in the Latin American context, one needs to think about the urban-slum dwellers and their struggles. This group of people, most of them women and children, are considered vulnerable not only to diseases and natural catastrophes but also to many kinds of physical and emotional abuses and discrimination. The crime rates are very high in these areas as a result of social disability. In most cases, these communities are located in the peripheries of the main cities; isolated, segregated, and set aside from the view of the "rich" and, often, from government aid.

According to a report presented by the General Assembly of the United Nations, the number of persons living in poverty in Latin America has risen considerably in recent decades. For instance, in the period of 1997 to 1999 the number of people living in poverty grew from 204 to 211 million. By the year 2000, the percentage of poor households was estimated to be around 34 percent and, of those, 14 percent were indigenous households (United Nations 2005). For these people, being poor means the lack of options, the absence of opportunities for meaningful participation in society, and inadequate support for capacity development.

Ethnic marginality is another part of the social marginality present in the continent. In countries such as Brazil, Guatemala and Bolivia, race and ethnicity continue to be a deterrent to opportunities as people of Indigenous and African descent have incomes that are 35 to 65 percent lower than those of European descent. This same population segment is much less likely to have access to education and housing than their Caucasian counterparts (United Nations 2005). According to *Cities in a Globalizing World: Global Report on Human Settlements* 2001, "78 million [Latin Americans] live in extreme poverty, unable to afford even a basic daily diet. The poverty rate is 80 percent among the region's 30 million indigenous people, who are concentrated in Bolivia, Ecuador, Guatemala, Mexico and Peru" (2001:17).

Pobre as the Economically Marginalized

In recent decades globalization has been a contributing factor for some of the economic marginality in Latin America and, as discussed in Chapter 2, this globalization has challenged the continent due to the misdistribution of wealth and resources that it has caused. "In Latin America, a quarter of all national income is received by a mere 5 percent of the population, and the top 10 percent own 40 percent of the wealth" (United Nations 2001:17).

In addition, the financially poor are the first to suffer the consequences of drastic budgetary reductions in education, health, housing, social security, retirement programs and so on, that are imposed by those in positions of power.

Pobre as the Politically Marginalized

Latin America has suffered from political marginality throughout its history. As addressed in Chapter 2, this marginality has been present in civil wars, dictatorial governments, and many kinds and scales of corruption. However, in recent years the main enemy of an open society is no longer communism but the threat of global capitalism. In the eyes of some global capitalism (or political neo-liberalism) has been exposed as the greatest threat not only to democracy but also to the environment and to the very survival of humankind and especially to the poor around the globe.

Neoliberalism subordinates the common good to the economic interest of a powerful elite for whom the meaning of life is defined in terms of material possessions. It presupposes, with no basis, that modern society will be able to achieve "the greatest happiness for the greatest number of people" by means of individual effort to satisfy private economic interest. (Padilla 1996:28)

Political laws have produced what Leslie Sklair has called a "class polarization," which is the emergence of a transnational aristocracy of materially wealthy and politically powerful people in comparison to increasing masses of poor and deprived people unable to satisfy their basic needs. The gap is widening not only between the rich and poor countries but also between the rich and the poor within the countries, including those belonging to the First World (2002:53). Global capitalism, therefore, is obviously benefiting the rich minority while leading the poor majority into deeper poverty. Immanuel Wallerstein in his book, *The Capitalist World-Economy*, provides a sustained critique of global capitalism. He points out that "without unequal exchange, it would not be profitable to expand the size of the division of labor. And without such expansion, it would not be profitable to maintain a capitalist world-economy" (1979:73).

Most of the Latin American countries are adopting the neopluralist democracy system; a system in which the main philosophy revolves around the belief that the best balance of interests and values within a given polity is produced by competition among individuals in the rational pursuit of one's own self-interest. Neopluralistic democracy has contributed to the fragmentation of civil society, widening the gap between the rich and the poor and leaving thousands and thousands in absolute misery.

Government laws are used in Latin America to persecute and oppress those who do not agree with the government's interests. Roman Catholic theologian Leonardo Boff points out that "since the 1960s Latin America has been the scene of the proliferation of so-called national security regimes, according to whose ideology anyone publicly questioning the dominant interest of the state is labeled a subversive, and becomes the victim of government surveillance, repression, torture, or even death" (1984:56).

Pobre as the Religiously Marginalized

Chapter 2 noted the spiritual dimensions of Latin America, exploring how, during the period of colonization, the natives suffered many kinds of persecution, exploitation and segregation. The chapter also demonstrates that throughout the history of the region those who did not profess to be part of the dominant religious institution of the Roman Catholic Church were also submitted to many kinds of persecution, segregation, and marginalization. Something that happened in the past and is happening in a lot of places today is that membership in an Evangelical or Protestant church is enough reason to be persecuted, segregated, and in some instances put to death.

Due to the intimate connection of the Roman Catholic Church with the dominant secular power, sometimes laws and social benefits (such as education, health services, job availability, and so on) only favor those who are part of the Roman Catholic Church. Those who belong to a different credo are cast out and are sometimes denied their rights and benefits. There are many cases like this to demonstrate that being *pobre* in Latin American sometimes means experiencing religious marginality.

In sum, the *pobre* in Latin America are those who are socially, spatially, economically, politically, and religiously marginalized. These people are poor not only for the lack of money or material resources but due to segregation, discrimination, and the subjugation of international and monetary laws that have made Latin America what it is today. "Poverty and oppression do not just happen. They are the result of deliberate decisions that the people of means make. Poverty and oppression, then, are not impersonal forces that are endemic to economic structures. They are human creations" (Hoppe 2004:17). Therefore, a better definition for the word *pobre* from the Latin American standpoint is: the socially, spatially, economically, politically and religiously marginalized; the oppressed, the outsider, the excluded and the needy. Clearly the Latin American definition of pobre or pobreza, "poverty," is much broader than the definitions offered by English dictionaries and Bible translations. How does this definition relate to the way that Luke and Acts use the words "poor" and "poverty"? How do these definitions challenge and in some ways help the church better understand its theology, ecclesiology and missiology within the Latin American context?

"The Poor" in the World of Luke-Acts

Scholars typically accept that Luke tells the story in his gospel as "good news to the poor." The vocabulary referring to "the poor" or "poverty" appears more frequently in the Gospel of Luke than any other New Testament book. There are three main words for "poor" used in the Luke-Acts literature: the word πενιχρός "poor" (used only once in the New Testament, Luke 21:2); the word ἐνδεής "needy" (used only once in the New Testament, Acts 4:34); and the word πτωχός "poor" (appears 10 times in Luke, 5 times in Matthew, 5 times in Mark, 4 times in John, 4 times in the Pauline letters, 4 times in James and twice in Revelation).

In order to understand the use Luke makes of the word πτωχός it is important to explore the social classification present in the Roman world and Israelite tradition. According to Green, "Luke's social world was defined around power and privilege, and is measured by a complex of phenomena—religious purity, family heritage, land ownership (for non-priests), vocation, ethnicity, gender, education, and age" (1997:60). This social classification was part of the Old Testament boundary between "pure," referring to those who were part of the Israeli people, and those who were considered "impure." These last ones were marginalized and categorized as "sinners"; they were the lepers and sojourners who were pushed to the sidelines in order to keep Israel pure.

One Old Testament example of the classification between pure and impure is found in the dietary rules. This dietary classification provided some degree of an educational basis that eventually developed into a conscious system of discrimination in the Jewish mentality as Mary Douglas points out

> The purity rules of the Bible . . . set up the great inclusion categories in which the whole universe is hierarchized and structured. Access to their meaning comes by mapping the same basic set of rules from one context on to another. In this exercise the classification of animals into clean and unclean, the classification of peoples as pure and common, the contrast of blemished to unblemished in the

attributes of sacrificial victims, priest and woman, create in the Bible an entirely consistent set of criteria and values. The table, the marriage bed and the altar match each other's roles in the total pattern. (1973:139)

In the process of learning what is clean and pure the Jews also learned to distinguish between people according to their occupation, gender, physical condition, and nationality.

Most of the purity rules are scattered through the first five books of the Old Testament. I will not provide details about all of the purity rules since this is not the purpose of this investigation but what I will do is highlight the most important concepts of "purity" and their implications for the Luke-Acts world.

The Concept of Wholeness as Purity

Douglas points out in her book *Purity and Danger* that wholeness/completeness and separateness are the two principles of purity observed in the priestly laws, the Holiness Code, and Deuteronomy (1966:52). She claims that "to be holy is to be whole, to be one: holiness is unity, integrity, perfection of the individual and of the kind" (1966:55). There were two main things that constitute the concept of wholeness in ancient Israel: avoiding mixing of classes and keeping the order of the creation.

The order of creation according to Genesis was divided into three main categories: elements that belong to water, air, and land. The Israelites categorized all animals into one of these main categories; those animals that did not clearly fit into one and only one of these categories broke the "order of creation," and were, therefore, considered unclean (Douglas 1999:134-75). Genesis 1:5-10 affirms Douglas' principle that is also further developed in Leviticus 11:1-8 (land); 11:9-12 (water); 11:13-23 (air); and Lev. 11:46-7. Once again the same principle of wholeness is in operation; everything must be maintained within its specific class.

The Concept of Separateness as Purity

Cleanliness in Israel played a very important role in their society. In order to consider something clean, it must be separated. This principle came from God's concept of order: in God's creation there was separation between order and chaos. Separateness is the second principle highlighted in the purity rules in all the priest laws, the Holiness Code and Deuteronomy. In these laws there was a separation (of animals, objects, and people) between two main kinds. Animals were divided into clean and unclean and humans were divided into those "under the covenant" and "the rest of humanity" (Douglas 1999:152).

There are several examples in Leviticus of the application of this rule. For instance, the sacrificial system entails separation from rules of uncleanness and the restoration of purity. Leviticus 16 points out that the purity rule was concluded with a full description of the rite for the Day of Atonement. On this day, the high priest made "atonement for the Most Holy Place because of the uncleanness and rebellion of the Israelites, whatever the sins had been" (Lev. 16:16).

The Holiness Code (Lev. 20:22-26) also reinforces the importance of separation and has implications for the Jewish ideology of the land (Lev. 20: 24b-25). As long as Israel is holy, the land, which is also holy, belongs to them. However, if they are contaminated, their claim to the land is threatened. Michael A. Rynkiewich in his article *Strangers in a Strange Land: Theologies of Land* makes five points that are relevant to understanding the biblical concept of the land (2001:219-220),

1. In the beginning, land became both symbol and substance of the relationship between God and humans.[6]
2. Land was an important marker of personal and social identity.[7]
3. Land was the measure of the health of people's relationship with the supernatural.[8]
4. But, if the relationship between people and spirit was unhealthy, the land would reflect the damage.[9]
5. One aspect of the personification of the land was that the land could wear down or be abused to the point that the land needed rest and renewal.[10]

The purity/impurity rules also emphasized the importance of Israel as a nation and their close relationship with God. In other words, the covenants were based on the relationship the Israeli people had with God. In this respect holiness has an ethical connotation. The phrase "you shall be holy for I am holy" defines holiness not only as separation from others but also as being set apart for God. Holiness means living a life of godliness (Milgrom 1990:187). Time after time the Israelite people were reminded that they needed to follow God's rule because of their close relationship with God (Deut. 7:1-5; 6; 14:21). Finally, for the Deuteromist, the purity laws were part of the covenant between God and His people and were connected with the promise of fertility (Deut. 7:12-15).

In sum, the Holiness Code and Deuteronomy provide standards that share two main principles: wholeness/completeness and separateness. Israel categorized any creature according to the creation order. As long as the Israelites stayed away from impurity, they would dwell in the land (the Holiness Code) and would be fertile (Deuteronomy). The purity laws draw a boundary between what is considered pure and impure. This boundary corresponds to the boundary of nationality (Israel as a holy chosen people and the rest of humanity). Jews learned to distinguish food, animals, people, and things based on purity and impurity at the table. This dietary classification provided in some degree the educational basis that eventually developed into the Jews discriminative consciousness. This background provides the framework for understanding how these laws became means of segregation, classification and discrimination during the "Second Temple" period which in turn may help put Luke's use of the term πτωχός into its proper context.

The Outcast Groups and the Jewish Hierarchy

Hierarchical stratification within the Israel system was ascribed by birth. Howard Eilberg-Schwartz in his book, *The Savage in Judaism*, defines ascription as the "assignment of status or prestige on the basis of qualities or attributes such as sex, age, certain physical characteristics, or kinship ties. By contrast, when status is based on achievement, it is determined by an actor's performance, by her or his effectiveness or success in achieving certain specified goals" (1990:196). In the Israelite system, a religious boundary of purity and impurity corresponds with one's status, and an individual cannot control it. The whole population of the Jewish world, including the Gentiles, was ranked and categorized according to pure and impure distinctions. The Jewish world is a good example of what Eilberg-Schwartz describes by saying, "when status depends primarily upon ascription, the idea of contamination takes a corresponding form in the religion system" (1990:197).

The purpose of this stratification was to keep the Israelites whole and set apart. In this respect, purity-impurity rules have the same objective quality that status does. "It is beyond a person's power to control and therefore experienced as coming from the outside. Furthermore, an individual's actions or intentions will have virtually no impact on the functioning of the system" (Eilberg-Schwartz 1990:197). There were three main norms or customs that separated Jews from the outsiders (Gentiles or non-Jewish people): (1) circumcision, (2) observation of dietary rules, and (3) observation of the Sabbath.

During the Second Temple period discrimination was already present within the Jewish community. Three examples of outcast groups during this period were (1) those who experienced discrimination because of their occupation, (2) those who experienced discrimination because of sickness, and (3) those who experienced discrimination because they were sojourners or resident aliens. Because these three groups endangered Jewish purity, they experienced discrimination.

Discrimination and Occupation

Louis Dumont in his book, *Homo Hierarchies: The Caste System and Its Implications*, points out that the correlation between discrimination and occupation is to some degree a common feature of discrimination in every culture throughout the ages (1980:92-108).

There are some jobs that were considered unclean and therefore despised in the Synoptic Gospels. For instance, the Pharisees criticized Jesus because he shared the table with tax collectors and sinners[11]. They regarded tax collectors as unclean and inappropriate to share the table with others Jews. The rabbinic literature, such as *M. Hagigah* 3.6 and *M. Tohoroth* 7.6, states that a house became unclean if a tax collector entered it. It also highlights that the tax collectors deserved to be labeled as unclean and sinful because they were dishonest and immoral.

It is difficult and out of the scope of this study to discern whether groups experienced discrimination because they held certain occupations or whether they were forced into certain occupations because of discrimination (1980:92).

Discrimination and Sickness

People who were suffering any kind of sickness were also objects of segregation and discrimination in the Jewish culture. According to the priest laws, impurity was caused by childbirth (Lev. 12:1-8), leprosy (Lev. 13-14), and discharges such as blood and semen from the vagina or penis (Lev. 15). The priestly laws categorized irregular discharge as being worse than normal discharge. For instance, seminal emission made a man unclean for one day (Lev. 15:16-18), but a chronic flow was more severe, requiring a sin offering (Lev. 15:1-15). Women suffered a longer period of uncleanness than men because menstruation made a woman unclean for seven days (Lev. 15:25-30).

The priest played an important role in declaring people who suffered from diseases as clean and unclean. Following is the criteria the priest used to determine if a person was considered clean or unclean: when symptoms appeared; for instance, in the case of a leper, the priest performed an examination and pronounced the person to be "a leper" under specific conditions (Lev. 13:1-43). Lepers had to announce their conditions and remain outside of the camp (vv. 45-46). Once the disease was healed, lepers were subjected to a rite of purification (Lev. 14:1-32).

Those who suffered from any kind of genetic defects were excluded from some social activities and positions. For instance, Leviticus 21:16-24 provides a list of those who could be excluded from the priestly status which includes those who were blemished, blind, lame, mutilated in face/limb, crippled foot or hand, hunchbacked or dwarfed, eye defect, festering or running sores, scabbed, or who had damaged testicles. According to the Rule of the Congregation by Qumranic texts, persons could be excluded from the congregation of the whole assembly as a result of injury or genetic fault (IQSa 2.5-7), some of these were: afflictions in the flesh, injured feet or hands, lameness, blindness, deafness, and dumbness. J. A. Sanders points out that the War Scroll (1QM 7:4-6) even excluded the following people from joining in the eschatological battle: boys, women, lame, blind, crippled, and persons with permanent bodily defects or bodily impurities (1974:245-71).

In sum, those who were sick or suffering from discharges were labeled as unclean and were therefore separated from the rest of the Jewish society. Those excluded from any kind of activity, office, and occupation because of their physical "defects" were socio-economically, politically and religiously marginalized. In most cases those who were suffering any kind of disease were segregated to live as outsiders.

Discrimination and the Sojourner

The purity rules, with the purpose of keeping the Israelites complete before God and separated from others, contributed to Israel's reaction against ethnic diversity. This was despite the fact that ethnic diversity was already a reality in Israel because when they took possession of the Promised Land it was already occupied.

The sojourners were also categorized as recipients of protection and as regular members of Israel; for instance, the Holiness Code[12] urged Israelites to protect the sojourner and the poor among them (see also Isaiah 56). In addition, the Israelites and the sojourners are the direct audience for the purity rules in Leviticus 17 and 20, which means that not only were the Israelites commanded to keep clean but the sojourners were as well.

In Deuteronomy the sojourners also received a special place within the Israelite community. The protection of the sojourner by the Israelites is mentioned in Deuteronomy.[13] This Israelite behavior was based on the fact that Israel was also a sojourner in Egypt.[14] Even though these laws provided special treatment for the guests among the Israelites, these laws also provided some classification for those people outside of the core members of Israel (Deut. 14:21) which, in one way or another encouraged segregation of and discrimination against outsiders.

The Outcast Groups and the Greco-Roman Society

G. E. Lenski in his book, *Power and Prestige: A Theory of Social Stratification,* used a widely-accepted diamond-shaped graphic to depict the social classification of the Greco-Roman world. James Malcolm Arlandson argues that Lenski's graphic is inadequate because the diamond shape minimizes the social gap between the rich and poor. Arlandson uses a different graph to demonstrate the reality of the wide gap between the elite and "all the rest" in the Greco-Roman world (Arlandson 1997:22).

According to Arlandson's depiction, the majority of the people lived just a little above or at poverty[15] level with little or no status and power while a very small minority benefited from great wealth, status, and power. Very few people lived in-between. The right side of the graphic represents the rural sphere, which is longer than the urban sphere in order to demonstrate that most Mediterraneans lived outside the large metropolis and in small towns and villages.

Few persons ever crossed boundaries. The lines above the unclean and degraded and the expendables are very porous because if social mobility existed at all, then it was almost exclusively downward. As previously discussed, the unclean and degraded were considered such because of occupation, heredity, or disease (Lenski 1966:280-81).

"Retainers" and "expendables" are merely tools to describe a historical reality: the first illustrates a class that the rulers employed to carry out their will and policies and the second, argues Lenski, describes people, found in every agrarian society, "for whom the other members of society had little or no need"

(1966:281). It was precisely to those who belonged to this category of people that Jesus ministered.

Even though Arlandson's graphic provides a complete social description of the Greco-Roman world, it is inadequate because it assumes that wealth is the key factor that describes the social position in the Luke-Acts world. The amount of possessions and wealth does not necessarily determine the status of a person in the ancient Mediterranean culture and the world of Luke-Acts. Describing the social situation in the Mediterranean and the Luke-Acts world, Green emphasizes that "in that culture, one's status in a community was not so much a function of economic realities, but depended on a number of elements, including education, gender, family heritage, religious purity, vocation, economics, and so on" (1997:211).

One example from the Lukan Narrative that demonstrates the inadequacy of Arlandson's graphic is found in the story of Zacchaeus (Luke 19:1-10). Zacchaeus was economically wealthy, but by popular opinion he was considered a "sinner." "Zacchaeus like a widow, a toll collector, children, and blind beggar, is a person of low social status" (Green 1997:666). Therefore, Arlandson's graphic is insufficient to describe the social situation of Zacchaeus in the Lukan world; clearly wealth was not the determining factor for social classification but rather inclusion or exclusion was based on other, more complex factors. "Luke's social world was defined around power and privilege, and is measured by a complex of phenomena—religious purity, family heritage, land ownership (for non-priests), vocation, ethnicity, gender, education, and age" (Green 1997:60).

In conclusion, discrimination during the Second Temple Judaism—the Greco Roman World as well as in the World of Luke-Acts—was based on laws of purity and impurity. Israelites avoided integration to remain complete/whole while at the same time maintaining their separateness. Their lifestyle included following dietarian norms, but also rules to segregate those who held certain social positions, occupations, had health issues, and those considered outsiders. This discrimination was engraved on the hearts of the Jewish people at the daily table. This segregation or discrimination was not a matter of economic or political status. In most cases this discrimination had religious connotations that permeated all of the social spheres. For instance, those who were considered unclean because of their occupation, diseases, or disabilities were expelled from the community and forced to live on the edges of the society. This also happens in Latin America, the πτωχός in the Lukan world are the socially, spatially, economically, politically, and religiously marginalized. The πτωχός are the outsiders, the powerless, the segregated; not because of their own negligence but due to injustice in the socio-political and economic systems that have forced them to live in the periphery of the society.

The images of Latin American *pobreza*, "poverty," and πτωχός in the Luke-Acts world are a good background to understanding some of the key texts in the Luke-Acts literature. Will the Lukan understanding of poverty, the mission and work of Jesus Christ among those who are socially, religiously, politically marginalized provide ecclesiological and missiological insights for the church in Latin America?

πτωχός in the Text of Luke-Acts

As mentioned before, Luke used the term πτωχός ten times in his gospel. Seven out of those ten times Luke used the word to refer to those who were excluded and suffered hardships and discrimination in the society. "Whereas the priestly and Qumranic texts list those who are impure and of low status because of disability so as to exclude them, Luke presents such a list in order to indicate the very people who should be included" (Green 1995:81). The following list shows the use of the term πτωχός in the Lukan narrative:

Luke 4:18	6:20	7:22	14:13	14:21	16:20, 21
Poor	Poor	Poor	Poor	Poor	Poor
Captive	Hungry	Lame	Maimed	Maimed	Ulcerated
Blind	Mournful	Leper	Lame	Blind	Hungry
Oppressed	Persecuted	Deaf	Blind	Lame	
		Dead			
		Blind			

As we can see in the previous list, in every case except for in Luke 7:22 the term πτωχός stands at the beginning of the list. In Luke 7:22 the term πτωχός appears in the final and emphatic position (Green 1994:68). Luke carefully chose the order of his words to emphasize who is now being included in Jesus' missional task. Seeing the list provided in the texts, the πτωχός appears to be more than those who are economically marginalized or belong to an economic classification. πτωχός interprets and is amplified by the others adjectives. "Apparently, Luke is concerned above all with a category of people ordinarily defined above all by their dishonorable status, their exclusion" (Green 1995:82). By connecting with these lists of the unclean people, Luke emphasizes the unclean and the marginalized dimension of the πτωχός. The πτωχός, as just the other persons mentioned on the list, illustrate those who stand on the margins of the respectable society yet are the unexpected recipients of salvation. Luke highlights that the unclean and the marginalized are those who have a dishonorable status; those who have positions outside circles of power and prestige; and those who have been excluded.

The list also shows those who are socio-economically alienated and experience socio-religious discrimination; yet, these groups are the recipients of the good news[16] and blessings[17]. They were once excluded but now are welcomed[18]. Green highlights that the "Lukan list points to the challenging dimensions of the new era Jesus proclaims, a reign that embraces those marginalized by religious leaders, those thus defined as outsiders" (1994:68). Thus, people are not to be predetermined as insiders or outsiders by the sex, family heritage, financial position, location in the city or in rural environs, religious purity, and so on. "The message of Jesus is that such status markers are no longer binding. Everyone may freely receive the grace of God. Anyone may join the community of Jesus' followers. All are welcome" (Green 1995:82).

Sanders offers a final observation; he saw the connection between the lists provided by Luke and the list of excluded persons at Qumran (1974:245-71). It is unclear whether Luke's intentions were to contradict this kind of segregation but what it is clear is that Luke intended to provide a new alternative that in some way overturned any overly narrow notion of election. Referring to this point Green highlights

> The Third Gospel emphasizes the inclusiveness of the community being created by Jesus. In this context, "the poor" has become a cipher for those of low status, for those excluded according to normal canons of status honor in the Mediterranean world. Although "poor" is hardly devoid of economic significance, for Luke this wider meaning of diminished status honor is paramount" (1994:69).

The following sections will study Luke 4:16-30; Luke 5:27-32; Luke19:1-10; Acts 2:42-47; and Acts 4:32-5:11 to explore if these texts provide insights about the mission of Jesus as the continuation of the *missio Dei* and the role the church has as part of this task in the present world, more specifically in Latin America.

Proclaiming Good News to the πτωχός (Luke 4:16-30)

To understand the mission of Jesus in the Lukan narrative, look closely at Luke 4:16-30 because this is the text that describes the opening of Jesus' public ministry. It also indicates the direction of his mission and the violent rejection by the people of Nazareth. Luke 4:14-15 summarizes a concrete representation of Jesus' ministry. Jesus interprets his baptism as a Spirit anointing for his mission. Later, citing the prophet Isaiah, Jesus provides the dimension of his missional task. The citing of Isaiah 61:1-2 and 58:9 in Luke 4:18-19 provides a framework to help understand this dimension. A more literal translation of the text illustrates its structure:

> The Spirit of the Lord is on me,
>   For he has anointed me;
> To preach good news to the poor. He has sent me:
>   To proclaim for the captives *release*,
>   and to the blind sight,
>   To send forth the oppressed in *release*;
>   To proclaim the year of the Lord's favor.

The emphasis of the word "me" at the end of the three lines highlights the identification of Jesus as "the anointed one, the regal prophetic figure who will work under the guidance of, and as empowered by, the Spirit of the Lord" (Green 1995:78).

The three subordinate clauses (to preach, to send, and to proclaim) describe Jesus' mission statement. These clauses are extensions of the statement: "To preach good news to the poor he has sent me." In other words, to preach the "good news to the poor" entails the next three descriptions that portray Luke's definition of the poor (the captive, the blind, and the oppressed) (Green 1994:73).

Luke also emphasizes the term ἄφεσις, "release," to categorize those who are "poor." The term ἄφεσις is used in a legal sense. In Luke-Acts, the term ἄφεσις entails "forgiveness or release from sin" and "freedom from the binding power of Satan" (Sloan 1992:397). Thus, "forgiveness" involves (1) the removal of the barrier that excludes sinners; providing in this way an entry back into the community[19]; and (2) "freedom from the binding power of Satan" that entails healing which also requires the removal of the social barrier excluding sinners. Therefore, "release" in Luke-Acts signifies the restoration of social status for the unclean.

As noted, the πτωχός in the Second Temple period were the unclean people, those who were cast out to the edge of society. Jesus emphasizes that to preach "good news to the poor" denotes restoring the purity of the unclean and their position in society. It also indicates embracing the widow, the unclean, the Gentile; those of the lowest status. Thus, the message of "good news" in Luke-Acts is directed to those who are socio-economically alienated and experience socio-religious discrimination; they are the recipients of this good news; they are blessed and included. Green ascertains

> It is thus evident that Jesus' mission is directed to the poor—defined not merely in subjective, spiritual or personal, economic terms, but in the holistic sense of those who are for any of a number of socio-religious reasons relegated to positions outside the boundaries of God's people. By directing his good news to these people, Jesus indicates his refusal to recognize those socially determined boundaries, asserting instead that even these "outsiders" are the objects of divine grace. Others may regard such people as beyond the pale of salvation, but God has opened a way for them to belong to God's family. (1997:211)

This reflects God's will: "God takes the side of the poor against their oppressors because God did not intend people to be poor" (Hoppe 2004:18). The πτωχός in Luke-Acts are those who, for whatever social, cultural or religious reasons, are marginalized and relegated to a place outside the boundaries of a nation; in the Luke-Acts case it was the Jewish nation.

When citing Isaiah 58:6 and 61:1-2 Luke also portrays Jesus' mission as the proclamation of the Jubilee law (cf. Lev. 25; Deut. 15). The term ἄφεσις (Hebrew יוֹבֵל *yowbel* or יֹבֵל *yobel*), twice cited in the text plus at the end of the Isaiah quotation, "the year of the Lord's favor" (that is, the year of Jubilee), shows Jesus' interest in recalling the Jubilee implications as part of his mission.

According to the Jubilee stipulation, every fiftieth year property would be returned to the original owners, debts would be canceled, and those Jews who had managed their debts by selling themselves into slavery would be released. This last point is important because it was possible for a person to "go so deeply in debt that he could negotiate no more loans because he had no possibility of repaying his outstanding debts. In such circumstances, Israelite debtors resorted to selling themselves and their families into bond slavery" (Hoppe 2004:28). According to the texts, the year of Jubilee was a reminder of the following:

God was sovereign over the land, Israel, and ultimately the whole world (Lev. 25:23). "The Year of Jubilee was a social and economic institution with a strong theological foundation. Its purpose was to bolster the economic viability of the family by ensuring that the land that had been sold would revert to the family whose economic circumstances necessitated its sale" (Hoppe 2004:32). It also implies rest for the land, allowing it to lie uncultivated. Through this practice the Israelites were taught to trust in God's provision: not by sowing, reaping, or harvesting, but by living by faith, always trusting that God will provide for their needs. This was the same teaching Jesus wanted to communicate to his disciples (Luke 12:29-31). Jubilee also has ecological implications not only to Israel but also to the church today; this is a reminder that we are stewards and caretakers of creation (the land was given to us to be preserved and cared for, not destroyed). As Howard Snyder pointed out, "the world belongs to God, not to private individuals, economic enterprises, or national governments. Therefore we have no right individually or corporately to mistreat it or claim it solely for our own interests. Human beings are stewards of what God has made" (2005:3). The Jubilee Law challenges the church to have a healthy theology of the land as Rynkiewich points out,

> (1) The church's theology would begin with the recognition of spiritual interest in the land; ultimately God owns it all and not even the church can disenfranchise God; (2) the inhabitants of the land, as well others, are admittedly a mixture of good and evil, but there is not warrant, Scriptural or cultural, for dispossession or displacement based on higher moral standing; (3) since . . . [Latin Americans] are the proper (God-given) human owners of the land, and always will be, the missionaries are guests; (4) hosts have a responsibility to seek care of guests, even uninvited guests; (5) guests have the responsibility to seek the welfare and good will of their hosts; (6) all tenure in land is based on establishing and building up relationships, not on abusing and breaking down relationships; (7) the life of the land is part of a more general system of peace and balance where healthy exchange relations exists between land (ecological care), people (social care) and God (spiritual care). (2001:228-229)

The reign of God entailed freedom or liberty from bondage (to all slaves and debtors); this was God's reminder to Israel that they were once slaves in Egypt but had been freed[20]. This also evokes economic and social implications. The restitution of each clan's patrimony as a kind of agrarian reform accompanied by a redistribution of wealth (this was a reminder of the conquest of Canaan and equitable distribution of the land as described in Joshua). Remitting all debts and redistribution of wealth are two topics that appear constantly in Luke-Acts[21].

Luke connects Jesus' mission with the Jubilee law not in its narrow sense of "releasing from debt," but in the wider sense, that is, restoring the positions of those who have once been excluded from society. The year of Jubilee was created by God in order to avoid extremes of wealth and poverty among his people. The Israelites, who were once slaves in Egypt but have now been freed by God, must not become the oppressors of the poor, but must take care of and include them into their society. The status of the poor as the discriminated groups among them must be transposed just as that of the Israelites was transposed through the Exodus. "The aliens and tenants who lived in Israel but were not native Israelites were completely dependent upon the Israelites for their economic well-being since they could not own land. They survived as farm laborers, artisans, and servants. Just so, the Israelites were to think of themselves as completely dependent upon God for their survival" (Hoppe 2004:33).

Luke's lists of people included in salvation[22] are those excluded from Israel under the Old Testament purity laws. The Old Testament Jubilee law, which is made up of Sabbath-year laws[23] and various royal decrees of amnesty or "release" involves the redistribution of real state, the cancellation of debts, the freeing of slaves, and the designation of an agricultural fallow year. Thus, the year of Jubilee that Jesus came to inaugurate has implications not only for Israel and the newborn church in Jerusalem but also for the universal church today. The kingdom expression of Jubilee has social, political, environmental, and spiritual dimensions. "Release" from captivity refers to release from "all the experiences of enslavement or imprisonment that characterizes human life" (Ringe 1985:30). Release is not just for Israel but also for all humanity who are suffering under oppression. "Release for Luke signifies wholeness, freedom from diabolic and social chains, acceptance" (Green 1995:78). In Jesus the final deliverance came not merely by freeing Israel from the oppressor's hand but also by reestablishing God's justice in Israel and, later, to the end of the world.

There are two examples in which Luke 4:21-30 helps to interpret Luke 4:16-20. First, the fact that Jesus' own town rejects him, in some ways confirms Jesus' prophetic mission and also affirms his missional message in Luke 4:16-30. Just as Elijah and Elisha were rejected as prophets, so Jesus is rejected by his people thereby confirming Jesus' status as a prophet. Second, the material used in Luke 4:25-27 is largely drawn from 1 Kings 17:8-27; 2 Kings 5:1-19 forming a parallel that Larrimore C. Crockett highlighted in his article "Luke 4:25-27 and Jewish-Gentile Relations in Luke-Acts."

> But the truth is,
> there were many widows in Israel
> in the time of Elijah . . .
> yet Elijah was sent to none of them
> except to a widow at Zarephath in Sidon.
> there were also many lepers in Israel,
> in the time of the prophet Elisha,
> and none of them were cleansed
> except Naaman the Syrian.

According to Crocket, the use of these parallel passages highlights Luke's primary concern to demonstrate Jew-Gentile relationships (1969:177-83). This parallelism shows also the neediness of the people in Israel, the divine mandate under which Elijah and Elisha worked, and the exceptional character of the recipient of their ministries (Green 1997:218). We also can see in these two texts that Elijah and Elisha are agents of healing to outsiders. Green points out,

> Elijah is sent to a woman, a non-Jew, a widow — surely a person of low status,
> Elisha encounters a non-Jew, too, a Syrian whose disease, leprosy, served as a

further marker of his socio-religious distance from the community of God's people (Leviticus 14). With these examples, Jesus underscores that "good news to the poor" embraces the widow, the unclean, the Gentile, those of the lowest status. (Green 1997:218)

Thus, Luke 4:21-30 reaffirms Jesus' missional purpose in 4:16-20 that is later extended throughout the Lukan narrative. As Crocket points out, "Not only Elijah and the widow but also Elisha and Naaman, joined in Luke 4:25-27, are models for the narrative in Acts 10-11" (1969: 81). The story of Cornelius in Acts 10 and the story of Naaman in Luke 4:25-27 has many parallels that reaffirms God's plan of salvation and inclusion to all. This shows that the inclusion of gentiles in the salvation of God along with Jews creates the necessity and the opportunity for fellowship together, including table fellowships.

In sum, Luke 4:16-30 provides Jesus' public and inaugural speech that introduces his missional agenda. It is this agenda that Luke follows by carefully selecting the right material to show throughout the rest of the Gospel of Luke and Acts how this message of "good news to the poor" is fulfilled in the person and work of Jesus Christ and later through the church. The next section will delineate what Jesus' embrace of tax-collectors as he preaches "good news to the πτωχός" implies about the church's theology, ecclesiology an missiology.

Jesus and the Tax Collectors (Luke 5:27-32; 19:1-10)

It seems ironic that Jesus, having been anointed to proclaim good news to the poor as his missionary agenda, is repeatedly found visiting the homes of the wealthy[24]. However, for Luke poverty is not necessarily related to economic stability. The πτωχοί are those who for some reason have been cast out, discriminated against or segregated from the core of the society. As previously stated, the Old Testament purity laws categorized sinners or the impure as those who had certain occupations, had some health problem, or belonged to a nation other than Israel. Therefore, it is obvious that in the Lukan world there were other factors besides money that made a person be an insider or an outsider, accepted or discriminated from the society. "Status honor is a measure of social standing, family heritage, ethnicity, vocation, religious purity, and gender. In the Greco-Roman world, then, poverty is too narrowly defined when understood solely in economic terms" (Green 1994:64). Jesus' vocation of "proclaiming good news to the poor" embraced not only the economically oppressed but also the excluded and disadvantaged in society.

The Romans contracted the collection of taxes to individuals by requiring contractors to pay the taxes that were due. These contractors or "tax collectors" were then free to use appropriate means to collect money to reimburse themselves at a profit (Stambaugh and Balch 1986:71). Most people assumed that the contractors enriched themselves at the expense of their fellow Jews (Luke 3:12-13). Therefore tax collectors, despite their wealth, were segregated from and discriminated against by the Jewish society (Luke 19:7). Pharisees and teachers of the law even categorized tax collectors as "sinners"[25].

In Luke 5:27-32 and 19:1-10 we have two stories that share a number of parallels. Both stories depict Jesus' encounter with a tax collector and both portray the low status of a tax collector, classifying them as "sinners" (5:30; 19:7). Both stories also describe behavioral changes in the tax collector as a result of the encounter with Jesus: Levi left everything, followed Jesus, and offered a feast in Jesus' honor. Zacchaeus made fourfold restitution to those he had defrauded and gave half of his goods to the poor. Finally, both accounts provide clear insights about Jesus' mission: "I have not come to call the righteous but sinners to repentance" (5:32); and "For the Son of Man came to seek and to save the lost" (19:10).

Jesus' ministry challenged the social structure of his time. A social structure that classified as sinful those who were outsiders, or those whose "behavior departs from the norms of an identified group whose boundaries are established with reference to characteristic conduct" (Dunn 1988:264-89). Jesus' inclusive attitude toward the so-called "sinners" and outcasts from the Jewish society (in this case the tax collectors) illustrates a status reversal in the society. Those who were excluded are now included; the outcasts from society are restored to their status. This reaffirms Jesus' missional goal that the gospel is directed to the groups who are cast outside of the boundaries of society as unclean. The gospel is the restoration of status for the outcast in society. The gospel also challenges the social structures that force the people off of their lands, and encourages the current land owners to: (1) return the land to those from whom it was taken, (2) care for the land in a responsible way, (3) care for the guests who are in the land, (4) build solid communities and relationships, and (5) establish healthy relations between the land, the people and God.

The Role of Possessions in Response to God's Visitation

In both stories (Luke 5:27-32 and 19:1-10) Levi and Zacchaeus' respond positively to Jesus' invitation. (Levi left everything he had and followed Jesus [5:28] and Zacchaeus gave half of his possessions to the poor and promised to make restitution for anything he had defrauded.) However, Luke-Acts also portrays several stories where the love of possessions stands in the way of following Jesus and, in some ways, to receiving salvation. The rich ruler story (Luke 18:18-29), for example, provides a negative response to Jesus' call.

There are also several parallels between the story of Zacchaeus and the rich ruler. Zacchaeus is a 'ruling" tax collector, the second man is a ruler. According to the story the ruler keeps the commandments, while Zacchaeus is considered a "sinner." The ruler is counseled to sell all he has and give to the poor; Zacchaeus sells half of his possessions and gives to the poor. The ruler is very wealthy; Zacchaeus is wealthy. We also see Jesus' point at the end of each story, "Who then can be saved?" (Luke 18:26) and "Today, salvation has come to this house" (Luke 19:9).

It appears that what makes the difference between Zacchaeus and the rich ruler was their response to their possessions. In some ways the role possessions plays in one person's life determines their self-identity, their worldview, and their salvation. Luke T. Johnson, in his book *Sharing Possessions: Mandate and Symbol of Faith,* affirms that "the way people regard owning things and the values they attach to possessions involve the ways they think about human nature (or human freedom in the world), about the place of humans within the world, and about the relationship of human beings and the Word of God" (1981:7). Luke portrays possessions as a symbol of human freedom and argues that the way a person disposes of possessions symbolizes the way he or she responds to God's call.

Even though Zacchaeus was wealthy, his wealth was not a source of security before or apart from God. "The chief characteristic of Zacchaeus is not that he is wealthy but, in contrast to the ruler, that he is (1) a social outcast who is (2) willing to put his money in the service of the needy through his generosity" (Green 1994:72). So, the problem is not to having possessions but it is instead the role that those possessions play in one's life. The real difficulty regarding possessions lies in what they mean to the bearer. Loving money can be an obstacle between people and God and this was precisely what happened with the rich ruler. His struggle was not with his wealth but that he identified his very existence with the security he thought came from having these possessions. It is the service to possessions that is the evil and it is that service which prevents people from responding to the call of God. In Luke 16:13, Jesus says, "you cannot serve God and mammon." Mammon became an idolatrous power, something to which the people's service was misdirected instead of serving God. "It is the self-aggrandizing use of money which renders it idolatrous. Currency is indeed a human invention, but only when it is worshipped does it become "the work of human hands" as an idol" (Johnson 1981:64). For Zacchaeus, salvation meant being set free from the slavery to mammon; his (partial) renunciation of wealth demonstrates that devotion to possessions would not rule his life (Powell 1998:106).

Going one step farther, what really made a difference in Zacchaeus' life was not only the place wealth had in his heart but also his generous response to care for the poor, the needy, and service to justice. In so doing, Zacchaeus enjoyed salvation through giving. Luke described the spiritual effects of giving earlier in the gospel when Jesus told the disciples to give alms with the expectation that this will bring "treasure in heaven" (Luke 12:32-33). Jesus was not merely expecting his disciples to have a proper attitude toward wealth and social position; Jesus was looking for action as a sign of repentance; for concrete acts of benevolence toward the poor (Luke 18:22; and also 3:10-14). In some ways, those who neglect their duty to care for the poor are expelled from salvation (as in the rich ruler's case). The salvation of Jesus is the divine status reversal: those who were excluded from the society are now included (in Luke 19:9 Jesus called Zacchaeus son of Abraham) and those who excluded them are now, themselves, excluded.

Luke highlights that "the good news to the poor" embraces the widow, the unclean, the Gentile, those of the lowest status. Luke 4:16-30; 5:27-32; and 19:1-10 point to Jesus' mission as opening the way for the inclusion of the people in God's dominion who otherwise had no apparent claim to God. They had been made outsiders in the social systems of the ancient Mediterranean world. They were the πτωχοί to whom Jesus proclaimed the good news (Green 1994:74). They became the included, accepted and blessed.

Almsgiving and Hospitality

In the Levi and Zacchaeus stories, Jesus was eating and sharing with tax collectors. In fact, some of the Lukan material portrays Jesus' table fellowship as the context in which he carried out social intercourse and teaching (Green 1995:87). Sharing a meal with them was a way Jesus included the outcast but it was also a way in which Jesus' cared for people's physical needs (providing food for the hungry). According to Douglas, however, sharing food encodes messages about hierarchy, inclusion and exclusion, boundaries and crossing boundaries. Therefore, mealtime was a social event whose significance far outdistanced the need to satisfy one's hunger (1975:249-75). To be refused at the table by others signified exclusion from an identified group.

The list of excluded people (maimed, lame, and blind) in Luke 14:13 and 21 (excepting the poor) has special significance since these are the types of "blemishes" found in Leviticus 21:18 as prohibiting participation in the cult of Israel. As I mentioned before, the Qumran also states that people with these characteristics were considered unworthy of and therefore were excluded from the eschatological and Messianic Banquet (1Qsa 2:5-6 and 1QM 7:4-5). Jesus challenges these exclusive notions by welcoming people to the table as a way of extending to them intimacy, solidarity, and acceptance. Once at the table, Jesus' companions were treated as part of his family (Zacchaeus was called "son of Abraham") and his kingdom (Zacchaeus received salvation in his house). This welcoming attitude of Jesus has ecclesiological and missiological implications. "Jesus gave his life so that persons could be welcomed into the kingdom and in doing so linked hospitality, grace, and sacrifice in the deepest and most personal way imaginable" (Pohl 1999:29). The church is the household of God and as such should embrace all people, especially those who society has segregated.

The early church understood that sharing meals was a common practice of welcoming strangers into fellowship, the community and the kingdom of God. There are several examples of sharing meals in Luke 11-15, demonstrating the importance of this practice in understanding Luke's view. It was a practice to remember that the Lord became the central social and religious activity of the early Christian community. While people of means within the community might provide the meal, the "guest list" was to be inclusive and no special places of honor were to be reserved for the elite. On the contrary, the host ought to provide a special welcome for the poor. Offering care to strangers became one of the distinguishing marks of the authenticity of the Christian gospel and of the church.[26]

It can also be said that the idea of redemptive almsgiving plays a key factor in the Lukan literature. For instance, in Luke 11:37-42, Jesus criticizes the Pharisees and urges them to "give for alms those things that are within" (v. 41). This phrase has implications with "justice and the love of God" (v. 42). Thus, what Jesus says in 11:40-41 is that purity is revealed by almsgiving. Later in 12:13-34, especially verses 33-34, Jesus urges almsgiving to avoid greed (v. 15). If one puts one's treasure in heaven, one's heart will be set on heavenly things. There is a similar urging to give alms in 18:18-30. The command to sell possessions and give to the poor in 18:22 is followed by "and come follow me" (18:22). In each case, 12:33 and 18:22, "to sell one's possessions and give is the mark of true discipleship" (Pilgrim 1981:135). Finally, in 19:1-10, the indication of tax collector Zacchaeus' turn to faith in Jesus is his distribution to the poor (v. 8). Jesus responded to Zacchaeus' behavior of alms giving by declaring him a son of Abraham (v. 9) although he had previously been marginalized at the edge of Jewish society. Thus, inheriting the Jewish idea of redemptive almsgiving, Luke grasps it as an act of purifying sins and a mark of discipleship.

Welcoming the stranger, caring for the poor and needy, giving alms, embracing the sinners, setting free the oppressed and healing the sick are all part of Jesus' missional goal and describe what the phrase "good news to the poor" means. Based on Acts 2:42-47 and 4:32-5:11, how should the Christian church use Jesus' missiological example as part of its ecclesiological identity.

One Heart and Soul as the Church's Characteristics (Acts 2:42-47 and 4:32-37)

There is a lot of discussion between scholars regarding the veracity of the events narrated in these texts

> All the believers were together and had everything in common. Selling their possessions and goods, they gave to anyone as he had need. (Acts 2:43-45)

> All the believers were one in heart and mind. No one claimed that any of his possessions was his own, but they shared everything they had...there were no needy persons among them. For from time to time those who owned lands or houses sold them, and put it at the apostles' feet, and it was distributed to anyone as he had need. (Acts 4:32, 34-35)

Scholars ask: Did the early Christians practice the sort of commonality described here, or is it a fictional reconstruction of the life of the early church on the part of the author? Some scholars affirm that what is described here is too close to the ideal community of certain Hellenistic traditions. It is not my intention to show the agreements or disagreements regarding the authenticity of the facts narrated in the texts studied. What I see in these passages is a community where people relinquished their possessions, not for the sake of renunciation, but for the sake of those in need. Study of the texts also shows that not everybody sold their house or all of their possessions since they continued using some of their houses for meetings and fellowship. "They broke bread in their homes and ate together with glad and sincere hearts" (Acts 2:46). I am suggesting that these passages portray not an ideal but in actuality depict the result of the Holy Spirit's presence in their community.

In Acts 2:42, "they devoted themselves to the apostles' teaching and to the fellowship, to the breaking of bread and to prayer." Here Luke used the word κοινωνία, "*koinonia*" that means fellowship, association, community, communion, joint participation, interaction, or brotherhood. In this passage, *koinonia* means not only fellowship toward each other, but also sharing. In most of the cases this expression is used in the New Testament in connection with material goods. *Koinonia* is not simply a spiritual sharing; it is a total sharing that includes the material as well as the spiritual. "Luke sees the sharing of all possessions as the natural and inevitable corollary of life together. In the perfect unity of mind and heart established by the Spirit, only a full sharing of goods could function as an adequate expression of that interior oneness" (Johnson 1997:187).

Koinonia as a Christian expression is not only present in the Luke-Acts literature but also in the Pauline and Johanine literature. "In Acts 4:34, Luke observes that the problem of destitution did not exist in the first Christian community of Jerusalem since the members of that community shared their food and possessions" (Hoppe 2004:155). In Acts, Luke does not focus on the destitute who need charity, but he describes the actions of the first Christians that eliminated poverty from their community. It looks like the Christian church assumed the *koinonia* practice as part of its ecclesiological identity that described not only the Jerusalem community, but something that, fully practiced or not, was still part of the self-understanding of the universal Church.

Acts 2:42-47 and 4:32-37 shows that their sharing all goods in common and calling nothing their own directly expressed the spiritual unity of the believers; exemplifying in this way an authentic Jubilee community. In doing that the church embraced the mission Jesus began in Luke 4:18-19. The church became an agent of justice, mercy and truth for their time. As an agent of justice the church became a place of belonging for the outcasts and the strangers; the church became a community of spiritual, emotional and physical support for the poor and needy. In doing that the church proved to be authentic communicators of Jesus' gospel of "good news to the poor." This good news has both eschatological and present implications.

A narrow reading of Luke's description in Acts 2:43-45 and 4:32, 34-35 will view these texts as ideal for an eschatological reality but not for the present reality of the Jerusalem and universal church. I disagree with such reading; I assume that what Luke is describing in these passages is an example of what salvation looks like in his own view. The other synoptic Gospels see the accomplishment of salvation in Jesus' death on the cross; in Luke's gospel, however, Jesus saves people throughout the story. Since the beginning of Luke's story, Jesus is introduced by the angel as "a Savior" (Luke 2:11). Jesus was already a Savior from the day of his birth. In Luke-Acts salvation is tied less to Jesus' death than to his life (Powell 1998:105). This is precisely what makes the Luke-Acts narrative unique, Luke affirms the Christian hope for eternal life in "the age to come" (18:30), but in general he places more emphasis on the life that is possible here and now. We can see this in several verses, uniquely in the Third Gospel, that make use of the word *today*. "Today . . . a Savior is born"

(2:11); "Today . . . this scripture is fulfilled" (4:21); "Today . . . we have seen strange things" (5:26); "Today . . . I must stay at your house" (19:5); "Today . . . salvation has come to this house" (19:9); "Today . . . you will be with me in Paradise" (23:43).

For Luke, salvation happens now and has future as well as present implications. The Gospel of Luke emphasizes the present consequences of God's saving action. Salvation for Luke is not limited to the spiritual sphere; salvation can mean reception of sight (18:42) or to a leper it means being made clean (17:19). To others it may mean the reception of such blessings as peace (2:14) or forgiveness (7:48) or the removal of various infirmities (6:10; 8:48). Salvation in Luke is essentially liberation. Luke makes no distinction between what might be construed as physical, spiritual, or social aspects of salvation. Forgiving sins, healing diseases, and feeding the hungry are all saving acts (Powell 1998:106).

Thus, the description of the Jerusalem community in Acts 2:42-47 and 4:32-37 is nothing other than the present exemplification of the saving power of Jesus operating in the community under the direction of the Holy Spirit. This is not an eschatological ideal; it was a present reality for the church of Jerusalem as well as a present reality for the universal church that includes us . . . today.

Summary

The words "poor" and *pobre* most often used in Bible translations of the Lukan literature do not represent the best choices of words to describe the social, political, economic and spiritual reality of either the Greco-Roman world or Latin America. Perhaps it is better to use words like the marginalized, the cast out, the oppressed, the captive, those who are segregated by the socio-economic, religious, and political systems, and those who are voiceless. Poverty in Latin America can mean social, spatial, economic, political and spiritual marginality. Like in the Bible, poverty in Latin America does not happen on its own; it occurs because people make it happen. The *pobre* in Latin America have only one choice and that is to depend upon God. This is where the Church, God's agents and own heart, must take an initiative to integrally address the questions and needs of a continent that suffers.

The Third Gospel and the book of Acts present the Gospel and mission of Jesus Christ as "good news to the poor." Luke defines πτωχός as the socially, politically and religiously segregated; the outcasts; the marginalized; those who live in social, political, and spiritual oppression and in the margins of society. In Jesus' mission he embraced them and welcomed them into the community and into his kingdom that he is inaugurating. Luke portrays God's salvation as a present reality that has present implications. Salvation can mean several things for different people: It can mean healing for the sick; freedom and liberation for the captive; forgiveness for the sinner; inclusion for the excluded; economic and physical well-being for the needy. The Christian Church in Jerusalem embraced Jesus' Gospel of "good news for the poor" and responded to the needs of the community by sharing their goods and eliminating poverty.[27] Luke presents this example not as an ideal for the Jerusalem church but as a true reality for the universal church, implying that once the church is filled with the Holy Spirit and understands its role in the world, it can become an agent of change, justice, mercy and truth.

Luke-Acts portrays missiological and ecclesiological implications relevant for the church around the world and specifically for the church in Third World countries. It is not my goal in this chapter to deal with these implications, as they will be studied more closely in Chapter 7; however, the International Congress on World Evangelism, held in Lausanne Switzerland in 1974, provided a confession that is compatible with these Lukan implications. Paragraph 5 of the Lausanne Covenant states

> We affirm that God is both the Creator and the Judge of all men. We therefore should share his concern for justice and reconciliation throughout human society and for the liberation of men from every kind of oppression. Because mankind is made in the image of God, every person, regardless of race, religion, color, culture, class, sex or age, has an intrinsic dignity because of which he should be respected and served, not exploited. Here too we express penitence both for our neglect and for having sometimes regarded evangelism and social concern as mutually exclusive. . . . The message of salvation implies also a message of judgment upon every form of alienation, oppression and discrimination, and we should not be afraid to denounce evil and injustice wherever they exist. When people receive Christ they are born again into his kingdom and must seek not only to exhibit but also to spread its righteousness in the midst of an unrighteous world. The salvation we claim should be transforming us in the totality of our personal and social responsibilities. Faith without works is dead (Padilla 1976).

Luke-Acts also presents an opportunity for response on the part of the wealthy nations (First World countries) and wealthy individuals within the Third World countries. A person's or a nation's response to God is the most fundamental of all responses, and thus a most important possession. If people are filled with the terror of nonbeing and the threat of worthlessness, and see their lives as that which must be constructed and then possessed; if the security given by things (no matter whether material or spiritual) becomes a god, then people have no choice but to cling to what they possess. It becomes very difficult for people to detach themselves from their possessions because they are what they own. On the other hand, if people are able to acknowledge that life comes at every moment from God and that identity and worth are established, not by what people can seize but by what has been given in grace, then people can escape from being defined by what they own (materially and/or spiritually). People can be free from the tyranny of possessing. People can be free from the distortion of idolatry and see all things as they really are—neither gods, nor the measure of human worth, but gracious gifts from the hand of God (Johnson 1981:80).

A more complete appreciation of "the poor" in the Third Gospel embraces Luke's concern for the economically destitute but also recognizes how economic concerns must be integrated more fully into an understanding of the human condition and social dynamics in the first-century Roman world. The mission of Jesus in Luke goes to those on the outside; this must be the mission of the church today as well.

This Lukan understanding supports this investigation in three ways: a). Luke-Acts provides an evaluation of the Latin American churches' theology of mission; b). Luke-Acts provides a model of mission for the Latin American churches; and c). Luke-Acts will question and challenge the actual Latin American churches and the way they are doing mission.

The next chapter, Chapter 4, will look at where the church in Latin America stands today in their missiological and ecclesiological response to the gospel and to the continent. Chapters 4, 5 and 6 will provide the basis for Chapter 7, which will provide a synergy between the reading of Luke-Acts and the analysis of the churches in Latin America. In one way Luke-Acts will evaluate how the church is doing mission and in another way, the church in Latin America's method of doing mission will provide new lenses through which to read Luke-Acts. The following graphic (Figure 4) illustrates this tension.

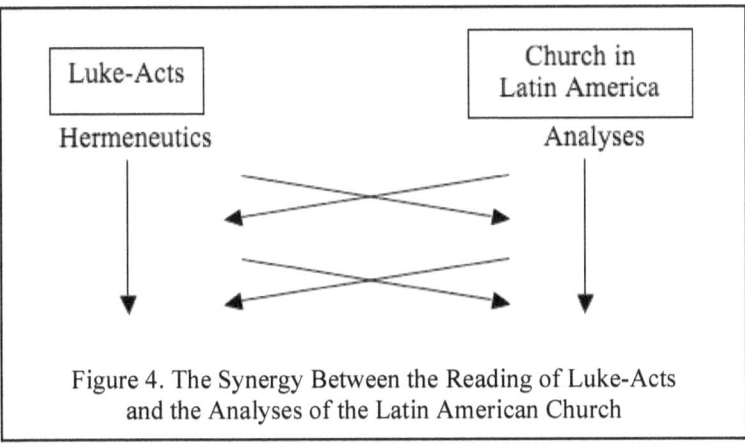

Figure 4. The Synergy Between the Reading of Luke-Acts and the Analyses of the Latin American Church

Notes

1. This is an anthropological dualism that compartmentalizes the person into body–soul entities. This dualism reduces the role of the church's ministry to a mere spiritual dimension, neglecting social, political, economic and environmental participation.

2. The Christian tradition is largely dualist (body vs. soul). There is a type of dualism that prevails in Latin America, one that derived from the philosophy of Descartes—the dualism between the human (the thinking subject) and the world (the object of thought). As this developed, there was less space for God as the transcendent being who has the power to act in history and in nature.

3. Luke 2:11, 26; 3:15; 4:41; 9:20; 20:41; 22:67; 23:2, 35, 39; 24:26, 46 and Acts 2:31, 36, 38; 3:6, 18, 20; 4:10; 5:42; 8:5,12; 9:22, 34; 10:36, 48; 11:17; 15:26; 16:18; 17:3; 18:5, 28; 24:24; 26:23; 28:31.

4. Luke 6:24-36; 10:29-37; 12:16-21; 13:10-13; 14:1-6; 15:8-32; 17:1-19; 18:9-14; 19:1-10.
5. Bible paraphrase written in "Contemporary Language."
6. Gen. 1:9; Ex. 14:21; Joshua 4:18,22; Isaiah 43:2; Neh. 9:11; Lev. 25:23; Jonah 1:13, 2:10
7. Gen. 24:7, 31:3, 34:1; Ex. 2:22; 14:3; 18:3; Ps. 137:4
8. Gen. 34:21, 45:18; Ex. 3:17, 13:5, 33:3; Lev. 20:24, 25:19, 26:4; Nu. 14:8, 16:14; Deut. 6:3, 11:9,17, 26:15, 27:3; Joshua 5:6; Jer. 11:5, 32:22; Deut. 33:28; II Kings 18:32; Isaiah 36:17
9 Gen. 8:14,24; Lev. 18:25, 19:29, 25:2, 19, 35:33, 35:34; Deut. 11:17, 21:23, 24:4, 32:43; Jer. 3:1, 3:2, 3:9, 4:20, 12:4; Eze. 14:13; Hos. 1:2, 4:3; II Chr. 7:14, 36:21; Judges 3:11; Job 31:38; Isaiah 24:11; Joel 1:10; Zech. 12:12
10. Gen. 13:6, 34:21; Ex. 1:7, 23:9; Lev. 25:2; II Chr. 7:14, 36:21; Eze. 39:1
11. Matthew 9:10,11; 11:19; Mark 2:15, 16; Luke 5:30; 15:1; 18:13
12. Lev. 19:9-10, 33-34 and 23:22
13. 14:22-29; 24:14-15; and 26:12-15.
14. Deut. 10:18-19; 24:22; 26:12-15.
15. "Poverty" was defined as the condition of a person who barely subsists from day to day, earns only enough money to feed himself and his family and to take care of a few basic needs, and lives without hope of setting aside some resources to improve his lot in life.
16. Luke 4:16-36; 7:18-23
17. Luke 6:20-26
18. Luke 14:12-14, 15-24; 16:19-31
19. Luke 5:31-32; 7:36-50; 15:3-31; 19:1-10; and Acts 15:8-9
20. Lev. 25:42-55; Deut. 15:15
21. Luke 6:33; 11: 42; 12:30-33; 16:1-15; Acts 2:44-45; 4:32-37
22. Luke 4:18; 6:20; 7:22; 14:13, 21; 16: 20, 22
23. Ex. 21:2-6; 23:10-11; and Deut. 15:1-18
24. e.g., Luke 5:29; 7:36; 14:1; 19:5
25. Luke 5:30; cf. 7:34; 15:1: 18:11; 19:7
26. See "1 Apology of Justin," ch.14, p.167 and ch. 67, p.186, ANF, vol.1. Also Aristedes, "Apology," ch. 15, ANF, vol. 9, p.277. Also, Tertullian, "The Prescription Against Heretics," ch. 20, ANF, vol. 3, p.252.
27. The integral understanding of salvation and the Christian response to human needs are conclusions that liberation theologians highlighted in the past. Some of the points describing this view are found in Gustavo Gutierrez's book *A Theology of Liberation*, Jon Sobrino's book *Christology at the Crossroads*, and Leonardo and Clodovis Boff's books *Introducing Liberation Theology* and *Salvation and Liberation*.

Chapter 4

Theology and Praxis of Mission among Selected Roman Catholic Churches

This chapter will explore the actual theology and praxis of mission of selected Roman Catholic Church in four Latin American countries: Mexico, Colombia, Peru, and Argentina. This analysis in this chapter is divided into four main sections: theology and praxis of mission of the Roman Catholic Church in Mexico, in Colombia in Peru and in Argentina, based upon 16 field research interviews made with Roman Catholic priests in those countries[1]. Some of the interviewees' names have been changed according to their request for privacy.

For the purposes of this report I have integrated the interview content in each country. I will first provide a general description of the church's structure in each country and then of each parish represented. I will then discuss the social and environmental involvement of each parish. I will share (1) the biblical basis from which each priest operates, (2) the order of work and (3) the way it addresses theological issues. I will conclude with general statements and observations based upon the interviews. Finally, I will attempt to compare and contrast my findings, highlighting similarities and differences between the countries.

Roman Catholic Church in Mexico

The Roman Catholic Church in the Archdiocese of Mexico City is divided into eight vicariates that are subdivided into 65 *decanatos*, "decant." Each *decanato* is comprised of ten parishes. A monsignor leads each *decanato* and the archdiocese is lead by an archbishop.

Structurally the Roman Catholic Church in Mexico follows a common missiological and evangelistic plan that comes directly from the Vatican.

However each parish is free to develop its own pastoral plan and strategy and is responsible for its implementation.

In Mexico City, I interviewed four Roman Catholic priests. The following chart (Table 4) summarizes the general information about each of the priests that I interviewed and their corresponding parish.

Table 4. Roman Catholic Priests/Parishes Interviewed in Mexico				
Name	José Antonio RAMIREZ	Manuel FERRER	Benjamin HERRERA	Sergio Oliba MARTINEZ
Experience/ Position	Priest	Theologian teacher Mexico & Loyola / Priest	Priest	Monsignor
Nationality	Mexican	Mexican	Mexican	Mexican
Age	Mid-forties	Mid-fifties	Early thirties	Early Sixties
Parish	Inmaculado Corazón de Maria	La Virgen de Guadalupe	La Asunción de Maria	La Santa Cruz de Jerusalem
Denomination	Roman Catholic	Roman Catholic	Roman Catholic	Roman Catholic
Social Background	Middle-low	Middle	Middle-high	Middle-high

I chose these dioceses because these were the priests that were willing to provide an interview. I also chose them because they represented different social backgrounds that in some ways provide a glimpse of Roman Catholicity in Mexico. It should be noted that several priests refused to be interviewed without prior authorization from their superiors.

According to Ramirez (*Inmaculado Corazón de Maria* Parish), Christians in Mexico, just as in other parts of the world, need re-evangelization. He said, "We have millions baptized but few believers who are practicing." He reports that 85 percent of the so-called "Roman Catholic believers" have no commitment to the church or to its mission. Most of the people are from a Catholic tradition and come to church just on the holy days. Ramirez thinks that the reason for this lack of involvement is based on a deficiency in their faith formation, especially within the family settings. Despite this, they have a few members who have a strong commitment to the church and to its pastoral work.

All four interviewees emphasized that their church is following *El Sistema Integral de Nueva Evangelización* called SINE,[2] "Integral System of New Evangelization," that started in the beginning of the1990s. The main goal of SINE is to bring the church to the people rather than to wait for them to come to the church. This is what Benjamin Herrera describes as "decentralization of worship." In addition to using their church building, Herrera's parish has established a tent where the church holds services, in this way providing a common place close to the people and their neighborhoods.

Manuel Ferrer from *La Virgen de Guadalupe* parish highlights the importance of the SINE. The vicariate in which the parish is part has implemented a local diagram of work called the *Plan San Marcos*, "Saint Mark Plan." He describes this plan as the intent to see the church and its work as *una iglesia organica*, "an organic church." This means that it is to be a community of fellowship. In order to accomplish this goal the parish provides spiritual retreats where they teach parishioners evangelistic skills to do their missionary work. In most of the cases, the work is done by visiting people in their homes. This is called *una Iglesia Domiciliaria*, "a Domiciliary Parish." This serves the same purpose of bringing the church to the people; ministering where the people are, in their own environment.

Ramirez's parish, *Inmaculado Corazón de Maria*, has implemented a similar system, utilizing a program aimed at teaching religious formation. *El Colegio Biblico*, "Biblical School," is a series of classes led by priests who prepare specific church members, who in turn teach the rest of the members. "The laity are the agents of evangelization," points out Ramirez. "In order to perform this task we need to spend time working on the foundation, so we need to have spiritual (charismatic) retreats." The retreats have three main focuses: Baptism, Renewal of Confirmation, and Communion. The main goal is to lead ordinary Christians into a personal relationship with Jesus, a living Jesus. Ramirez continues, "We introduce the Son of God incarnated, made as one of us, for us; he is a Lord of love, mercy, and forgiveness." The retreats focus on changing the parishioners' image of a God: from an image of *un Dios policia*, "a police God," to a God who is loving and kind, the one with whom a relationship is possible. Ramirez said he and his workers are conscious that changes are not instantaneous; they know that conversion is a process. What they are hoping to do is provide believers with a practical faith, a faith that can be shared through intensive evangelism. This intensive evangelism is played out when believers set out in pairs (one to share and the other to pray) for door-to-door evangelism twice a year. Evangelism is understood here as sharing in person what God has done in the life of the believers, inviting the people to be part of the small groups of the Christian community.

The *Inmaculado Corazón de Maria* parish is comprised of small groups where the believers can be integrated and find a place of belonging, following the model of the Base Communities in Brazil. "Most of these communities are successful because people know each other," reports Ramirez. The church began to work with this system six years ago and they now have 17 small groups that meet every week. They follow this plan: 30 minutes of fellowship and prayer (worship and thanksgiving) followed by 60 minutes of biblical classes where they go deep in their faith and doctrinal formation. These groups are led by committed members of the parish who are willing to take the classes provided by the church *programas de estudio biblico*, "Biblical Study program." These smalls groups have been effective in reaching the community; they began with three groups and now they have 17 groups (each group is composed by no less than eight members and no more than 15). "The goal to have this size of group is to promote participation and fellowship among the members," Ramirez said.

Ramirez believes that the key to the success of his parish is its focus on the new generation, in other words its work with young parents. According to Ramirez, some measurements of success in his parish are: the numerical growth and the level of involvement of the parents within the church family and fellowship, plus the commitment of the members in the life of the church.

It should be pointed out that not all the parishes are involved in the SINE. For example, of the ten parishes that make up the *decanato* to which the *Inmaculado Corazón de Maria* parish belongs, only three are working on the process of intense evangelism and the formation of small communities. "The others are just content with the traditional Church and Sacraments," says Ramirez, "but we need to live out our faith in a practical way."

Social Involvement

In response to my questions about the involvement of the churches in social issues, the interviewees agreed that this was an area that belongs to the government, and the church should be careful about being involved in areas that are not its own. As Ferrer from the *Virgen de Guadalupe* parish pointed out, "The church should be about its business and the government about theirs. The church in Mexico is very clear in what its role is." Ferrer explained that experiences in the past have shown that when the church was involved in some social and political issues, the image of both the church and the gospel deteriorated. In some cases the church succumbed to corruption by sometimes misappropriating funds and similar activities. In other cases, the church has been categorized as communistic and supporting subversive practices.

Ferrer points out that some theologians, like Arturo Pauline in his books *The Person, the World and God* and *Dialogue of Liberation,* write about the aspects of sharing goods. According to Ferrer, this is a strong topic in Latin America because this view can result in a person taking a political position as happened in archbishop Oscar Romero's case in El Salvador[3], whom Ferrer claims was the only one allowed by the pope to take this view. When Pope John Paul II came to Mexico "he told us to be careful with liberation theology."

Ferrer states that there is a Latin American version of the Bible that is written in a social language that is not totally theological. This can be dangerous because it can lead to political areas rather than biblical ones. Martinez of *La Santa Cruz de Jerusalem* parish agrees. According to Martinez, "Economic and political power were the main problems of the church in the past." Today, there is fear that the church can become involved in issues that do not relate to it. It is for this reason, Martinez claims, that liberation theology was blocked in Mexico. It has not been allowed to flourish.

Despite this understanding, Ferrer affirms that there is room for the church to provide social, economic and spiritual support but this must happen in the core of the Christian community. For instance, there is a community in Guadalajara called *Santa Cecilia* where people share everything; similar with a community in Taize, France, where people share all their possessions. "These communities are one hundred percent what a community should be like and are models for us today," he said.

Ferrer's own parish has established a medical service. They also are working on putting in place other social development projects where the main goal is more than providing one-way economic help, but attempting to create a conscience of self-improvement and development.

Some parishes have established a few programs that deal with social issues. For example, the parish *Inmaculado Corazón de Maria* led by Ramirez has a program that helps with issues of social justice. The church provides relief to those who have been victims of social injustice. For instance, a young man from his parish was mistakenly accused of stealing a car; the church took up a collection to economically help his family. With the money collected the family paid the lawyers allowing the young man to be freed. There have been more cases like this where the church was directly involved. "Our main goal is not only to support the people with prayers but also to help them economically or materially according to their need," Ramirez remarked.

Herrera from the *Asuncion de Maria* parish sees the church as a living community, a dynamic agent, a promising entity, and an evangelistic force, whose main goal should be to help people in an integral way. He believes that salvation should deal with the whole person, covering all the human dimensions. "We cannot pretend to save the soul and forget the body. Salvation must be integral." However, when I asked about the involvement of the church in social issues, he admitted that this is an area of weakness in his parish.

All of the people interviewed agree that just providing material assistance is not enough to meet the needs of the people. "The essence of the social life is love," affirms Herrera, so to provide support to the needy without helping them develop some skills to support themselves would be more damaging than helpful.

Environmental Involvement

None of the churches interviewed have an established environmental plan. Some of the priests believe that it would be good to be involved in this area but their parishes are not working directly on it. Some adhere to the idea that this is an area that belongs to the government and not to the church.

Biblical Basis for Their Work

Although most of the parishes interviewed have theological and biblical convictions, they do not have a specific biblical foundation that describes their philosophy of work; instead they follow some basis and philosophy of work that is provided by the Church of Rome.

When I asked about their understanding of "the poor" in Luke 4:18-19, most of their answers referred to "poor" as a spiritual dimension. For instance, Ramirez, sees the "poor" as more than disadvantaged economically but poor religiously and culturally as well. In his parish, he points out, "we have many people who are poor economically but also very poor in faith. We also have a lot of people who are economically rich but poor in the religious culture."

Ferrer from the *Virgen de Guadalupe* parish thinks that the Luke 4 text has relevance in the sacerdotal ordination. He said the text made reference to the "anointed one" and it also talks about the course of justice. "The grace of God cannot be given in a world where Justice is not present." In fact, Ferrer claims that this text provides dignity to the priesthood. Herrera from *Asuncion de Maria* parish, however, believes that the text has missiological implications: "As Jesus has been sent, we are also sent. This has implications not only for the priest but also for all believers." He believes in the *sacerdocio de todos los creyentes*, "priesthood of all believers," as agents of mission and change in the society. Martinez from *La Santa Cruz de Jerusalem* parish similarly claims that "the text provides a summary of Jesus' mission and this is the mission the church needs to fulfill."

In regard to the understanding of Acts 2:42-47 and Acts 4:32-5:11, Ramirez from the *Inmaculado Corazón de Maria* parish thinks that these texts are "the grand utopia of the faith." Explaining this statement he points out, "If you do not work, you do not appreciate. We cannot give people help unless we teach them how to work and appreciate what they have. Otherwise, giving can result in more damage than benefit." Referring to these texts Herrera comments, "Love is the characteristic of the first community. We are trying to find the same model, not necessarily in a literal sense, but in something that can be applicable in principle." For Martinez, these texts represent "a model for our churches. This is our ideal, to create small communities where the love of God is present." Martinez says the church plays a key role in the community. "If we try to change the structure we need to remember that the gospel has deeper dimensions. We need to provide the means to change people's lives first and later the social structures will be changed as well." In other words, creating small communities like those described in Acts 2 and 4 will eventually bring change to larger social structures.

Theological Issues

Ferrer from the *Virgen de Guadalupe* parish believes that the mission and a theology of the church must begin with the leadership. Physical health plus emotional health equals spiritual health is an equation that every minister and layperson must follow. In addition, the church needs to be aware of the changes taking place within the society in order to provide a realistic and relevant pastoral plan that deals with the needs and questions the society is raising. "Christian identity in all the areas of life should be the goal of every priest and member of the church. Living what they preach must be a reality every priest must follow," Ferrer concluded.

The pastoral plan of the *Inmaculado Corazón de Maria* parish led by Ramirez intends to provide new believers with an encounter with the person and work of Jesus Christ. This encounter takes place in the heart of the community expressed in small communities where people can find a place of acceptance, respect, love and encouragement through fellowship and the study of the Bible and church tradition.

General Statements

All of the Mexican respondents stressed the role of Vatican II as an instrument that changed the churches' understanding of mission. Ramirez from the *Inmaculado Corazón de Maria* parish said, "Vatican II opened a new evangelistic dimension for the Roman Catholic Church, providing renewal of the church." He contends that there are three ways in which Vatican II renewed the church: (1) It changed the language of the mass, allowing it to be understood by the people; (2) it allowed a rediscovery of reading the Bible, putting the Bible in the people's hands; and (3) it allowed theology to be accessible to the laity. However, despite the accomplishment of Vatican II, Martinez from the *La Santa Cruz de Jerusalem* parish thinks "most of the stipulations of Vatican II have been on paper alone. What we have accomplished is minimal."

Finally, all the interviewees agreed that the future of the church depends upon the work the church can do as a living community and the work of the pastors and leaders. They also agree that the future of the Roman Catholic Church in Mexico is dependant upon the younger generations and they are worried because the newer generations are leaving the church. The interviewees realize that there has not been a very good evangelization system in the past so the goal of the church is to provide a new evangelization force that targets the younger generation.[4]

Conclusion

In conclusion, the Roman Catholic Church in Mexico City today seems to be focused on evangelization and following SINE, a continuation of the force that Vatican II provided to the renewal of the Roman Catholic Church. This new evangelization's focus on small groups seems to be successful in reaching the younger generation through re-evangelization. Even though most of the Mexican population consider themselves Catholic, the vast majority does not have a commitment to or participate in the church; therefore this re-evangelization is necessary to reach them. The leaders are attempting to bring the church to the people rather than having the people come to the church. Still, not all churches have adopted this mission and some continue with the traditional plan of waiting for the people to come to their services without any social or evangelistic initiative.

The involvement of the Roman Catholic Church in social issues seems to be minimal. It seems that social or political involvement has been prohibited by the hierarchy of the church. The church has attempted to define which areas belong specifically to the church's realm of influence and which belong to the government. Steps have been taken to keep the two areas from mixing. This is one reason why the church is completely uninvolved in environmental issues even though, as demonstrated in Chapter 2, Mexico City has tremendous problems with air and water pollution.

Finally, the Roman Catholic Church in Mexico City seems very tied to hierarchical decisions, not only for their plan of work but also in their theological and ecclesiological mission. The fact that some priests refused my interview without prior approval made the church seem very closed and distant to outsiders.

Roman Catholic Church in Colombia

I interviewed four Roman Catholic priests in Colombia: two belonging to the traditional Roman Catholic structure and two belonging to the ecumenical groups. Even though Catholic priests lead these two ecumenical groups, they are considered independent from the Roman Catholic structure. In other words, the two ecumenical groups interviewed for one reason or another have been separated from the Roman Catholic Church yet their services follow a liturgy and style which is very similar to those of the Roman Catholic Church. I decided to interview these two ecumenical groups and record their insights under the Roman Catholic subdivision because they are growing substantially in Latin America and in some ways represent what many consider to be the Roman Catholic population today.

The following chart (Table 5) summarizes the general information about each priest and their corresponding parish.

Table 5. Roman Catholic Priests/Parishes Interviewed in Colombia				
Name	Luis Maria Carreño PEREZ	Herbert Monsalve VILLAVONA	Nelson Javier PABÓN	Fredys Samanca DAZA
Experience/ Position	Priest	Part of direct body of the Archdioceses/Priest	Priest	Priest
Nationality	Colombian	Colombian	Colombian	Colombian
Age	Early thirties	Early fifties	Late thirties	Mid-forties
Parish	*San Jeronimo Emiliani*	*Nuestra Señora de la Providencia*	*Comunidad Ecumenica Los Santos Apostoles*	*La Tierra de Provisión*
Denomination	Roman Catholic	Roman Catholic	Ecumenical	Ecumenical
Social Background	Middle-high	Low	Middle-low	Middle
City	Bogotá	Bucaramanga	Bucaramanga	Bucaramanga

The Roman Catholic Church in Colombia follows a specific missiological and evangelistic plan that to some extent attempts to unify the mission of the church as a whole. This project is called *Projecto Diocesano de Renovación y Evangelización* or PDRE, "Project Diocesan of Renovation and Evangelization." This project has been implemented in 24 diocesis of Colombia. The archdiocese of Bucaramanga has implemented this program as their philosophy of work yet, as we saw in Mexico, not all of the Colombian parishes are following this plan step-by-step. For instance, both of the Roman Catholic Churches interviewed have their own missiological and pastoral goal and plan.

A good representation of the PDRE project is demonstrated by La Providencia parish, under the leadership of Villavona, who has been working in this project and in this parish for the last six years. According to Villavona, "the project's goal is to be the church God wants; a church of community inspired by Scripture and with the structure established by the Vatican II counsel."

La Providencia parish took three years to evaluate the reality in which their community was living when they began using the PDRE plan. They arrived to the conclusion that *comunión*, "fellowship" was the key area they wanted to target as a pastoral plan. Once they determined the goal, they established ways to achieve their goals, which are in many ways similar to the PDRE guidelines. The following are the steps they are currently pursuing:

1. The Kerigma, First Announcement, consists of sensitizing people to the values of the Word of God. In order to reach this first step the parish promoted some activities each month during the services. For example: to achieve fellowship and closeness, they found ways for people to look at each others and to achieve reconciliation, they promoted respect and acceptance in the relationships. This first step was periodically evaluated.

2. Growing in Faith. The goal of this step is to deepen one's faith according to, as Villavona implies, "the encounter with Jesus, with the faith and with the Word of God."

3. Commitment and Ministering. This consists of helping the participants discover their role in the church so that they are then able to create small communities.

4. The final goal of the PDRE is to create small communities that move from a conglomeration to a real representation of God's people.

La Providencia parish counts on a small group of leaders that joined with Villavona to oversee the whole project. They have divided the parish into nine zones. Each pastoral zone has a layperson that is its leader. Each zone is also divided by streets, which also has a leader. The zones are comprised of approximately 12 families. Villanova reports that this structure has resulted in positively reaching the community and offered a closer and more personal evangelization.

This plan to create small ecclesiological communities is similar to the plan the Mexican Roman Catholic Church is implementing. These too are modeled after the Base Communities in Brazil. According to Villavona, "the project is attempting to reach everybody, which underlines the golden rule that is evangelization." Who does the evangelization? Villavona continues, "All the baptized have the responsibility to evangelize all."

San Jeronimo Emiliani Parish led by Perez has its own missiological plan. This parish began seven years ago and now they have five services on Sunday with a total attendance of approximately 2,000 people. The parish counts on a *Concejo Pastoral*, "Pastoral Council;" a group of 12 people who help address the needs of the community and develop programs for the church.

Most of the programs of the *San Jeronimo Emiliani* parish were created to address the needs of the people. As Perez points out, "the programs are made with the people for the people. We try to provide answers to the needs of the parishioners." Most of the time, the needs of the people are ascertained through pastoral visits and listening to the people.

On the other hand, the *Comunidad Ecumenica Los Santos Apostoles* led by Pabón focuses more on spiritual matters such as the laying on of hands, prayer, and signs. For Pabón, "the key reason people like to come to our church is that people had received healing and blessings from the Lord here." Since beginning as a community three years ago, the role of signs and manifestations of the Spirit have been a reality of the community. Pabón says, "One day I dreamed that God was telling me that the parish is not limited to a place. God was telling me," Pabón continues, "that the world is the parish."[5] Since that day Pabón has worked with this ideal and today they have 450 people that meet together regularly.

Pabón came to understand about healing through prayer and the laying on of hands when he was in seminary. There were several instances where Pabón prayed for people and people receive healing and/or a response to their needs. Later a teacher explained the role of prayer and laying on of hands to bring healing. Pabón learned that many of the physical diseases are caused by psychological factors. Prayer helps people deal with the psychological factors. Pabón concludes, "spiritual warfare is an issue that the church is dealing with and we must address."

La Tierra de Provision parish led by Daza also focuses on prayer, healing and liberation. When Daza was in school, he was interested in issues related with prayer and healing. Six years ago Daza received an invitation to lead a group whose primary focus was prayer and healing. Around 200 people attended and began what they have today. Today the attendance is between 600 to 800 people and every service focuses on prayer and healing and spiritual manifestations through signs such as healing, speaking in tongues, liberation, etc.

Social Involvement

In contrast to the lack of social involvement on the part of the Roman Catholic Church in Mexico, the Colombian Roman Catholic Church seems to be very much interested and involved in social issues. Three of the four churches interviewed have a pastoral plan in place that deals with social issues in the parishes where they serve.

San Jeronimo Emiliani parish provides pastoral care for sick people. The parish has lay people who visit the sick and share with them communion and prayers. In addition the parish sometimes provides economic help to those who are most needy.

San Jeronimo Emiliani parish also has a lay outreach program that focuses on the protection of high-risk children. The idea for this outreach program was taken from the Padres Somazcos[6] (*Carisma de San Jeronimo*, "Charisma of Saint Jerome") who was the founder. At the time of the interview they had 120 local children in the program, including children from different parts of Colombia. Their main focus is to provide safe houses for these children who have come to them due to abuse, homeless, etc. The parish works jointly with a government organization called *Bienestar Familiar*, "Family Well-Being."

San Jeronimo Emiliani parish already has a team of psychologists, social workers, and educators in place. The church contacts the child's family to determine his/her situation and then they begin a process of counseling, education, and rehabilitation in the child's life. According to Perez, the length of rehabilitation varies depending upon the case however, when the child turns 18 years old he/she must leave the institution. This program has also been extended to others parishes in Bogotá and there are now five houses in Bogotá (especially fulfilling the role as a place of protection and support).

La Providencia Parish, led by Villavona, has about 30 pastoral groups that help with the development of the church: worship, ministerial leaders, people who are in charge of the social areas and needs, etc. Actually, the parish has two groups in place that are in charge of providing social support to the community (*San Vicente de Paul* and *Madres Mercedarias*, "Merciful Mothers"), comprised primarily of youth and adults. They visit and verify the specific needs of the people they serve and then, not only provide physical and economic assistance but also look for ways to help improve people's quality of life. Sometimes they provide loans to help the needy begin their own micro enterprise (small business). They usually help people develop their own skills after assessing their capabilities and interests.

The way that *San Vicente de Paul* gets its support is through fund raising activities throughout the year and, in some cases, through the economic and material support of a specific group of people. The *San Vicente de Paul* group does not limit themselves to provide only social support but they also provide spiritual and evangelistic assistance, depending upon the need. *Las Madres Mercedarias* and the *San Vicente de Paul* groups basically conduct the same work but *Las Mercedarias*, which is a group of women, is self-supporting using the resources of the group members themselves.

In an effort to equip the community with skills that can be used to support its members, *La Providencia* parish provides training workshops such as: baking, beauty, crafts, etc. However, the primary program of *La Providencia* parish is running an elder home, which opened its doors in the year 2000. At the time of my interview, they had 25 internal and 10 external elders, most of which are either homeless or from very poor backgrounds. One hundred percent of the support to run this place comes from the parish.

In contrast to the strong social involvement of the two Roman Catholic Churches already mentioned, the two Charismatic groups interviewed have few social programs in place. For instance, *La Comunidad Ecumenica Los Santos Apostoles* parish has a project called *Pan con Queso*, "Bread with Cheese," that consists of providing homeless people with refreshments like bread, cheese, and hot drinks once a week. The objective of the program was to show a new dimension of the church. According to Pabón, "we want to show that the church is not a place where people go to simply to receive for themselves, instead we want to teach the people to go to church and give a little of what they have in service to others."

Based upon his own experience, Daza, from *La Tierra de Provision* parish, does not think that the church's social involvement is a solution to the needs society is facing. He used to work in areas of Colombia where violence was strong. In these places programs and alternatives given by the Red Cross and the Church were limited and did not provide concrete solutions. Daza emphasizes that, "the problems of violence and insecurity come from very deep in the people's hearts. What we need to do is change the heart, because this is where the wrongdoing originates. Therefore, our target is the hearts of men and women and not their stomachs." Clearly, this church focuses primarily on the spiritual sphere.

Environmental Involvement

Only one of the interviewed parishes in Colombia has established an environmental plan. The others believe that this is an area where the government should take the initiative. Villavona from *La Providencia* parish reports that, "the church's structure has been very clear that it needs to be involved in the conservation of nature." Villavona continues, "*La Providencia* parish, for example, has created a micro enterprise project of recycling." Through this program they encourage the community to care for the conservation of the environment, and of plants and animals as well as provide jobs for the program organizers. "This enterprise that was born in our parish six years ago has been growing and flourishing," stated Villavona. At the time of the interview this company was producing composted fertilizer as well.

Biblical Basis for Their Work

Perez from *San Jeronimo Emiliani* parish affirms that Saint Jerome's commitment to "living and dying with them" provides his parish with its motivation and model for ministry. "This means the we must follow the road of the crucified and serve the poor." Perez highlights, "Our work is focused on working with the children in a world where the lack of love, where injustice and where violation of human rights prevail. Therefore, we assume that these children are our own; we work to make sure that their rights are taken into consideration and we strive to grant them a new opportunity for life with the hope that tomorrow's society will receive them as humans worthy of value and honor."

According to Villavona from *La Providencia* parish, the basis for their understanding of evangelization comes from the Vatican II, especially the encyclical by Pope John Paul VI, *Evangelius Anunciandi*, "Evangelization of the Peoples." Villavona mentioned that documents such as Rio of Janeiro, Medellin, Puebla, Santo Domingo, and the Church in America assisted in developing this new plan of evangelization. "Those documents are very relevant to the Roman Catholic Church in Latin America because those are properly made by Latin American theologians to Latin America," Villavona emphasized.

In response to my questions about their understanding of "the poor" in Luke 4:18-19, Perez from the *San Jeronimo Emiliani* parish, pointed out, "We are in this world with a call. We are small instruments of God. The mission we have as Father Somascos is a gift from God who has given us his Spirit to respond to others, especially to the poor." This statement is lived out in the way that his parish welcomes the poor. Perez affirms that the church should have a correct concept of the poor, "they are people who have dignity and the potential to succeed if we give them the opportunity. The "good news" we proclaim is that God has not forsaken the poor and we are here to help them in any way that we are able."

Villavona from *La Providencia* parish thinks that the Luke 4 text, especially the phrase "the good news of the gospel," describes not only the mission of Jesus but also also the task of the church. "Jesus demonstrates the way we can do the work and this means working in an integral manner to promote healthy evangelization," Villavona said.

Regarding the understanding of Acts 2:42-47 and Acts 4:32-5:11, Perez from the *San Jeronimo Emiliani* parish thinks that, "We are not alone; we have the Holy Spirit and Jesus in the Communion." These texts also show that the kingdom of God is manifested every day through justice, loving our neighbor, in an equal society where everybody has an opportunity. Perez continues, "We are part of a community and for this reason we should be open to share and tolerate others. We need to be open to others because it will help us purify ourselves. It is in the heart of the community that we learn how to live plainly." For Perez the answer for the society is found in giving alms. For example, he mentioned that in the story of the rich man found in the gospel it was not enough to fulfill all of the law but he also needed to give all he had. "In the same way we need to give up all we have, in doing that our walk will be easier and true," Perez said.

Theological Issues

The PDRE provides the basis upon which the Roman Catholic Church in Colombia understands its theology and mission. According to Villavona, "the way *La Providencia* Parish evangelizes is with the intention of bringing the Gospel alive in the community, just as Jesus did. In order to do that it is not necessary to offer an exposition of doctrine but rather to create a living community of participation."

The Gospel itself is the motivation that stimulates *La Providencia* parish to offer its programs. According to Villavona "the evangelization needs to be integral. In many churches there is a concept of evangelization that is too spiritualistic. We need to recognize that *humanidad es más que espiritu*, "humanity is more than spirit." In order to have a correct Christian anthropology we need to see humanity in an integral way. Therefore, a correct evangelization needs to deal with *toda la persona*, 'the whole person.'" For Villavona, evangelization has to deal with both preaching the word and providing social assistance. It is not only about offering a spiritual dimension but also about being concerned with the material needs of the people. These two dimensions are fundamental parts of *el Reino de Dios*, "the Kingdom of God." Villavona stresses that "we cannot minister to the spiritual needs of the people and be blind to *la tragedia social en que viven*, 'the social tragedy in which they are living.'"

For the *San Jeronimo Emiliani* parish, theology must address the questions society is raising. For instance, talking about social injustice that is present in Colombia, Perez points out, "The church cannot be passive toward the situation we are facing. As a church we need to say or do something. The answer is not to just give economic relief to people, but we need to create ways to help the people improve their lives and self-esteem."

For *La Comunidad Ecumenica Los Santos Apostoles* parish a correct theology comes by way listening to people through counseling and dialogue. Pabón affirms that people in their community have three primary types of need: (1) economic, (2) labor, and (3) emotional. For Pabón, the philosophy of the church's mission is to focus the gospel on the present needs of the people in a practical way. This is why their services are very participative: the parish is looking for ways for people to express their ideas and emotions. In doing that, Pabón points out, people will escape religiosity and find within the gospel a profound truth that is applicable to their lives.

General Statements

All the respondents in Colombia stressed the key role of liberation theology in the missiological understanding of the church. For instance Villavona, from *La Providencia* parish, points out that liberation theology deals with the reality Latin America is facing. "We recognize that there have been some extremist positions manipulated by communism and some of our leaders have been manipulated by this teaching and take this extremist position. On the other hand, there have been some ministers who truly have identified with the poor, oppressed and the needy of the society. These ministers have been persecuted and wrongly identify as communists or guerillas," Villavona said.

All the interviewees agree that there are too many sects, or what they called *iglesias de garaje*, "garage churches," spreading in Colombia. According to Villavona, these groups are characterized by having a very poor theological and doctrinal foundation. "These churches are anti-social; in other words, they do not believe that social issues are also part of and fundamental to the gospel. Their faith is too spiritualistic and narrow." Villavona believes that what unified the continent of Latin America was a Catholic faith but Protestantism has created division. Every day there is more division in the community and in the society. Pabón, from *La Comunidad Ecumenica Los Santos Apostoles* parish, agrees with Villavona. "Unification," states Pabón, "is one of challenges the church in Colombia is facing."

Conclusion

The Roman Catholic Church in Colombia today seems to be focused on the PDRE (Project Diocesan of Renovation and Evangelization). In some ways this missiological and evangelistic project tries to unify the mission of the church as a whole.

In contrast to the Church in Mexico, the Roman Catholic Church in Colombia seems to be very much involved in social issues affirming that this sphere is a crucial part of the gospel as a whole. Only one parish has an established environmental plan, which also serves to provide a source of income to several families.

In contrast to what we learned in Mexico, the Roman Catholic Church in Colombia sees liberation theology as a good contribution to the missiological understanding of the church. In addition, the Roman Catholic Church in Colombia welcomed me, a stranger, without needing permission from their superiors to talk to me.

Roman Catholic Church in Peru

In Lima, Peru, I interviewed four Roman Catholic priests. Table 6 on the following page summarizes the general information about each priest and their corresponding parish.

All of the parishes interviewed have in place a specific pastoral and social plan that more or less has been determined by the needs present in the society in which they minister as well as by the influence of the Peruvian headquarters of the Roman Catholic Church. The parishes interviewed have ministries to children, to young people, to the family, to couples (premarital classes), of the sacraments (first communion and confirmation), to the sick (visitation and assistance) and biblical formation.

In order to accomplish this pastoral task two of the parishes, *San Diego-Dios Caraballo* parish led by Barrios and *El Sagrado de Corazón de Jesus* parish led by Thorndike, have divided their parishes into *pequeñas comunidades*, "small communities." At the time of the interview, Barrios' parish had fourteen base communities groups, which had been in operation since the year 2000 and enable him to empower the laity to do the pastoral work.

Table 6. Roman Catholic Priests/Parishes Interviewed in Peru

Name	Wilson **BARRIOS**	Marco Antonio **LOLI**	Luis **SARMIENTO**	Ricardo Wiesse **THORNDIKE**
Experience/ Position	Priest	Police Chaplain	7 years/ Ordained Priest	Monsignor
Nationality	Peruvian	Peruvian	Peruvian	German
Age	Early fifties	Early sixties	Mid-thirties	Mid-seventies
Parish	*San Diego-Dios Caraballo*	*La Capellania General de Lima*	*Santiago Apóstol*	*El Sagrado Corazón de Jesus de Barranco*
Denomination	Roman Catholic	Roman Catholic	Roman Catholic	Roman Catholic
Social Background	Middle-low	N/A	Middle-high	High

In the same way, Thorndike's parish has small biblical centers led by *los consagrados*, "the consecrates." According to Thorndike, *los consagrados* are people who have a deeper commitment of service to the church. Started by the Vatican II, the requirements to be a *consagrado*, "consecrate," are: (1) a deeper Christian life, (2) an intellectual formation, (3) an understanding of the history of the church (3) a knowledge of theology. A *consagrado* is allowed to serve communion. For Thorndike, *los consagrados* play a key role in the ministry of the church. It is impossible for a priest to minister to all of the members and therefore *los consagrados* provide new dimensions and an extension of the ministry life of the church. Meetings led by *los consagrados* take place twice a month at the group leader's house that has previously been prepared by the parish. These groups are divided by blocks and their main goal is to decentralize the pastoral work of the parish. Each member has their own Bible, allowing them to study the Scriptures individually.

Social Involvement

According to Thorndike (*Sagrado Corazón de Jesus* parish) the parishes of Lima are implementing a program called *Remar Mar Adentro*, "Go Deep Into the Sea," that consists of reviewing the religious (spiritual) life of the parishioners and the social conditions in which they live (number of family members, education, salary, etc.). This information provides them with a better social understanding of the inequalities and the needs of the people while offering insight into how the parish can provide a solution to those needs.

At least two of the parishes interviewed seemed to be very involved in social issues. For instance, the *San Diego-Dios Caraballo* parish has a social ministry that includes food services, support for the elderly, work in green areas, and more. The parish offers seminars on hygiene, health, parenthood, family relationships, respect and the dignity of life. "There are many young people in our community who are not prepared to be parents; therefore, our parish is providing them with some basic skills that will help them get started in this important task of life," Barrios said. The parish has provided seminars to the community on human rights issues, especially against child abuse, violations, and spouse abuse. According to Barrios, "these seminars serve the purpose of making the community aware of their rights and responsibilities as parents and children."

The *Santiago Apostol* parish is also somewhat involved in social programs. Every month a youth group visits a nursing home where they help in serving and cleaning up after a meal and every two months a group of youth visits a homeless shelter. In addition, the church has annual campaigns to collect clothing for several families and homeless shelters in the city. Sarmiento affirms that the needs of the society have motivated them as a church to implement these programs. "The church does what the government should be, but is not, doing." Sarmiento continues, "we have learned that the key is not to supply all of the people's needs, but rather to teach them to get the things and resources they need. We follow the slogan: Don't give them a fish but rather teach them how to fish."

Environmental Involvement

Two of the parishes interviewed have programs in place to deal with the preservation of the environment. For instance, the *San Diego-Dios Caraballo* parish led by Barrios has implemented a campaign against the burning of garbage near residential areas because, according to Barrios, "the smoke caused by burning has produced several respiratory infections in the inhabitants of the area." Thanks to the participation of the parish, the local government became aware of the problem and is involved in notably reducing this type of activities. Also the parish started a campaign against raising pigs because of the practice's contamination in the community. The parish also has been involved in several reforestation programs, encouraging the whole community to conserve and plant new trees in the area.

El Sagrado Corazón de Barranco parish, led by Thorndike, at the time of the interview was protesting against a violation of the beaches of Barranco. According to Thorndike, "they are building restaurants and recreational areas on these beaches, violating the public space. The protest specifically goes against the building of a concrete wall along the beach, destroying the public space and environment." The community, lead by the parish, has sued these companies and at the time of the interview the trial was in progress. Thorndike states, "the role of the church is to defend the elements that have been violated; in this respect the church needs to take the side of justice and defense of God's creation."

Biblical Basis for Their Work

All of the interviewees agree that the basis for their work comes from the needs of the society where their parishes are located. They also agree that the motivation for doing their task comes from Scripture as a whole. Police chaplain Loli points out that his motivation comes from *Santa Rosa de Lima*, "Saint Rosa of Lima," who inspired the police force as well as the chaplains to serve those who are in need.

On the other hand, Barrios, from the *San Diego-Dios Caraballo* parish, commented that "their motivation for work as a parish comes from the importance of being together as a community as a means of evangelization based on the instruction in the gospel of John which states that we should be one for the world to believe in Christ" (John 17:21).

In response to my question about their understanding of Luke 4:18-19 Barrios, *San Diego-Dios Caraballo* parish, responded, "As Jesus began his apostolic life, we as a community are called to follow Jesus' example. The good news is Jesus himself. We need to note that humanity is religious by nature. The church has the responsibility to provide humanity a space where they can find spiritual and material fullness. Jesus Christ takes the side of the poor and needy in the Luke 4 text." Sarmiento from *Santiago Apostol* parish emphasizes the concept of Jubilee present in Luke 4:18-19, "Jubilee is a time of grace (freedom, forgiving of debts). Jesus does not only focus on social issues, he is the mark of grace and the year of jubilee. Jesus is the healer of humanity's heart. Therefore, the person and work of Jesus liberates anything that oppresses humanity. This is our pastoral task to share a message that provides salvation to the whole person." For Thorndike, *Sagrado Corazón de Jesus* parish, "Luke 4:18-19 points out Jesus' revelation to the Jews; however, his revelation does not end there, Jesus continues to reveal himself to us today."

I asked about their understanding of Acts 2:42-47 texts. Barrios, *San Diego-Dios Caraballo* parish, responded, "this text provides a model of the church as a community of fellowship. Our identity is found in that community which implies our communion with each other--*una fé, un bautismo*, "one faith, one baptism." The focus of the church should be communion, as a bride of Christ."

Theological Issues

Sarmiento from the *Santiago Apostol* parish affirms that the church's main goal should not be to simply provide social assistance; it should go a step farther and take care of the people's spiritual needs. Faith involves the whole person, body and soul. The starting point is spiritual but it must move to solid and concrete fruits. In other words, salvation is *integral*. Sarmiento affirms that the involvement in social issues helps the younger generation to be close to God. They find identity in the society and in their own life.

For Barrios, *San Diego-Dios Caraballo* parish, the church is a family that shares community, friendship and suffering. It is not possible to conceive a Christian apart from *la Comunidad*, "the community:" Community is a key to evangelization and discipleship. Community represents God's nature because the only way to conceive God is in the Father, Son and Holy Spirit. In other words, *Dios es comunidad*, "God is community." Thorndike affirms that the church has a prophetic role in denouncing the injustice in society. At time of our discussion, his church was denouncing the materialistic society.

General Statements

Analyzing the situation of the spiritual life of the Peruvian people Thorndike, *Sagrado Corazón de Jesus* parish, stated that the spiritual situation of Lima and Peru is better than when the Roman Catholic Church was the state religion. He said, "since there is freedom of religion in Peru, people willingly choose to go to the services and to live a deeper life with the church and with the sacraments." On the other hand, Sarmiento from *Santiago Apostol* parish is more pessimistic. He commented, "right now there is relativism in the society of Lima, where people call what is sinful good. There is no *consciencia biblica*, 'Biblical conscience.'" All of the interviewees agreed that the church should not be involved in politics or any related activity.

Answering the questions about their thoughts on liberation theology, Sarmiento, affirms that "most of the time liberation theology has been looked at only partially or overlooked altogether. It does, however, have good things to offer to the missiological and ecclesiological task of the church." According to Thorndike, "since the beginning the liberation theology interpretation was a Marxist interpretation. This theology starts with poverty we gain nothing with only words. We need action."

Reflecting upon the importance of Vatican II, Sarmiento believes that it helped to put the Bible in the hands of the people. Vatican II also opened the venue to ecumenism as did the goals of Pope John Paul II and the Roman Catholic Church. However, this ecumenism depends on the head of the church. For Barrios, *San Diego-Dios Caraballo* parish, "Vatican II provided new air to the church; it is not a new way to be a church but it is a relevant way to see the church and the society."

Conclusion

The Roman Catholic Church in Peru seems to have a specific pastoral and social plan have in place that more or less has been determined by the needs of the society in which it ministers as well as by the influence of the Peruvian headquarters of the Roman Catholic Church. Like the churches in Colombia, at least three of the Roman Catholic parishes interviewed in Peru seem to be very involved in social issues, confirming that this sphere is a crucial part of the gospel as a whole.

In contrast with the churches in Colombia and Mexico, the Roman Catholic Churches in Peru seem to be very involved in environmental issues. They affirm that the role of the church is to take the side of justice and defense of God's creation. Despite this environmental commandment, the city of Lima seems to be struggling with air and water pollution, overwhelmed by the accumulation of garbage and lack of a proper sanitation system.

Finally, the Roman Catholic Church in Peru seems to be divided with regard to the theology of liberation. On the other hand, the Roman Catholic Church in Peru agrees that Vatican II has provided key elements that have brought renewal and vitality to the church.

Roman Catholic Church in Argentina

In Buenos Aires, Argentina, I interviewed four Roman Catholic priests. The following chart (Table 7) summarizes the general information about each priest and their corresponding parish.

Table 7. Roman Catholic Priests/Parishes Interviewed in Argentina

Name	Pablo VERDEGAL	Pablo Ignacio ARAGON	Jorge Eduardo ARSAINE	Fernando JULIECER
Experience / Position	Priest	Thirty three years / Priest	Nine years / Priest	Five years in this parish / Priest
Nationality	Argentinean	Argentinean	Argentinean	Argentinean
Age	Late thirties	Sixty	Late forties	Early forties
Parish	*San José Obrero*	*José Leon Suarez*	*Nuestra Señora de Aranzaso*	*Purisima Consección de Pacheco*
Denomination	Roman Catholic	Roman Catholic	Roman Catholic	Roman Catholic
Social Background	Middle-high	Low	Middle-high	Middle
Average Attendance	400 people		1,400 people	

Like the churches in Peru, the Roman Catholic Churches in Argentina are encouraged in their ministry by the reality that they effect the society where they minister. All of the parishes interviewed have a well-established pastoral ministry including the liturgy, biblical formation, and teaching of confirmation and first communion; they minister to the family, the elderly, single parents, children, young people, and sick people (visiting and helping them). For instance, the *San Jose Obrero* parish led by Verdegal generally has first communion classes with an attendance of around 150 children. The *Purisima*

Consección of Pacheco parish led by Juliecer has an established pastoral work in which the main emphasis is on ministering the sacraments. According to Juliecer, a lot people from the community come wanting to be baptized, have first communion, be married, etc. *Nuestra Señora de Aranzaso* parish has an elementary, middle, and high school for about 1,300 students. There is also a functioning radio station as part of the parish.

Social Involvement

The Roman Catholic Church in Argentina seems to have a strong commitment to social issues. As is the case in Colombia and Mexico, the parishes in Argentina have adopted a social plan from *Caritas*[7] that are shaped according the needs where each one operates.

The *San Jose Obrero* parish led by Verdegal has three main social areas: (1) After school support for children 3-5 years old. At the moment the parish has around 90 at-risk children participating in this program; (2) Pre-school children and infants. This ministry is located in the *barrio Juan Diego*, generally considered to be one of the riskiest neighborhoods in the city. This program has been in operation for twenty years and approximately 120 children currently take classes there Monday through Friday; (3) In the year preceding the interview, the parish has changed from mere assistance to promotion through the influence of Caritas. This means that the parish is now offering workshops for painting, sewing, literature, and so on. Most of these programs target women and so the parish has also started workshops relevant to women and families.

According to Aragon from the *Jose Leon Suarez* parish, the condition of life and the lack of a good sanitation system have produced a series of physical diseases in the area. Governmental medical assistance takes place only a few times a year and most of the time people do not have the money needed to buy their prescriptions. For this reason, the parish provides some help for this medicine. Aragon emphasizes that the State expects the parish to provide what they neglect to provide for the people. In the last twenty years the parish has supported several programs that, good or bad, have helped meet the community's needs.

One example is a home improvement plan. The *Jose Leon Suarez* parish provided the supplies and the people themselves provided the labor. The plan worked and supported the community for a while but it later failed due to the lack of resources. Later the parish tried to start different kinds of micro-enterprises but it has been difficult to create a cooperative mentality among the people. Aragon points out, "the main problem is that people have a mentality of dependence and it is difficult for them to depend upon their own support." At one time the parish also created a *cooperativa*, "cooperative," with a capital of almost $4,000 dollars. The parish bought machines that produced pantry products that could be sold to generate income for several families of the parish. Sadly this cooperative only lasted four years because it could not compete with other products on the market.

Today, the parish has an operation called *el Banco de los Pobres*, "the Bank of the Poor." This bank loans money to mothers who organize themselves in groups of forty persons and that invest the money in projects. They pay back this money in moderate parts during the year. In addition, through Caritas the parish sells prepared food at half price twice a week. This food is given to those who do not have any money. The parish also feeds around 150 school children and distributes clothing from Italy to the needy.

Likewise *Nuestra Señora de Aranzaso* parish led by Arsaine works with Caritas. The parish has two feeding programs that serve two impoverished neighborhoods. Most of the economic support to run these programs comes from private donations and some government support. They also have a dental office that cares for those who are more needy. The parish collects food, clothing and distributes it to *los pobres*, "the poor." They also serve breakfasts and offer showers to homeless people everyday. The parish periodically visits the hospital in which Arsaine is also the chaplain. *Nuestra Señora de Aranzaso* parish has a big building and lots of help from its people. In contrast to *Jose Leon Suarez*, *Nuestra Señora de Aranzaso* parish has a well-structured program for young people.

Like the other churches in Argentina, the *Purisima Consección de Pacheco* parish led by Juliecer has adopted Caritas as the main social program. Thus, through *Caritas* the parish offers free weekly lawyer consultations (family and penal) to the community. They also distribute food once a month and once a week they distribute medicine. They have a center for school support. In addition, the parish hosts support groups such as Alcoholics Anonymous (AA) and *Gordos Anonimos*, "Overeaters Anonymous (OA)."

Environmental Involvement

In contrast with the church in Peru, the Roman Catholic Church in Argentina does not have an established environmental program yet Buenos Aires is experiencing serious problems with water and air pollution. Verdegal from *San Jose Obrero* parish claims that this is a new topic in Argentina. He points out, "we as a society do not have a conscience for the preservation of the environment. This is an area that we are just beginning to think about."

Biblical Basis for Their Work

Most of the priests interviewed agree that there is no particular text in the Scriptures that motivates their work. They claim that the Roman Catholic Church in Argentina takes the initiative for their work based on *toda la Escritura*, "the Scripture as a whole." Some of the parishes, however, have specific biblical texts that provide some insight to their work. For instance, according to Verdegal, *San Jose Obrero* parish, "in the last years *La Palabra de Dios*, 'the Word of God,' has become the main encouragement to exist and meet." Verdegal continues, "our main goal was *empezar desde la misma Palabra de Dios*, 'to begin from the Word of God itself,' something that was not previously in the Roman Catholic perspective." Thus, starting with the Bible itself, the parish began its pastoral and ministerial project. The following are the texts and the topics the parish discussed for their ministerial plan: John 13 (strengths and weaknesses in the service); 1 Corinthians 12 (strengths and weaknesses in communion and diversity); Philippians 2:1-11 (strengths and weaknesses in the closeness of Jesus' feelings for us. Jesus became one of us and worked faithful to his call. This is our task and inspiration); Acts 2:42-44 (strength and weaknesses toward the Word that unites us and the bread we share). Verdegal added, "The life of Joseph inspires us as a congregation. He was a man who was a second stage person yet he lived and served the Lord faithfully without making too much noise."

The veneration to Mary continues to play a crucial ecclesiological and missiological role for the Roman Catholic Church in Argentina. For instance, according to Arsaine, "*Nuestra Señora de Aranzaso* parish is a community that is very devoted to Mary—the Mother of God."

In response to my questions about their understanding of Luke 4:18-19, Verdegal, *San Jose Obrero* parish, affirms that "we are living in the year of the Lord's favor, and as such we need to live this reality in our daily life. To heal and to save are the same verb. We need to be liberated from the spiritual blindness regarding to the person of Jesus."

For Aragon, *Jose Leon Suarez* parish, "since the beginning of my ministry in this parish 20 years ago, our main goal has been to work among the poor. Our foundation was and is to show concrete love, meaning to treat others with respect and dignity. There are more poor, more oppressed, more blind, and more captive everyday. It is our task to support them as much as we are able. The style of our teaching goes in this direction."

Analyzing Luke 4:18-19 Arsaine, *Nuestra Señora de Aranzaso* parish, points out that the Word of God is the fountain of life and the fundamental fountain of the community, but "it is not the only fountain from which we drink. This is a fundamental passage to the pastoral program of Jesus but we need to interpret what this means for us here in Latin America and more specifically here in Argentina. For instance," Arsaine says, "we need to find out what 'the poor' means and who the poor are. The poor today are not the same as the poor15 years ago. The poor are those who are *afuera del Sistema*, "out of the system (marginalized)" (i.e. health, retirement, etc.): those who are excluded, the sick, the lonely, the drug addicted, the alcoholic and so on. There is nobody that is not poor; everybody in one or another way is a poor. *Con el pobre es donde Dios habla*, 'With the poor is where God speaks.' Jesus said, I needed clothes and you clothed me, I was sick and you looked after me, I was in prison and you came to visit me (Matthew 25:36); Jesus is with the poor."

Responding to my questions about their understanding of the first chapters of Acts, Aragon, *Jose Leon Suarez* parish, pointed out, "Acts reminds us that we need to look for the support and fullness of the Holy Spirit. We also look at our community to be a living community; this means that the community shares the faith and the goods in such a way that it shows that Jesus Christ is present. In this way we provide the means (human and spiritual) in which people can find the person of Jesus Christ." For Verdegal, *San Jose Obrero* parish, "Acts highlights that discipleship roles have male and female faces. We also can see the importance of domestic communities—where each one cares for the needs of the other. Sharing the bread and the Word with a sincere heart is a reality that describes our community." For Arsaine, *Nuestra Señora de Aranzaso* parish, Acts shows the influence of the Holy Spirit. The church needs to dirty itself by working with the poor and sinners. The role of the church is not the center; the center is Jesus himself.

Theological Issues

The strength in the relationship of the *San Jose Obrero* Parish in some ways represents the picture of the Trinity—Father, Son and Holy Spirit as a family. According to Verdegal, "*el ejemplo de la Trinidad*, 'the example of the Trinity,' is what the parish as a whole is trying to live."

Based on studying the books of Ruth and Nehemiah, Verdegal points out that the parish is challenged "*resistir el imperio*, 'to resist the empire' from their own house. This means that they, as a local community, can resist the hegemony of the empire or, in other words, the authoritarian Roman Catholic structure that says that you can be Catholic only from one point of view; or the neo-liberal system that made the people objects and depersonalized the crowd." The church must become a place of personalization and welcome.

General Statements

Verdegal, *San Jose Obrero* parish, reports that in the time of the crisis and dictatorship in Argentina the church promoted human rights. Although this was a time of confusion, it was during this period that the church was one of the few places where people could express their own ideas and disagreements. The parish was the place of gathering and discussion about issues related with social justice and human rights." Verdegal highlights that in the Jubilee 2000, the Bishops of the Roman Catholic Church in Argentina asked for forgiveness for their silence, their lack of involvement, and their ambiguity during the time of dictatorship.

All of the interviewees agreed on of the importance of Vatican II for the ecclesiology and missiology of the Roman Catholic Church in Latin America. According to Verdegal, *San Jose Obrero* parish, "Vatican II opened the door to other Christian styles that enriched the Roman Catholic Church. It helps to understand the church as a sacrament and not as a mere reality." This means it helps to see the church as the symbol of salvation and not as the salvation itself; the church is the symbol of Christ and not Christ himself. Vatican II helped the church recover the road to humanity, by helping the church be incarnational. "Just as the Word of God became incarnate; we are to be incarnate and show the way to salvation. The church should have the attitude of a servant and not an owner: a church that is a servant of the gospel and not an owner; a church that is a servant of the people and not an owner of them; a church that is a servant to truth and mercy and it is not an owner of truth and mercy."

According to Arsaine, *Nuestra Señora de Aranzaso* parish, Vatican II has produced fundamental ecclesiological changes, however these changes have been founded on Christological and anthropological changes. Vatican II looked differently at God, humanity and the church. For Juliecer, *Purisima Consección* parish, since Vatican II the Roman Catholic Church has changed a lot. For instance, it is an open community willing to talk with others; the function of the priest changed from being office work to being more participatory with and in the needs of the community.

Responding to my question regarding ecumenism in Argentina, Verdegal, *San Jose Obrero* parish, pointed out that ecumenism happens in Argentina only on local levels. When it happens, he says that this dialogue and relationship takes place with main line denominations and not with Pentecostal groups. This great separation between the Roman Catholic Church and Pentecostals is caused, according to Verdegal, by the fundamentalism on the part of the Pentecostals. "The majority of Pentecostals criticize the Roman Catholic Churches and Mainline denominations. In general or national levels ecumenism is reduced only to meetings of good education." For Arsaine, *Nuestra Señora de Aranzaso* parish, "in order to have dialogue with other denominations (ecumenism) we need to have a correct identity. There are many Protestants whose identity is still in formation; their main focus in this moment is growth; this makes the dialogue difficult."

Almost all the interviewees spoke openly about areas of weakness of the Roman Catholic Church. For instance, for Verdegal, *San Jose Obrero* Parish, there is a distance between the hierarchy of the Roman Catholic Church, and the reality with which every priest is living. "Most of the time we as a priest accept everything that comes from the head of the church as the word of God; but things are changing, right now we evaluate and see what is true and relevant and what is perhaps not relevant," points out Verdegal.

Juliecer, *Purisima Consección* parish, agrees with Verdegal. He adds that there are several areas in which the Roman Catholic Church struggles: (1) It is too tied to tradition; (2) People who are in high positions and write the decrees lack contact with reality; (3) As a whole the church is too vertical rather than democratic in making decisions; (4) Celibacy is another issue the Roman Catholic hierarchy needs to rethink. Juliecer points out, "celibacy should be an option for those who have the gift, it should not be a rule. There are several examples of priests who have left the ministry because they fell in love with a girl. If you want to minister to the family in a more effective way, being married will open your experience and provide you with relevant and realistic advice;" and (5) The segregation of divorced people needs to be revised. According to Juliecer, "it is too sad to deny communion to a divorced person."

Juliecer points out, "the structure of the Roman Catholic Church needs to change starting with Rome itself. The main problem is that Rome expects the world to be conformed to their point of view and it is not willing to listen to the world. The Roman Catholic Church of Latin America is completely different than the church in Rome. I believe the Roman Catholic Church will change as whole when we have a Latin American pope."

Finally, Arsaine, *Nuestra Señora de Aranzaso* parish, points out that in the past the Roman Catholic Church has failed by looking indoors rather than outdoors and being aware of the Kingdom of God and its surroundings. By looking indoors the church has lost track of the reality that society is facing. He thinks that the future of the Roman Catholic Church is very interesting; "the church will not be the church of the majority; therefore, it will have others challenges and opportunities." Arsaine points out, "we will have small communities allowing us to renew our message and our relationship with the people. This will be a long but positive process that is already happening in the Roman Catholic churches in Europe."

Conclusion

Like the churches in Peru, the Roman Catholic Church in Argentina seems to have in place a specific pastoral and social plan that more or less has been determined by the needs present in the society in which they minister. Like the churches in Colombia and in Peru, the Roman Catholic parishes interviewed in Argentina seem to have a strong commitment to social issues. As is the case in Colombia and Mexico, the parishes in Argentina have adopted a social plan from *Caritas*. Also as is the case in the previous three countries, the women's role in the life of the Argentinean society and in the ministerial task of the Roman Catholic Church is crucial.

While quite involved in social issues, the Roman Catholic Church in Argentina is not involved in environmental issues. Much unlike the priests from Mexico, Colombia and Peru, the priests from Argentina were very open and honest about their opinions and even about their opposition of their own church.

Summary

The Roman Catholic Church in Latin America seems to structurally follow a common missiological and evangelistic plan that comes directly from the Vatican. However each parish in each country is free to develop its own pastoral plan and strategy and its implementation; in this respect, the Roman Catholic Church seems to be a very localized organization.

Socially the Roman Catholic Church seems to be very involved, especially supporting the needs of those who are most needy. Caritas is one of the major social programs within the Roman Catholic Church that is implemented throughout Latin America. It seems that the preference to minister among the poor and needy in society comes from the influence of Vatican II on the continent.

Although there are serious environmental issues affecting the principal cities of Latin America, the Roman Catholic Church as a whole does not seem to have a specific environmental plan in place. Of the 16 priests interviewed only two local parishes (The Colombian *Providencia* Parish led by Villavona and the Peruvian *Sagrado Corazón de Jesus de Barranco* parish led by Thorndike) are specifically involved in environmental issues.

On the whole, it seems that the priests interviewed are committed to the study of the Scripture and how it relates with their ecclesiological and missiological task. Also it seems that as parishioners are more exposed to the Scripture it is awakening an interest to know how the Scripture speaks to them personally. It should be stated that this is present now only in a minority of the people and the popular religiosity is still alive in the majority of Latin American population.

Theologically speaking, the Roman Catholic Church in Latin America seems to be more aware of the socio-political, economic and spiritual structures that are oppressing the people. Slowly but surely the church is recognizing the crucial role of the priesthood of all believers; the laity is being more and more empowered for pastoral and social work throughout the continent. As a whole, the Roman Catholic Church is recognizing the gospel is integral, meaning that it deals with the whole person and all of their needs. It seems that this integral understanding comes from a biblical and anthropological understanding and perhaps is influenced by Vatican II and its implementation in the last four decades.

In summary, the Roman Catholic Church still has a strong influence on the Latin American society although; today the church is listened to but not necessarily obeyed. Chapter 5 will explore the theology and praxis of the mainline Protestant denominations in Latin America, focusing specifically on these same countries of Mexico, Colombia, Peru and Argentina.

Notes

1. As mentioned in Chapter 1, I spoke to four priests from four Roman Catholic churches within each of the four main Latin American countries that I visited. The interviews with these priests were coordinated by my local contacts, after they had done research to find out which priests were open to interview me. I purposely interviewed priests belonging to parishes of different socio-economic backgrounds in order to achieve a better representation of the actual reality that describes each city and country. The information collected was audio-recorded and handwritten in Spanish which I then translated into English and interpreted the data in a coherent way. Rather than translating each interview word-for-word, I wrote up interpretative notes in English, looking for meaningful and relevant answers to describe the theology of mission and praxis of the Roman Catholic Church in these countries (I used the same process with the mainline Protestant, chapter 5, and Pentecostal, chapter 6, interviews as well).

2. The SINE was the result of the Special Assembly for America of the Synod of Bishops, which was held in the Vatican from November 16 to December 12, 1997. This gathering was a continuation of the dialogue started during the Fourth General Assembly of the Latin American Bishops in Santo Domingo that took place on October 12, 1992, in

commemoration of the five hundredth anniversary of the first evangelization of America. According to John Paul II, the main theme of the Assembly was "the encounter with the Living Jesus Christ: The Way to Conversion, Communion and Solidarity in America. Put this way, the theme makes clear the centrality of the person of the Risen Christ, present in the life of the Church and calling people to conversion, communion and solidarity. The starting-point of such a program of evangelization is in fact the encounter with the Lord. Given by Christ in the Paschal Mystery, the Holy Spirit guides us towards those pastoral goals, which the Church in America must attain in the third Christian millennium" (John Paul II 2006).

3. Salvadorian archbishop Oscar Arnulfo Romero Y Galdames' ministry among the poor and "his condemnation of the right-wing government, the army, and the leftist guerillas, who collectively brought misery to his small, densely-populated country" are thought to have prompted his assassination in 1980 (Collins and Price 1999:212).

4. This was also a concern of Pope John Paul II who in the post-synodal apostolic *Ecclesia in America* highlights: While many young people in America are searching for true meaning in life and are thirsting for God, quite often they lack the conditions needed to take advantage of their abilities and realize their aspirations. Unfortunately, unemployment and the lack of prospects for the future lead them at times to withdrawal and to violence. The resulting sense of frustration not infrequently leads them to abandon the search for God. Faced with this complex situation, "the Church is committed to maintaining her pastoral and missionary commitment to young people, so that they will encounter today the living Jesus Christ." (2006:Internet)

5. It is ironic that this is the famous and much referenced claim of John Wesley, the founder of the Wesleyan Movement in his struggle to preach revival in the Anglican Church.

6. The Community Fathers Somascos is a community founded on April 29, 1537 by Saint Jerome Emiliani: universal father of the orphans and homeless. Their goal is to work with the young generation specially the orphans and homeless. They provide an integral support to the young men/women: -Studies, -Life skills workshops and technical preparation (carpentry, welding, computing, mechanics, etc). They also have some schools for children who are poor.

7. Caritas is an international organization of the Roman Catholic Church as a whole. Caritas began in Argentina around 50 years ago and it collects clothing, food, and medicine from the people of Argentina and worldwide then puts them in a common pool that is later distributed to those with the greatest need.

Chapter 5

Theology and Praxis of Mission among Selected Mainline Protestant Churches

In this chapter, we will explore the theology and praxis of mission of selected mainline Protestant churches in four Latin American countries: Mexico, Colombia, Peru, and Argentina. This analysis is based on 16 field research interviews made with Protestant pastors belonging to historically mainline churches.[1] Just as in chapter 4, the information obtained from the interviews is divided into four main sections: theology and praxis of mission of mainline Protestant Churches in Mexico, Colombia, Peru and Argentina.

Mainline Protestant Churches in Mexico

In Mexico City, I interviewed four pastors from mainline Protestant circles. Table 8 on the following page summarizes the general information about each pastor and their corresponding church.

The mainline Protestant churches in Mexico seem to have their own particular pastoral programs, history and inclinations that show how diverse the church is in Mexico. For instance, there are fourteen *Anabautista Menonita* churches in Mexico City and their preference is to work with the poor. The church's major emphasis is in discipleship, the goal is for each person to become a disciple.

The *Nazarena* Church led by Perez has several areas of focus. These include: the youth, children, evangelization, discipleship and compassion. The *Nazarena* Church in Mexico began in 1903. According to Perez, because of its strong doctrinal emphasis (holiness) the church does not grow fast. There are approximately 750 *Nazarena* churches in Mexico today.

Table 8. Mainline Protestant Pastors/Churches Interviewed in Mexico				
Name	Victor Pedroza CRUZ	Eli Gamas PEREZ	Jorge GUARILLO	Samuel Fernandez TOXTLE
Experience/ Position	National Director/ Pastor	5 years as National Director	Director Missionary District/Pastor	34 years as a Minister/Pastor
Nationality	Mexican	Mexican	Mexican	Mexican
Age	Mid-forties	Mid-fifties	Early fifties	Late-fifties
Church	*Anabautista Menonita*	*Iglesia Nazarena*	*La Iglesia Metodista Libre*	*La Casa de Él*
Denomination	Anabaptist Mennonite	Church of the Nazarene	Free Methodist	Independent Christian with mainline roots
Social Background	Low		Middle-low	Low
Average Attendance	50 people		35 members and 15 children	140 members

The *Nazarena* Church led by Perez has several areas of focus. These include: the youth, children, evangelization, discipleship and compassion. The *Nazarena* Church in Mexico began in 1903. According to Perez, because of its strong doctrinal emphasis (holiness) the church does not grow fast. There are approximately 750 *Nazarena* churches in Mexico today.

The *Metodista Libre* Church in Mexico City led by Guarillo began four years ago in a wealthy area of the city. Most of the people who attended were professionals. However, when the church bought property in a poor neighborhood two years ago most of the attendees decided to continue meeting at the first location and the church split. Therefore, Guarillo had to restart a new program in the present area.

La Casa de Él Church began 34 years ago motivated by Toxtle and a group of friends who belonged to historical churches in the downtown area of Mexico City. Their main idea was to form a coffee place where musical groups could come and share the gospel in a non-religious way to drug addicts, homosexuals, prostitutes, alcoholics, and so on. As the years passed the group grew to the point that the Mexican laws required them to formally become a Christian organization, which is how *La Casa de Él* Church was born.

Social Involvement

The mainline Protestant churches in Mexico appear to be very much involved in social issues. Pastors agree that tradition, legacy and overwhelming social needs are the principal motivations for their social involvement. For instance, according to Cruz, "the *Menonita* Church does their work based on a long Anabaptist theological heritage. Concern for and practically showing mercy to the poor and needy has been a fundamental value, beginning during the sixteenth century. It continues to be a fundamental value of the church today."

Cruz points out that 60 percent of the members of his church are single women with one to three children. Therefore the *Menonita* Church began a project for women primarily to provide spiritual and social liberation. According to Cruz, "through this project we hope to dignify the person; saying that women should not be exposed to violence, exploitation, or oppression. The gospel of Jesus Christ comes not only to liberate the person from their sin but also from any emotional and physical oppression." The *Menonita* Church offers women an entire ministry plan which includes spiritual, emotional, intellectual and skill training (in English and computer) support. The church also has a center for savings and credit in order to teach people to save and also to serve those who have an emergency need. Cruz points out, "we want to develop a preventative saving culture among the people. This program has helped us face the problem of poverty in a practical way."

The *Nazarena* Church led by Perez has a social program called Compassion, which provides economic and skills training assistance to people in need. This program includes both micro-enterprise projects and relief aide. For example: in view of the fact that the water in Mexico is not safe to drink, the *Nazarenos* have installed machines to make it potable. These water purification plants are micro-enterprises that produce income for the impoverished families who process the water and for those who distribute this water in containers. The *Nazarena* Church also has a home for the elderly and has provided relief in the wake of a natural disaster. In the Guazteca zone of Mexico, the *Nazarena* Church created a community bank where they lend money to people so that they may begin their own micro-enterprise projects. At the time of the interview, this project has been in operation for five years.

In 2005 the *Metodista Libre* Church led by Guarillo began a series of mini-workshops for women in the community. According to Guarillo, "The main goal with these workshops is to provide the church's neighbors with skills to help them develop as human beings." The church offers weekly haircutting workshops, which are open to anyone in the community; most of the participants are not church members. Guarillo points out, "in this way we are empowering the women of the community to be better people. Some of them already have their own hair salons in their houses, in this way providing an income for the family." The *Metodista Libre* Church also offers training workshops on decorating candles that can be sold to produce income for the participant's families. "This has helped improve the women's self-esteem and their economic situation at the same time," Guarillo said. Each workshop had approximately 12 people attending. In addition, once a week the church offers English classes for adults, youth and children; and computer classes. Soon they will begin a welding workshop.

Thirty-four year ago *La Casa de Él* Church began working with elderly people in addition to providing a home to support homosexual people. According to Toxtle, "*La Casa de Él* church's main work is among those who are most needy." Throughout the years they have supported drug addicts, alcoholics, prostitutes, and homeless children. The church provides food, shelter and other basic needs, especially, providing a new alternative for life through Jesus Christ. "We try to share the news of the gospel through appropriate songs and celebrations." Toxtle continues, "One of our goals is to share the gospel without involving any common religious proselytism. The Mexican church is too religious[2] and this, rather than being a positive point, has distanced the church from those who are more needy." Toxtle contends that a strong structure exists among the Protestants in Mexico and, as is the case with the Roman Catholic Church, it has built a wall that blocks the movement of the Holy Spirit. "We have received lots of criticism from many Protestants groups but today we are accepted and we are supporting projects in many parts of the country and throughout Latin America." He says that several well-known Latin American leaders have come from the *La Casa de Él* Church program and now serve throughout the world.

Environmental Involvement

Although all four mainline Protestant churches interviewed do not have an established environmental plan, some of them have been sporadically involved in some environmental taskforces. For instance, the *Menonita* Church planted 10,000 trees in some zones that had experienced disforestation. Sermons frequently emphasize everyone's responsibility to be good stewards of God's creation and the positive and negative implications this has. Some of the mainline Protestant pastors agree with Toxtle's point of view that, "the first task of the church is the transformation of the person rather than dealing with the consequences of environmental concerns."

Biblical Basis for Their Work

Each church interviewed has its own particular biblical passage that in one way or another determines their philosophy of work. For instance, for Cruz from the *Menonita* Church, Matthew 5-7 (The Beatitudes) describes the principles Jesus gave to his people to be lived out in their time. Cruz proposed, "We, as *Menonitas*, believe that it is possible to live the Sermon of the Mount right now."

Guarillo reported that Acts 1:8 summarizes the vision that the *Metodista Libre* in Mexico City are following. Guarillo points out, "We begin our task with our Jerusalem (the local church), but our goal as a *Metodista Libre* church is to plant more churches in Mexico City."

La Casa de Él Church relies upon 1 Peter 3:15 for its order of work. "This text affirms our purpose to be prepared to produce fruit as our identity," Toxtle claimed.

In response to my questions about their understanding of Luke 4:18-19, Cruz, the *Menonita* pastor, points out, "For us this is a key text because here Jesus' project is exposed to us as a church. Just as it happened with Jesus, the Holy Spirit has anointed us to bring good news to the poor. This is why the *Menonita* Church of Mexico has an inclination to serve the poor. We believe in *una liberación integral*, "an integral liberation": it begins in the heart of the people but goes beyond that to impact the social dimensions. We do not interpret the text in a narrow spiritual sense; we see that this text has social implications. The church should be where the needy are; the church should go to the people and not expect the people come to the church."

Perez, of the *Nazarena* Church, claims that the interpretation of Luke 4:18-19 has been polemic in Latin America. It has motivated the beginning of revolutions thereby losing its principal focus. "The *Nazarena* Church in Mexico believes that we should be involved in social arenas but not to the extreme of taking up weapons." He believes that people should be free from sin but also of any area that is a struggle in their lives which can be social, economic, psychosocial, etc.

For Toxtle of *La Casa de Él* Church, Luke 4:18-19 provides the example of how to follow Christ. These texts are imperative for the church today. Toxtle insisted, "We do not have a choice; we need to be involved if the Spirit of the Lord truly lives in us."

When I asked about their understanding of the texts in Acts, Cruz of the *Menonita* Church, pointed out, "the *Menonita* Church believes in the mission of the church with the Holy Spirit being our guide and our director." Acts 2 and 4 reveals the purpose of church growth; to expand the kingdom of God that is not yet fully present.

Perez from the *Nazarena* Church opined, "We believe in the presence of the Holy Spirit in believers as a power that purifies and sanctifies; activating the believers for God's work in the world."

For Guarillo of the *Metodista Libre* Church, "the texts of Acts are a reality for us today. We are looking for *un discipulado integral*, 'an integral discipleship.'"

According to Toxtle, La Casa de Él Church, "We use a literal interpretation of the Acts texts. However, we are very careful not to over-emphasize the experiences with the Holy Spirit. Nowadays, there are too many manipulations among Protestant groups about experiences which result in reducing the work of the Holy Spirit to simple emotions."

It seems that among the mainline Protestant churches there is an emphasis on ministering integrally. There is the notion that the ministerial work should focus outside of the church, challenging the old concept that people need to come to the church. Apparently, they believe that the presence of the Holy Spirit in the church is measured by their social involvement in the society.

Theological Issues

According to Cruz, "we as *Menonitas* see salvation from up but also from down; from the inside but also from the outside. The kingdom of God fills all dimensions: it is from heaven but also has earthly connotations. It is spiritual but also material. Therefore, the mission is an extension of the kingdom of God that has a visible manifestation in this world."

Perez points out, "the *Nazarena* Church believes that the person needs to be attended to integrally." Perez believes that the strength of the church is in the younger generations and so the church is targeting those generations.

La Casa de Él Church's main goal is to share God's love for humanity in an unconditional manner. As Toxtle said, "we pick up the trash others do not want but whom God loves. Our main goal is to express God's love to the prostitutes, alcoholics, homosexuals, homeless, drug addicts, etc."

In summary, it seems that theologically speaking the mainline churches interviewed in Mexico see the role of the church as an agent that ministers integrally to the whole person. In doing that, they are extending the kingdom of God especially among those more marginalized by the Mexican society.

General Statements

Evaluating the Protestant church in Mexico, Cruz, the *Menonita* pastor, points out, "when missions arrived from the United States they brought a gospel combined with a Western understanding of development and progress that in its time was good and produced good results. Today, however, we see a Mexican church that is too fundamentalist, excessive, arrogant and rude. This means that the church is still under the influence of a political-economic and socially capitalistic mindset that is not Mexican but rather that of a dominant nation like the USA." He continued, "the Protestant Church of Mexico, has done good things, however, lately the church has been interested only in gaining political appointments and power. This can be very dangerous to the church's prophetic role."

Perez of the *Nazarena* Church made a similar statement saying that in Mexico there is a commercialization of churches. People are looking for a better product or a church where they feel more comfortable. What is happening in the globalized market is happening in the church as well. This also shows the lack of a stable and deep discipleship program resulting in people that move from one place to another. This is permitted due to the lack of ethical pastoral behavior.

According to Cruz, "Influenced by the United States church, most of the Mexican pastors dream of having a mega church. Theologically speaking, these churches are too superficial." He says that these immature churches are open to any kind of theology and movements such as: theology of prosperity and so on. Most of the time, people go to these churches looking for emotions; they want to "feel good without having any commitment." These churches that promote the mega churches are called neo-charismatic churches. Cruz makes the distinction between neo-charismatic groups and historical Pentecostals. His comparison of the two groups is as follows: The historical Pentecostal movement is among the poor when the target of the neo-Pentecostal movement is the high class. Many of the historical Pentecostals reject many of the points taught by neo-charismatic groups. Neo-Pentecostals reject any kind of theological preparation because "you do not need to be prepared; it is enough to just feel the call of God."

Perez, of the *Menonita* Church, agrees with Cruz. He affirms that although the Christian church has grown in Mexico, the social change in the society has been minimal because: (1) *La Iglesia Evangélica*, "The Evangelical church," has forgotten its social responsibility; (2) *La Iglesia Evangélica* is looking for a space in political circles at the cost of losing their prophetic role in society and compromising their own identity. "Our prophetic role is to communicate and denounce the injustice in the system," claims Perez.

Sadly in Mexico, Perez points out, "The mainline and Pentecostal Protestant church is not an agent of change. The Protestant churches in Mexico are fighting for one-another's members; competing for their money and showing how powerful and successful they are in their mega churches." The church has forgotten its true task: to reach new members and minister to them integrally. "Protestants have organized several events in the city with the main goal of each event sadly being profit and prestige for the organizer at the expense of the Protestant communities," Perez said.

Perez is also concerned about the religious persecution that is still present in some areas of Mexico (especially rural areas). The government says that there is no religious intolerance but Perez says that there is, resulting in some families being displace from their homes by the Roman Catholic Church.

Cruz sees an uncertain future for the Protestant Church in Mexico. Mexican churches are more fundamentalist. The church is becoming more and more spiritual, isolating itself from the social and human needs of the people. He also sees a church that is increasingly seeking positions of power.

All of the pastors interviewed agree that women play a key role in the church. There is a sense of equality even within a male dominated society like Mexico. They claim that women are equal to men; "there is not difference for us as a church. We as a church are to destroy any walls of discrimination." According to Guarillo, "the macho tendency in Mexico is just a superficial facade. The fact is that Mexico has a strong matriarchal inclination."

Conclusion

It seems that the mainline Protestant churches in Mexico have their own particular pastoral programs, history and ministerial inclinations that show how diverse the church is in Mexico. These churches as a whole have a strong commitment to social issues, which seems to be based on denominational traditions and the desire to be an authentic Christian witness in the society. The churches seem to be very effective in developing workshops and micro enterprises to alleviate the social needs of the people. On the other hand, the mainline Protestant churches in Mexico do not seem to have a clear commitment to the environment.

Pastors agree that two things describe the church in Mexico: 1) the influence of theology that is Western and fundamentalist and 2) the adoption of an economic and political neo-liberalism that is reflected in some of the neo-Pentecostal churches. These politics are also reflected in the movement of members from one church to another, illustrating the lack of a deep discipleship.

Finally, the mainline Protestant Church in Mexico seems to be very small in number compared with other Pentecostals and Neo-Pentecostal groups. Pastors agree that the slow growth rate is the result of a deep commitment to providing a solid discipleship emphasis.

Mainline Protestant Churches in Colombia

In Colombia I interviewed four pastors from mainline Protestant circles. The following chart (Table 9) summarizes the general information about each pastor and their corresponding church.

Table 9. Mainline Protestant Pastors/Churches Interviewed in Colombia				
Name	Cesar Arturo **GARCIA**	Oswaldo **ARENAS**	Eduardo **BARAJAS**	Luis Alfonso **RAMIREZ**
Experience/ Position	National Director/Pastor	26 years/Pastor	5 years at the present church/ Pastor	Pastor
Nationality	Colombian	Colombian	Colombian	Colombian
Age	Mid-thirties	Early-fifties	Late fifties	Mid-sixties
Church	*Iglesia Menonita Torre Fuerte*	*La Primera Iglesia Bautista*	*La Iglesia Reformada Presbiteriana Sinodo*	*Iglesia Interamericana*
Denomination	Anabaptist Mennonite Brothers	Baptist	Presbyterian	Independent
Social Background	Middle-high	Middle-high	Low	Middle
Average Attendance	80 adults and 20 children	85 members	25 members	80 members
City	Bogotá	Bucaramanga	Bucaramanga	Bucaramanga

Similar to the Mexican churches, the mainline Protestant churches in Colombia have their own particular pastoral programs determined by their own historical and doctrinal affiliations. All of the churches interviewed have had internal conflicts that in one way or another have affected their healthy growth. For instance, the *Torre Fuerte Menonita* church in Bogotá began 6 years ago in the Garcia's home. They began offering Bible studies with a group of 13 adults. In the last six years the *Torre Fuerte* church has moved 12 times to different locations making it difficult for some people to remain in the church. However, the people who stayed have good relationships with one another, which is very positive to the spiritual and social life of the church. The ministries of this church are one-on-one discipleship and Bible study groups. Fellowship dinners and other services and programs are driven by and improve relationships.

According to Arenas, *La Primera Iglesia Bautista* has experienced several conflicts between the people and pastors, resulting in division and the loss of several people. Currently the church is working with cell groups as a way to reach the community where it is. Some of the programs the church is implementing are: leadership training; discipleship for the whole church; preaching training; outreach programs; and programs for youth, children and women.

The *Presbiteriana* Church of *La Cumbre* led by Barajas also has experienced several divisions in the past influenced by theological differences. The church offers Bible study groups every Wednesday; they have a children's program every Saturday and regular services on Sunday.

Ramirez from the *Interamericana* Church has experienced several conflicts as well. The *Interamericana* church in Bucaramanga has a historical, traditional inclination but Ramirez' inclinations are more Pentecostal. These differences have produced serious friction between him and the congregation. Describing the vision and goal of the church, Ramirez points out that the main vision of the *Interamericana* church is to be a big, strong and influential church in the society. Some of the spiritual activities of the *Interamericana* church are fasting, prayer and watch night services.

Social Involvement

At least three of the four mainline churches interviewed in Colombia are seriously involved in social issues. For instance, the *Menonita* Church led by Garcia is supporting approximately 15 children from a poor neighborhood (*El Progreso*) located in the south of Bogotá through scholarships (education and food). Once in a while the church also provides groceries for families in the same community. This church also works together with other *Menonitas* to support Colombian missionaries in Lima, Peru; Guadalajara, Mexico; in the Guaunan tribe in Panama; Uzbekistan; and in a native community in Ecuador.

As a denomination the *Menonita* church in Colombia has created an organization called MECOLDES (Menonite Colombian Organization for Development) and *Paz Justa*, "Fair Peace." Garcia states, "because we have few members in our churches and in order to accomplish something tangible in the society, the *Menonita* churches joined forces and created this organization. Approximately 40 *Menonita* churches form part of MECOLDES and *Paz Justa*." The main focus these organizations are: community development, social work, and being a prophetic voice in the country. Through MECOLDES, the *Menonita* Church built an entire neighborhood after the 1999 earthquake in Armenia, Colombia. Now there is program to support people who have been displaced by the war.[3]

Although not on the same scale as the *Menonita* Church, *La Primera Iglesia Bautista de Bucaramanga* is also involved in social projects. For instance, since 2004 the church has been involved in an outreach program to one of the poorest areas of the city. Primarily the church provides continuing education for marginalized children. They also provide workshops about parent-children relationships.

According to Barajas, when the *Presbiteriana* Church began 25 years ago in the *Barrio La Cumbre,* World Vision worked through the church to provide support to many of the community's families. At that time, church attendance was around 250 but when World Vision left, the people also stopped coming to church. In 2002 the church realized that many children, whose families had been displaced by the Civil War in Colombia, were suffering from lack of food, clothing, and schooling. Therefore the church began a new social project to help alleviate these needs. This program consists of providing lunch each week day, school supplies and clothing to 60 children. This project is supported by some non-governmental organizations (NGOs), among them the *Programa Mundial de Alimentos*, "World Food Program," led by the United Nations and a Roman Catholic organization. When applying for assistance with the Roman Catholic Church, he was told, "Hunger does not have a religious affiliation." In 2005 Barajas also began a feeding project in another area of the city where people have been displaced by the war. Within a year the *Presbiteriana* Church was feeding approximately 150 children. Barajas reports that they were also reaching the children's parents through this project.

Environmental Involvement

The mainline Protestant churches in Colombia, like those in Mexico, do not have any established environmental programs in their churches. Most of the pastors interviewed stated that this is an area on which they do not spend time.

Biblical Basis for Their Work

The mainline Protestant churches in Colombia agree that there are three main areas that compel them to do their work: (1) practical; (2) biblical; and (3) theological or doctrinal. For instance, according to Garcia, of the *Menonita* Church in Bogotá, "there are needs in the societies in which we live that demand a practical and concrete response. At the same time these needs point us to a biblical teaching to love our neighbor. As *Menonitas*, we see the involvement in the society, the resolution of conflicts, non-violent resistance, loving others and working towards peace as our theological basis which is very relevant to the violent society in which we live."

Barajas, the *Presbiteriana* pastor, says, "the primary motivation for our work is the belief that the gospel is integral, meaning that it targets all areas of the individual. Second, we have seen the needs of the children in the area. Finally, we as Presbyterians believe that caring for those that are in need is a fundamental part of who we are."

In response to my questions about specific biblical text that describe their philosophy of work, Garcia from the *Torre Fuerte Menonita* church stated that his church emphasizes the Gospels because they focus on the life of Jesus, his dependence on the Spirit, and his communion with the Father. In other words, their focus is *Cristocentrico*, "Christ-centered." Garcia explains this notion by saying that "we do not see the Bible as a flat book where Deuteronomy has the same authority as Luke. We interpret each book of the Bible in the light of the Gospels. Our goal is to imitate Jesus and not King David or Solomon. We understand the Trinity based on the life of Jesus; in other words, our pneumatology is based on the relationship the Spirit has with Jesus." Another key text for them is John 17:21 "that all of them may be one . . . that the world may believe that you have sent me." "For the *Torre Fuerte* Church *unidad*, "unity," is a key evangelistic tool," Garcia points out, "We have unity not to become a social club but rather in order for the world to believe in Jesus."

In response to my question about their understanding of Luke 4:18-19, Garcia points out, "when Jesus says 'the Spirit of the Lord is upon me' it is not because Jesus speaks in tongues, not for his miracles, but because He helps the poor, heals the sick, sets free the captives, and so on. Therefore, what we teach in our church is that if you have the Spirit, this needs to be translated into concrete deeds and many of them should be social." For Arenas of *La Primera Iglesia Bautista*, Luke 4:18-19 describes the agenda of the pastor as well as the members of the church. Jesus defines his agenda based on the Word of God itself.

Barajas, pastor of the *Presbiteriana* Church, says that Luke 4:18-19 summarizes the mission of the church, particularly in a country like Colombia where there are so many needs and people, who in one way or another, are oppressed and captive. "The true vision of the church," he says, "is to leave the four walls of the church and reach the people in a integral manner. The Christian church has made mistakes by being too egocentric. When the church spends too much time looking at itself it immediately loses focus on the true commitment and the goal of the gospel." Many churches in Colombia, according to Barajas, are worrying about building their own kingdom and not the kingdom of God.

On the other hand, Ramirez' *Interamericana* Church sees Luke 4:18-19 as fundamental for their mission, especially in the area of liberation. They use this verse when they minister in liberation services.

In response to my question about their understanding of the first passages of the book of Acts, Garcia from *Torre Fuerte Menonita* Church, points out that Acts shows that being a witness also means being a martyr and therefore we need to be willing to sacrifice ourselves for the sake of the Gospel. For Arenas of *La Primera Iglesia Bautista*, Acts shows that the presence of the Holy Spirit is fundamental for any kind of project. "The Bible defines humanity as an integral entity therefore we need to minister to the person in an integral way." For Barajas at the *Presbiteriana* Church, Acts shows the beginning of a church that is full of power but through time this power has been misunderstood. For instance, for many the power of the Holy Spirit and Pentecost is reduced to only speaking in tongues. "However the *Presbiteriana* Church believes that this fullness of the Spirit comes to do concrete social and spiritual things."

Overall, it seems that the motivation for social involvement among the mainline churches interviewed in Colombia comes primarily from the Scripture itself and more particularly from the Gospels. The hermeneutics used for one of the pastors is to interpret the Scriptures based on the life of Jesus presented in the Gospels.

Theological Issues

Talking about the passive resistance of *Menonitas* in serving the Colombian Army Forces Garcia points out, "the biblical teaching of loving one's neighbor is not negotiable; thus, we cannot love our neighbor if we have a gun in our hands. It is proven in Colombia that stopping the violence with violence produces more violence."

For Garcia, each Christian church in Colombia says that Jesus is the center of their Christian life however that looks different in every church. "For us that Jesus is the center means that we are looking to imitate Jesus in a practical sense. It means that we should love and pray for our enemy; it means that we should forgive our brother and sisters seventy times seven; it means that we are to follow a Jesus that invites us to reconciliation, and so on. As a church we are trying to imitate who Jesus is and what Jesus does." Garcia continues saying that when Jesus said, "I am the road and the way to the Father," he was showing us both the direction and the means to get to the Father. "In this respect," stated Garcia, "Jesus is the model we should imitate to get to the Father and that begins here on earth."

The fellowship of the community of believers is a key theological, ecclesiological and missiological factor in the life of any Christian organization. The *Torre Fuerte Menonita* Church puts a strong emphasis on relationships; people should be able to know each other, share their needs, and behave as a united family. All the meetings target this relational purpose. Garcia claims that the fact that their church has no building of its own but instead rents neighborhood clubhouses or similar buildings to meet, illustrates in a very tangible way that it is the people who make the church, not the building. As such, strong personal relationships play a very key role for this church.

According to Barajas at the *Presbiteriana* Church in *la Cumbre*, it is important to preach an integral gospel that not only cares for the spiritual needs of the people but also the physical needs, as the book of James instructs. Barajas points out that the goal of the gospel is not to have a full church but rather that the church will be an instrument of the Lord to make disciples. At the end, it is the Lord who produces growth. Barajas says, "we as a church need to stop being worried about bringing people to our church. I believe that our goal as a Christian church is to be out and be present in the society. The church needs to be in the society where the people are."

Theologically speaking, the mainline Protestant church in Colombia takes Jesus' life as a missiological model and goal. They understand that numerical growth should not be considered a measure of spiritual vitality. This understanding is perhaps because many of the mainline Protestants churches in Colombia are relatively small in number.

General Statements

As the interviews turned to the topic of liberation theology, Garcia of the *Menonita* Church, was quick to establish that liberation theology says good things but not new things. In some respects liberation theology puts into practice what Jesus says in the Gospels. However, some liberation theology ideas are dangerous because of their emphasis on making social changes without having an encounter with Jesus. In some ways, conversion for them is understood only in social terms. "I think it goes far deeper than that," Garcia said. He also pointed out that discussions using the term "liberation theology" are not relevant anymore and we should make more emphasis on *mision integral*, "integral mission," now.

For Arenas of *La Primera Iglesia Bautista*, liberation theology is a subject of study for a seminary class but it is not much present in the life of the church anymore. Arenas thinks that liberation theology is a gospel interpreted socially.

For Barajas of the *Presbiteriana* Church, liberation theology's main fault is its extremist contextualization of the Word of God. "Changes are not effective if we only change the social structures, effective change takes place only if Jesus lives in people's heart and changes it." Barajas continues, "The spiritual dimension comes first and as a result of changes there, the social realities will also change."

Ramirez, *Interamericana* Church, does not know what liberation theology is about because he has not had any good experiences with people who were involved in this theology. Ramirez points out that this theology is too humanistic and not biblical.

The mainline Protestant churches in Colombia have been forced to change by the biggest Pentecostal and Neo-Pentecostal churches. According to Ramirez, *Interamericana* Church, "these big churches are planning one program after another with internationals speakers and inviting others churches. Once the pastors attend these events most of the leaders end up leaving to attend these big churches." There is competition between the churches and Ramirez claims that the big churches are growing at the expense, in terms of membership, of other churches.

Conclusion

Like the churches in Mexico, the mainline Protestant churches in Colombia have their own particular pastoral programs determined by their own historical and doctrinal affiliations. Three of the four churches interviewed were dealing with internal conflicts that in one way or another affected healthy growth.

Like the churches in Mexico, most of the mainline Protestant churches in Colombia have a deep commitment to social issues. It seems that their desire for social involvement is motivated by (1) practical; (2) biblical; and (3) theological or doctrinal understandings. On the other hand, like the church in Mexico, the mainline Protestant churches in Colombia do not seem to have a clear environmental commitment.

Finally, like the church in Mexico, the mainline Protestant churches in Colombia seem to be very small in terms of membership when compared with Pentecostal and Neo-Pentecostal groups. Pastors agree that there is competition between the churches and that the biggest churches are growing by taking members from other small churches.

Mainline Protestant Churches in Peru

In Lima, Peru, I interviewed four pastors from mainline Protestant circles. Table 10 summarizes the general information about each pastor and their corresponding church.

Like the churches in Mexico and Colombia, each mainline Protestant church interviewed in Lima has its own pastoral plan determined by its own denominational affiliation and the needs of the people to whom it ministers. Every church interviewed has an established program for children, teenagers and youth; women, music, and prayer ministry. All of the interviewees agree that discipleship is one of the main focuses of their churches. Only the *Bethel Presbiteriana y Reformada* Church led by Puell has done door-to-door evangelistic campaigns to distribute Christian literature. Two of the pastors interviewed (Prada and Miuler) mentioned the importance of sharing the Word of God in an integral way; meaning to minister to the physical, emotional, and spiritual needs of the people.

Social Involvement

It seems that only two of the four mainline Protestant churches interviewed in Peru have an established social plan that deals with the needs of the community. The *Menonita* Church led by Prada is helping one of the poorest areas of the city called the Guican, a neighborhood whose inhabitants were displaced by a war against the *Sendero Luminoso,* "Shining Path."[4] Prada points out that in this area hundreds of children are in need. The *Menonita* Church is joining forces with an already existing independent congregation that has a good

Table 10. Mainline Protestant Pastors/Churches Interviewed in Peru				
Name	Roque Felix PUELL	Jose Manuel PRADA	Klaus MIULER	Jose Luis LOPEZ
Experience / Position	15 months at present church/ Pastor	Missionary since 1999/Pastor	Missionary/ Pastor	Pastor
Nationality	Peruvian	Colombian	German	Peruvian
Age	Mid-fifties	Late-forties	Late-forties	Early thirties
Church	La Iglesia Presbiteriana y Reformada del Peru, Bethel	La Iglesia de los Hermanos Menonitas	La Iglesia Libre Luterana Vida Nueva	La Iglesia Metodista Libre
Denomination	Presbyterian	Mennonite Brother	Free Lutheran	Free Methodist
Social Background	Middle	Middle-high	Low	Low
Average Attendance	100 people/40 baptized	50 people	30 people	35 people

support program for children. These churches provide lunch and after school support to approximately 150 children.

Beginning in 1998 and ending in 2002, the *Vida Nueva* Free Lutheran Church led by Miuler organized soccer tournaments among gang groups of the Pamplona Alta area. Miuler points out that this resulted in reducing the violence in the area. "In the early years the tension was very high, but later it was better," Miuler said. Close to 240 people participated in each tournament. It is thanks to these tournaments that the people of the community know the church very well and are comfortable asking for the church's help in times of difficulty, like the death of a loved one. Miuler points out that nowadays the *Vida Nueva* Church has a lot of access to many families in the community.

Another area in which the *Vida Nueva* Church has been involved in the Pamplona community is with its ministry to poor children. Miuler believes that the first six years of life are the years in which the spiritual embryo of the person is developed; therefore this time is fundamental to plant the seed of God. With that in mind, one of the church's main focuses is on providing a program that helps in the spiritual, social, emotional, and physical development of children. The main goal is to teach children to face their problems rather than escape from them. Miuler points out, "We do not want to give money to the people; we want to empower them so that they can find their own destination."

The *Vida Nueva* Free Lutheran Church has a musical program that offers classes for children or adults to learn a typical instrument. Miuler claims that many people have come to know the Lord through that music. "There are so many talents in the people but there are no resources to help develop these talents so the church is providing the means for people to develop their own musical talents." Miuler thinks that the people with more talent are also those who cause more difficulty in society because nobody challenges them. "A lot of these children are just looking to be valued and accepted." Miuler continues, "When learning an instrument (1) the student learns discipline and perseverance; (2) the student also learns to use his/her time wisely; (3) the church gains trust with the families; and (4) the environment in the family changes. The children who play an instrument also participate in the church services. The philosophy we are using is that we help you to learn an instrument; you help your neighbor in return."

The *Presbiteriana* and *Metodista Libre* churches do not have an established social plan however they have some sporadic social involvement once or twice a year. For instance, the *Metodista Libre* Church led by Lopez raises funds to get Christmas gifts for children of the area. Lopez points out that most of the children who come to the church are very poor and many of them only have a mother. The church also distributes clothing for needy families. The *Metodista Libre* Church collects groceries to give to families that sometimes do not have anything to eat. Sometimes the pastoral family also provides support or food from their own home.

Environmental Involvement

Like the churches in Mexico and Colombia, the mainline Protestant church in Peru does not have much participation in environmental issues. Only the *Menonita* Church has had minimal participation against the deforestation of one area of the city of Lima.

Biblical Basis for Their Work

Pastors interviewed agree that the basis for their pastoral work is planted in the Scriptures. Prada of the Menonita Church says that the Beatitudes (Matthew 5-7) represent the core values for their ministry. For Miuler at *Vida Nueva* Free Lutheran Church bases his ministry on Matthew 11:28, "Come to me, all you who are weary and burdened, and I will give you rest." In the violent society where he ministers he wants to show that peace is found in Jesus. Lopez, of the *Metodista Libre* Church, says that Matthew 28:19 represents their commission and direction for their pastoral work; especially the significance of the words "Go" and "make disciples." Lopez points out, "being and making disciples is our goal as a church. In order to achieve this goal, we need to go and be with the people, we cannot wait for the people to come to our church." Finally, Puell of the *Presbiteriana* Church, says that the vision of the church is to be a missionary church; big, stable, and faithful to the Word of God with revival. The mission is to give testimony of God through evangelization, teaching, love and service to others. Puell points out that both the mission and vision of the church are based on the Scriptures.

In response to my questions about their understanding of Luke 4:18-19, Puell, of the *Presbiteriana* Church, points out, "we need first to know, in the context of the text, who are the poor? Are these people poor spiritually or materially?" Puell affirms that the gospel needs to address these two dimensions. For Lopez, the *Metodista Libre* pastor, the text is basic to understanding that God can use and empower the church to do his work.

In regard to their understanding of the first chapters of Acts, Prada of the *Menonita* Church, points out, "these texts show that the Christian life is practical, reinforcing *el sacerdocio de todos los creyentes*, "the priesthood of all believers." We want to have the characteristics of the church of the first century where we can share friendship, love, and unity." For Miuler, at *Vida Nueva* Free Lutheran Church, Acts shows that the Holy Spirit gives power to the church. "We need to be careful not to fall into activism (doing and doing) because others will ask what the difference is between our church and a NGO. We need to remember that it is the Holy Spirit that makes the difference. The nature of the Holy Spirit does not depend on the number of people in a congregation or if everything goes well. I believe that the Holy Spirit is revealed in good times as well as in times of difficulties," Miuler said.

Generally, there is a notion among the mainline Protestant churches interviewed in Peru that numerical growth is not necessarily the measure of spiritual vitality. It seems that community plays a key role for the mainline church and, as the Roman Catholic Church points out, the notion of the priesthood of all believers is also a key point for the mainline church. By this they mean the empowering of the laity for pastoral work.

Theological Issues

According to Miuler, of *Vida Nueva* Free Lutheran Church, "the idea to start the soccer tournament was not my idea but the idea of a gang. I believe that God speaks to us in a very quiet way and sometimes through non-Christian people."

Miuler highlights that the church has a prophetic role that it needs to fulfill. It is through the church where God speaks and criticizes what is wrong in the society. Social involvement and evangelization are two sides of the same coin and this coin is called the gospel; neglecting one would be neglecting the fullness of the gospel of Jesus Christ.

Talking about liberation theology, Prada, pastor of the *Menonita* Church, points out that there have been many criticisms against it in the past, perhaps for the lack of a serious study. "Liberation theology is something we as Christian need to look at carefully. Liberation theology rediscovers the Jesus of history that encourages us to live immersed in the society," said Prada. Miuler from the *Vida Nueva* Free Lutheran Church agrees that there are aspects of liberation theology that are very good; for instance, the questions about relationship between sin and the system. Liberation theology has raised questions that are worthy of consideration.

Giving a personal analysis of the churches in Peru, Miuler from *Vida Nueva* Free Lutheran Church said that, "Many churches in Peru determine their spiritual level based on the number of people who attend their churches."

According to Miuler there are two forms of social involvement: One is diaconal (providing material relief) and other is political (where we can denounce violations of human rights and provide an alternative to the problem). Miuler continues, "Most of the Evangelical churches in Peru are learning to provide diaconal assistance; more and more we see churches involved in this area." On the other hand, the Evangelical churches are still afraid to be involved in the political arena. There is an understanding among Protestants that a Christian should not be involved in politics. "I agree that perhaps joining a political party will not be the solution, but the word politics come from *Polis* that means the "caring of and for the city". Therefore, the answer to the question of what the role of the church in this world is will provide our mission, ecclesiology and theology," Miuler said.

In sum, theologically speaking there is the understanding of God's presence working outside of the church and even speaking through non-Christians channels. The gospel is seen as an integral form.

General Statements

All of the pastors interviewed agree that women play a key role in the life and ministry of the church. According to Prada, of the *Menonita* Church in Lima, women are fundamental for the pastoral and social work of the church. Women in the *Menonita* Church of Peru have to face a lot of resistance from the male members who have difficulty seeing them in leadership roles. Lopez from the *Metodista Libre* Church mentioned that the majority of the church's pastoral team are women. "Obviously," he said, "women play a crucial role in this church."

Analyzing the Lutheran church in Peru, Miuler says that the church in Peru depends too much on foreign practices. For example: he believes that the church in Latin America copies too much music, hymns, and liturgy from the United States and Europe.

Talking about the situation of the Peruvian church, Lopez from the *Metodista Libre* Church mentioned that there are too many conflicts between pastors and churches; most of these conflicts are caused by fighting for members. Lopez said, "In the last two years that we have been in ministry in this area, our crises and conflicts have come from other Christian churches. There is envy and condemnation among Protestants." Miuler also commented on this situation, "If the Protestant denominations do not start respecting each other (membership affiliation and theology), the church will receive the consequences in forty or fifty years. People will be confused and at the end people will believe in nobody." He said this is exactly what has happened in Europe.

Conclusion

Like the churches in Mexico and Colombia, the mainline Protestant churches in Peru seem to have their own particular pastoral programs determined by their own mainline and doctrinal affiliations. Like the church in Colombia, the mainline Protestant church in Peru is also struggling with the issue of departing members.

In contrast to the churches in Mexico and Colombia, only two of the four mainline Protestant churches interviewed in Peru have a deep commitment for social issues. However, like the churches in Mexico and Colombia and despite the increased environmental contamination caused by the accumulation of waste, air pollution, and a lack of an appropriate drainage system in Lima, Peru, the mainline Protestant churches in the city do not appear to have a clear environmental commitment.

Finally, like the churches in Mexico and Colombia, the mainline Protestant churches in Peru seem to be very small in numbers compared with other Pentecostal and Neo-Pentecostal groups. Pastors agree that there is competition between churches with larger churches often attracting members from the smaller churches.

Mainline Protestant Churches in Argentina

In Buenos Aires, Argentina, I interviewed four pastors from mainline Protestant circles. Table 11, on the following page, summarizes the general information about each pastor and their corresponding church.

The mainline Protestant churches interviewed in Argentina seem to have adopted an integral ministry model as their main pastoral plan. They also focus on small groups in which discipleship takes place. Like the churches in Mexico, Colombia and Peru, the mainline Protestant churches in Argentina have their own particular pastoral programs determined by their own Mainline and doctrinal affiliations.

For instance, the *Fé y Vida* Baptist Church, led by Baspineiro, is part of a renewal project based on integral mission. The first step toward this goal was to move from a vertically structured church to a more horizontal or base structure. Three elements that characterize this church are (1) creating a sense community (2) ecclesial environment and (3) base characteristics, meaning that the church wants to be involved in the destiny of the community where they minister. Thus, the main goal as a church is to redefine the concept of mission and incarnation in the neighborhood. The *Fé y Vida* Church has three main commitments: to God, to humanity, and to creation. Baspineiro worked with C. Rene Padilla at the Kairos Organization for several years, which is where he got his ministerial initiative.

For almost 33 years the *Alianza Menonita* Church, led by Gutierrez, maintained the German language and cultural tradition. "This was positive in its time because it helped the church establish as a community," said Gutierrez.

Table 11. Mainline Protestant Pastors/Churches Interviewed in Argentina

Name	Arturo Humberto BASPINEIRO	Juan Angel GUTIERREZ	Marcelo ROBLES	Jorge GALI
Experience/ Position	Pastor	Senor pastor of the present church since 2001	Senor pastor of the present church since 1998	Senior Pastor
Nationality	Argentinean	Argentinean	Argentinean	Argentinean
Age	Died on March 18, 2006 (late-fifties)	Early sixties	Late-thirties	Early sixties
Church	*Iglesia Bautista Fé y Vida*	*Iglesia Alianza Menonita*	*La Misión Presbiteriana*	*Iglesia Bautista La Lucila*
Denomination	Baptist	Alliance Mennonite	Mission Presbyterian	Baptist
Social Background	Middle-low	Middle	Middle-low	Middle-high
Average Attendance		60 people	170 regular attendance	150 people

However, the church felt the need to extend to the Argentinean community where they were. Therefore, 14 years ago the church changed its services from German to Spanish. More recently the church built a gym to try to welcome the community. Therefore, it can be said that the *Alianza Menonita* Church's programs developed out of the process of discovering who they are as a Christian community and in service to the kingdom of God.

The *Mision Menonita* Church, led by Robles, emphasizes small groups. Robles said, "Each small group is an expression of the kingdom of God in each neighborhood." This year the church has about 40 small groups. Together with these groups, the church is also working on discipleship training. In addition, the church has seven ministerial candidates that soon will be named pastors. Every month the church has a retreat with new members where the leadership shares about the vision of the church and ministers to the people's needs.

The *Lucila* Baptist Church led by Gali has three main areas of pastoral work: (1) the life in community, (2) service to the society, and (3) spiritual areas that include the liturgy, an ecumenical group, and spiritual retreats. According to Gali, discipleship takes place through small, in-home groups (the church has around 20 such groups that began 15 years ago and meet once a week) and brotherhood takes place through retreats (family camp and fellowship lunches in groups).

Social Involvement

It seems that the mainline Protestant churches in Argentina have a strong social commitment. For instance, the *Fé y Vida* Baptist Church led by Baspineiro has several activities in place that promote social justice, integration, and social relief. The church provides the setting for dialogues about topics of social interest such as: violence in the area (insecurity), single mothers, abortion, addiction, etc.

The *Fé y Vida* Church also promotes the participation of folkloric activities as a means for social interaction and discipleship. For instance, the church is in charge of keeping the instruments for folkloric musical groups of the community. By doing that the church has access to speak with the members of the groups as well as participate in the activities of the community. According to Baspineiro, in the process of picking-up and returning the instruments from and to the church, "we as a church have time to share about Jesus. This is what we call *discipulado en el camino*, "discipleship on the road." As Jesus did, so we do today." This discipleship on the road method has been very effective with young people in particular.

Since 2004 the *Fé y Vida* Church has also offered a discipleship program to women of the community through exercise, dancing and folklore. According to Baspineiro, "the road we chose is the long way, meaning that we do not choose to gain members quickly but are rather thinking of being incarnational." Thus, the *Fé y Vida* Church has become the space where the neighbors discuss and explore their life and their faith.

After surveying the community where it is located, the *Alianza Menonita* Church led by Gutierrez, found out that there were two major needs: the number of elderly people was increasing and there was a need for a program that involved the children and younger generation. The *Alianza Menonita* Church decided to start a project called CEDECRI -Centro Deportivo Cristiano (Sport Christian Center). This project began in 2005 and its main goal is to extend the invitation of relationship to the people of the community; especially children, teenagers and youths. The church built a new gym next to the main sanctuary that is open to the community for sport activities. People play basketball, volleyball and ping-pong as well as participate in mini-soccer tournaments, activities that are organized and led by members of the congregation. The main focus is to establish dialogue and relationships with people of the community who do not attend the church.

A year ago the *Alianza Menonita* Church also began an activity called Fellowship Sundays where they share a day with the non-Christian community. What the church is trying to do is open their door to the community through non-religious activities such as a lunch (potluck), fellowship, sharing, and usually they finish by repeating The Lord's Prayer. Gutierrez points out, "We are trying to help the people discover, through us, the God of life."

For the past ten years this church has also been economically supporting a Pentecostal organization that runs a house for abused children. On special occasions, such as Christmas, Children's day and others, the women and youth groups of the *Alianza Menonita* Church help with the celebration through activities and gifts for these children.

The *Mision Presbiteriana* Church led by Robles has elementary and high school programs for adults. It also offers a micro-enterprise program where the church provides loans to people who want to start a business. So far the church has provided loans to 15 people. The church also has two feeding programs in a marginalized neighborhood; one that serves a meal to more than 400 children (Monday through Friday), and another that provides snacks for 50 children. The church also has an office that supports people in finding jobs and legal documents.

The *Lucila* Baptist Church led by Gali has a drug rehabilitation program that began 15 years ago. The program offers a house where the participants live, professional counseling, technical skill workshops that encourage micro-enterprise, and reintegration into the society. The program has a maximum capacity of 12 people that have a time of recovery between 2 and 4 years. The church also offers an after school support program for children from an area of risk in the city and it provides food for homeless people once a week.

Through an ecumenical partnership, the *Lucila* Baptist Church supports a shelter for homeless people and it has participated in campaigns to help the voiceless. For instance, two years ago the local government issued an edict that did not allow the poor to collect and recycle boxes in the Lucila area. The *Lucila* Church joined with other churches in the area and spoke with the government superintendent in favor of people doing this kind of work. The result was positive and the government changed the law.

The *Alianza Menonita* Church led by Gutierrez has also participated in dialogue with others Christian churches and organization in Buenos Aires. Periodically Gutierrez attends a group meeting called *Red del Camino*, "Road Connection," that is comprised of people from several denominations, which meet to discuss issues concerning integrally serving the communities where they serve. Gutierrez said, "Listening to each other is one of the most constructive learning experiences we as leaders and church members can have."

Environmental Involvement

Like the church in Mexico, Colombia and Peru, the mainline Protestant churches in Argentina do not seem to have an established environmental plant. However, as isolated groups there is some involvement. For instance, in 2004 the *Fé y Vida* Baptist Church and neighbors from the area began a campaign to request that the government install a sewage system. They were successful and, at the end of that year, the government did the requested work. In the same way, one of the small groups from the *Mision Presbiteriana* Church led by Robles was concerned about and cleaned up the streets and the neighborhood. "In doing that we were demonstrating that the kingdom of God has environmental connotations," said Robles.

Biblical Basis for Their Work

Like in the other countries, the pastors interviewed in Argentina agree that the basis for their ministerial work comes from the Scriptures. For instance, for Gutierrez of the *Alianza Menonita* Church, Deuteronomy 8:11a "Be careful that you do not forget the Lord your God," shows that loving God has two dimensions: one is horizontal and one is vertical. "As a community we look everyday at how to love God and our neighbor as ourselves. This motivates our ecclesial life."

For Robles, of the *Mision Presbiteriana* Church, there are four main biblical texts that provide the foundation for their ministerial work: Luke 4:18-19 describes the mission of the church; Habakkuk 3:2 describes the spirituality of the church; 2 Timothy 2:2 describes the formational area of the church; and Acts 5:42 describes the church strategy: in the temple and in the house.

For Gali of the *Lucila* Baptist Church, Mark 12:30-31 "Love your God . . . and your neighbor as yourself," describes the ministerial role of their church. He says that this text describes three dimensions of the *Lucila* Church: worship and communion, mission, and service.

Responding to my question about their understanding of Luke 4:18-19 Baspineiro pointed out, "I think this text has a practical sense in which those who become disciples of Christ need to have the same vision that Jesus had about the Kingdom of God. This text means the commandment God has through Jesus for the community." This text points out a series of challenges for the building of a new humanity where equality, justice, solidarity, and fraternity among humanity is a reality for building the kingdom of God. This text ratifies the compromise of the church for the present epochs. "As a church we identify ourselves with this text because it describes who we are as a church and it also defines our task," Baspineiro said.

According to Gutierrez, *Alianza Menonita* Church, Luke 4:18-19 has two dimensions: a social/human and a spiritual dimension. Both things are crucial and the church cannot ignore either one. Gutierrez, said, "we as a church see "the captives" as both those who are immersed in sin and also those who do not have a voice in society." Those who are blind, as the text mentions, are those whose ambitions are focused on wealth and those who are egocentric. This is a text that needs to be interpreted and applied both consistently and constantly.

According to Robles, pastor of the *Mision Presbiteriana* Church, the name of their church is "the Mission" because their key text is Luke 4:18-19, and is the inspiration for the church's work. Every year Robles preaches on these key texts so that people can understand the church's mission. Robles said that this text demonstrates the mission God has for the church; it is spiritual as well as integral (in other words it covers the whole person). "The Spirit plays a key role; Jesus applied this text to himself but it also is applicable to the church. In the same way that God sent Jesus, God is also sending us as a church through the power of the Holy Spirit. Without the intervention of the Spirit we cannot accomplish anything." He continues that the mission of the church is first of all spiritual; this means, that unless God does a miracle to make the people free (those who are captive to drugs or any kind of addiction), then the church cannot accomplish anything.

In regard to their understanding of the first chapters of Acts, Baspineiro points out that these texts are an ecclesiological model for the *Fé y Vida* Baptist Church. This is practiced through love and justice. "We as a church feel satisfaction to be able to recover the concept of the Kingdom of God among our neighborhood. For instance, we talk freely about God without marking the dualism between the world and the church. There is a genuine dialogue about what faith is and what life is among the people of the neighborhood. *Fé y Vida* Church is a center for meetings in addition to gathering in several different places like a neighbor's house, in the streets or in the parks."

For Gutierrez of the *Alianza Menonita* Church, Acts provides a model in which the church needs to live in a way that provides a daily testimony in the world. The Holy Spirit plays a key role in this process of being a witness. "We need to be careful to not reduce the action of the Spirit in a particular action or expression," claimed Gutierrez.

For Robles, at the *Mision Presbiteriana* Church, these first texts of Acts are, "fundamental for the direction of the church and we need to go back to them time after time." He said that in most of the revivals of the past one of the main focuses was to go back to the model presented in these texts. For instance, "to have all the things in common" should have practical implications for people today.

For Gali of the *Lucila* Baptist Church, the events described in the book of Acts took place in specific time and setting and should not be taken as ideal for us today. He said that one thing that we need to take from Acts is that God worked in history. "Today, we need to discover how God is working in our time. Nevertheless, Acts 4:32 provides some parameters that describe how the church should live in community," said Gali.

In sum, it seems that like the churches in Peru, community plays an important ecclesiological and missiological role for the churches in Argentina. For most of the pastors interviewed the Scripture has present relevance for their ministry, yet one pastor believes that some of the biblical principles are not relevant for the church today.

Theological Issues

According to Baspineiro of the *Fé y Vida* Baptist Church, *ministerio integral*, "Integral ministry," implies hard work and commitment with God and the society where the church is ministering. He says, "It would be easy to continue with the old evangelistic style that promotes a dichotomy between the church and the world." However, in doing an integral ministry the church is being a Christian witness where the values of the Kingdom are presented and available to the society. He goes on to say that incarnation is the price every church needs to pay if it really wants to be Christ-like in the world.

Robles, the *Mision Presbiteriana* Church, points out that the main goal as a church is to be where the people are. Therefore, the majority of his church's work takes place in the neighborhoods. The church meets only in the sanctuary on Sundays, the rest of the week the church's activities take place with the people.

In sum, perhaps the reason most of the churches in Latin America are not involved in an integral mission is because it takes time and knowledge not only of the Bible but also of the social reality in which the church serves; this is an extra effort that many of the pastors are not willing to make. Another reason is that, in many cases, one needs to sacrifice numerical growth in order to truly become involved and most of the Christian denominations and mission societies do not operate with this philosophy.

General Statements

Discussing the role of the Protestant church in Argentina, Baspineiro of *Fé y Vida* Baptist Church says that there are several Protestant ethnic groups in Argentina. There are those who came from Europe and have their own pastoral focus. There are also churches that came from the United States through missional work and they have their own pastoral and ministerial agenda. During the time of the cold war in Argentina this final group decided to stay out of any social involvement because they did not want to be linked to the Marxist groups. These churches limited themselves to spreading the gospel through evangelistic campaigns. Baspineiro said, "this kind of evangelization is superficial and does not communicate the true values of the Kingdom of God. It only targets the spiritual needs that any religion can satisfy." The challenge of the church today is to know where they come from, where they are now, and where they are going.

According to Baspineiro, because many missionaries have economic commitments with their home denominations, their main goal is to produce a numerical result, which reduces their missional work to superficial results. He said that this system supports the dualistic view (church and world) where the social life depends on political decisions and the spiritual life is the church's responsibility. Baspineiro said that it is not possible to divide humanity because by doing that it deteriorates our anthropology and produces a wrong theology.

When analyzing the role of the mainline Protestant church in Argentina, Gutierrez, pastor of the *Alianza Menonita* Church, points out that he sees the church as being apathetic to social needs where in reality it should be leading. He says, "The new generations are not strong enough to continue the Christian role of the past generation. The church needs to assume the prophetic role in the society but it seems that instead the church is always behind the times and the events that the society is facing. This reality causes the church to be ineffective at times." Gutierrez points out that when a mainline Protestant church is divided and segregated; it makes it very difficult to be an effective and prophetic voice in Argentina.

Analyzing the mainline Protestant church in Argentina, Robles of the *Mision Presbiteriana* Church, said that the church has grown in recent years and that the impact of the church in the Argentinean society is bigger than before. The church is more involved in social issues today. "On the other hand," Robles points out, "the gospel that was brought to Argentina was a gospel that preached about individual salvation, lacking concern for the needs of the neighbor. For many years the Mainline Protestant church in Argentina limited their work to the middle social class thereby losing the opportunity to impact a more integrated and ethnic population." He states that there was no understanding of the gospel as integral and part of the kingdom of God. According to Robles, "Among mainline Protestant churches, there is a lot of reflection about social issues but very few actions. We need to speak and think less and act more, in concrete ways."

Speaking about the situation of the mainline Protestant church in Argentina, Gali, of *La Lucila* Baptist Church, mentions that the church has little impact on the Argentine society. He says that the Roman Catholic Church has more impact on the general society because it is facilitated by the media. However, when speaking about changes in people's lives, Gali believes that the Protestant church has had a greater impact. However, he claims that many pastors who have gained wealth using the church, particularly by espousing the theology of prosperity have tainted and damaged the reputation of the Protestant church in Argentina.

According to Gali, there are changes in the society that the church needs to interpret in order to minister effectively to the society. The mainline Protestant church is still influenced by a rational paradigm that has not produced much fruit in society when, on the other hand, the Neo-Pentecostal churches (the fastest growing church in Argentina) are using a paradigm based on senses (emotions and feelings) that is attracting thousands. Gali points out that this Neo-Pentecostal paradigm is targeting the most postmodern society of Argentina.

For Gali, in order for the Christian church to impact the society, the church needs to be more involved in ecumenical relationships. "However," he says, "we are too far away from this reality, because there is too much disrespect among the churches and among pastors. The vision of the Protestant church is still too individualistic. This attitude is based on an individualistic theology as well." In 2005 *La Lucila* Baptist Church was burned by vandals. At 10 pm that same night a Roman Catholic priest called to express sympathy and offered their cathedral for the Baptist services. *La Lucila* Church met there for a while. Later a Presbyterian pastor made the same offer so the congregation moved there. In January 2006 *La Lucila* Church had been meeting in the Presbyterian church for last 4 months. This is a good example of ecumenism in action.

Gali states that the ecumenical group in which the *Lucila* Church participates began in 1982 by responding to a call for prayer in favor of *La Guerra de las Malvinas,* "the Falklands War." "The desire for prayer was the key motivating factor and I think it was the work of the Lord. After that the communion (sharing, services together) was making this movement stronger. One of the keys to success was the changing of the proselytism attitude; this means, that the ministers understood that we all are Christians without worrying about what group one belongs to (Roman Catholic, Baptist, Lutheran, etc.)."

Reflecting on the role of liberation theology in Latin America, Robles, pastor of the *Mision Presbiteriana* Church, points out that it has fulfilled an important role in the church in Latin America. He claims that liberation theology is a critique to the theology made in the First World.

Conclusion

Like the churches in Mexico, Colombia, and Peru, the mainline Protestant church in Argentina seems to have its own particular pastoral programs determined by their own Mainline and doctrinal affiliations. The mainline Protestant churches interviewed in Argentina seem to have adopted a holistic ministry model as their main pastoral goal. They also focus on small groups in which discipleship takes place. Like the other churches on the continent, the mainline Protestant church in Argentina has very small congregations but, unlike the church in Mexico, Colombia, and Peru, it seems that the churches in Argentina are not competing among themselves for members or losing members to other congregations as much. In fact, they seem to be espousing more ecumenical tendencies.

Similar to the church in Mexico and Colombia, the mainline Protestant churches interviewed in Argentina have a deep commitment to social issues. Although there is increased environmental contamination caused by the accumulation of waste, air pollution, and the lack of an appropriate drainage system in the city, the mainline Protestant church in Argentina does not seem to have clear environmental commitment just like the churches in Mexico, Colombia, and Peru.

The mainline Protestant pastors interviewed agree that the motivation for their pastoral work comes from the Scriptures themselves. They also agree that there are too many social, economic and spiritual needs in the society where they minister and therefore, they are trying to address these needs through their ministerial work.

Unlike the church in Mexico, Colombia, and Peru, the mainline Protestant church in Argentina seems to be very involved in ecumenical dialogue and partnerships that have produced good results in creating social assistance and a good witness in the Argentinean society.

Summary

The mainline Protestant church in Latin America seems to have its own particular ecclesial and missiological programs determined by their own mainline and doctrinal affiliation. Even though the mainline Protestant church was the first Protestant group to come to Latin America, its numerical growth is very slow. Most of the churches visited average 89 members. It seems that, at least in three countries, the mainline Protestant church is competing among themselves for members or losing members to other congregations. It also seems that because of its reduced membership, the mainline Protestant Church's social impact in the general Latin American society is minimal.

Like the Roman Catholic Church, the mainline Protestant church seems to be very involved in social issues affecting the continent. The degree of involvement varies from denomination to denomination. Tradition (theological inclination), legacy, overwhelming social needs and the economic resources available to each group determine each denomination's involvement.

Although there are serious environmental issues affecting the principal cities of Latin America, neither the mainline Protestant Church as a whole nor the Roman Catholic Church has a specific environmental plan in place. It should be pointed out that despite having an established environmental plan, some of the mainline Protestant Churches interviewed have been sporadically involved in some environmental taskforces.

The mainline Protestant churches in Latin America seem to have three main areas that compel them to do their work: (1) practical, (2) biblical, and (3) theological or doctrinal. Like the Roman Catholic Church, the mainline Protestant churches are committed to the study of the Scripture and how it relates with the ecclesiological and missiological task.

Theologically speaking, and again similar to the Roman Catholic Church, the mainline Protestant churches in Latin America seem to be aware of the social-political, economic and spiritual structures that are oppressing the people. The mainline Protestant churches in Latin America are aware of the challenges that the economic and political systems are bringing to the continent. They believe that an effective way to respond to the present challenge is through an integral missional plan that reaches those who are in need in the society.

Unlike the Roman Catholic Church, the mainline Protestant churches in Latin America do not have a strong influence on the general society. This perhaps is caused by the segregation among them. Although the continent has great numbers of small congregations with good theological understanding and with good ministry programs to be Christ's witnesses, they are unfortunately working virtually alone. There were only a few cases of ecumenism seen in Argentina. It seems that in the rest of the continent churches are competing amongst themselves for members or losing members to other congregations.

There is another Protestant group in Latin America that will help to continue answering the main questions of this investigation. Compared with the mainline Protestant church, the Pentecostal Protestant churches perhaps have a bigger influence in the continent due to their numerical growth? The Pentecostal Protestant churches form part of the spiritual reality of the continent. Chapter 6 will study the theology and praxis of the Pentecostal denominations in Latin America, focusing again specifically in Mexico, Colombia, Peru and Argentina.

Notes

1. As previously discussed, in order to accomplish my research goal, I collected data through an interview process. I selected four pastors from four mainline Protestant

churches from major cities within four main countries in Latin America. I purposely interviewed pastors belonging to churches of different socioeconomic backgrounds in order to achieve a better representation of the actual reality that describes each city and country.

2. Meaning that the church has focused only on spiritual matters, neglecting social involvement.

3. For the last 50 years, the Colombian military has been fighting guerrilla groups who in more recent years have gained economic power and munitions through the cultivation and production of cocaine and other drugs that are exported primarily to the United States. Throughout these years of war thousands of Colombians have died and many more have been affected, especially women and children who have been forced to flee their homes in the countryside to seek protection in the cities.

4. Shining Path is a Maoist guerrilla organization in Peru. The communist Peruvian group's main focus is to replace Peruvian bourgeois institutions with a communist peasant revolutionary regime. Since the capture of its leader Abimael Guzman in 1992, it has only been sporadically active. The Shinning Path is widely known for its brutality, including violence deployed against peasants, trade union organizations, popularly elected officials and the general civilian population.

Chapter 6

Theology and Praxis of Mission among Selected Pentecostal Protestant Churches

In this chapter, we will explore the theology and praxis of mission of selected Pentecostal Protestant churches in four Latin American countries: Mexico, Colombia, Peru, and Argentina. As in the previous chapter, this analysis is based on 16-field research interviews made with Pentecostal Protestant pastors in these countries. The conclusions in this chapter are divided into four main sections: theology and praxis of mission of Pentecostal Protestant Churches in Mexico, Colombia, Peru and Argentina.[1]

Pentecostal Protestant Churches in Mexico

In Mexico City, I interviewed four pastors from Pentecostal Protestant circles. Table 12 on the following page summarizes the general information about each pastor and their corresponding church.

It seems that each Pentecostal Protestant church has its own pastoral plan that in one way or another is determined by its denominational affiliation. For instance, the ICIRMAR church led by Aguila has established pastoral programs for children, youth, men and women. On the other hand, the *Vive* Church led by Peña bases its pastoral program on the following topics: fundamental doctrine; justification; new creation; baptism in the Holy Spirit, baptism in water; repentance; the church as the body of Christ; Trinitarian understanding and the relationship between the believer and the church; spiritual gifts and ministries; and Jesus as the only church builder.

Table 12. Pentecostal Protestant Pastors/Churches Interviewed in Mexico

Name	Armando **AGUILA**	Benjamin **PEÑA**	Cutberto **OBISPO**	Noé **MARTINEZ**
Experience/ Position	44 years of pastoral experience/Pastor	Pastor	Pastor	Since 1981 at this church/ Pastor
Nationality	Mexican	Mexican	Mexican	Mexican
Age	Late sixties	Late sixties	Mid-sixties	Late forties
Church	*Iglesia Cristiana Interdenomino - cional de la Republica de Mexico (ICIRMAR)*	*Asociación Religiosa Vive*	*Iglesia Cristiana Independiente Pentecostes*	*Centro de Fe, Esperanza y Amor*
Denomination	Independent	Independent	Independent	Independent
Social Background	Middle-low	Middle	Low	Middle-low
Average Attendance	4,000 churches and more than 60,000 members	1,200 people	100 members	6,000 members

For Obispo and the *Independiente Pentecostes* Church, the pastoral programs are focused on restoration and liberation. Obispo points out that *Independiente Pentecostes* denomination is a Mexican denomination that began in Pachuca Idalgo through the manifestation of the Holy Spirit. The main focus of the church is prayer because, Obispo says, "this is where the power comes from." Obispo's ministerial preparation comes from the Scriptures, not from vocational or theological education. "Our primary preparation is found on our knees," said Obispo. The church is located in an area where there is a lot of witchcraft, so spiritual warfare is a reality in this church. According to Obispo, many people have come to the church possessed have and have subsequently been set free through prayer. Similarly, Obispo's pastoral life has been accompanied by miracles, spiritual warfare, prayer, and fasting.

Martinez from the *El Centro de Fe, Esperanza y Amor* works with children, young people, and adults through cell groups. The cell groups take place once a week and the pastors meet with cell group leaders weekly to discus the teaching topic. This year the church has approximately 400 cell groups, utilizing the same system that it has used for the past 15 years with relatively few changes. According to Martinez, the cell group model is a combination between the South Korean model and the Colombian model (G-12).[2]

Social Involvement

It seems that, in general, the Pentecostal Protestant churches in Mexico do not have established social involvement programs because all of the interviewees agree that the church's main focus is *evangelistico,* "evangelistic," rather than *social,* "social." Despite a general consensus that this is not a ministerial priority, there are some groups that are working in isolated social programs.

According to Aguila from ICIRMAR church, "the reality is that the priority of our movement is evangelistic. This is one of the biggest movements of Mexico. We have churches in the United States: California, Chicago [perhaps this is where some of their theology originates]; and in Central America: Nicaragua, Cuba, and the Caribbean islands." Sometimes the church offers support to single mothers and children if they have problems but the main focus of this church is evangelistic.

The *Vive* church led by Peña and *El Centro de Fe, Esperanza y Amor* Church led by Martinez sporadically support rehabilitation centers for drug and alcoholic addictions, and adult education programs. In the same way, Obispo and the *Independiente Pentecostes* Church occasionally provides food and clothing to a mission field that they have in the Guerrero area. Martinez points out, "The church does not have an established social relief program. The social support takes place more specifically in the cell group level."

Environmental Involvement

None of the Pentecostal Protestant churches interviewed have a commitment to environmental issues; most of them agree with Aguila's (ICIRMAR Church) comments that their church is not interested in environmental issues.

Biblical Basis for Their Work

According to Aguila, ICIRMAR Church, "the church programs come motivated by our directors. They are the people who construct our goals and programs. We do not accept external help and we do not let people come in from other groups to preach in our congregations." As a local church, Aguila states that Acts 2 describes the ideal for them as a church. "We want to be as close as we can to *La Iglesia Primitiva,* "the Primitive church." It is from there that we get the emphasis to the Holy Spirit, the Sanctification, and church growth," said Aguila.

For Peña (*Vive* Church) there are two main factors that motivate them to have the church programs: first experience, and second knowledge of the needs of the people. "We take into consideration the integral development and harmony of the person." Peña continues, "The Holy Spirit lives among the people and continues functioning in the church. Some key texts we use are: Galatians 2:20; Ephesians 5:25-27; and Revelation 21:5-6."

Obispo says that 1 Timothy 3:15 is the main text of the *Independiente Pentecostes* Church because it shows that the church is a pillar and foundation of the truth. Other texts they use often are Ecclesiastes 5:1-5 and Acts 2. Deuteronomy 22:5 is a text that Obispo uses to justify his point that women are not allowed to wear pants. Obispo's interpretation of the Deuteronomy text demonstrates how literally he and his church interpret the scriptures.

According to Martinez from *El Centro de Fe, Esperanza y Amor*, there are two main motivations for their work: (1) primarily, evangelization to gain souls for the Lord; (2) and secondly, to make the people feel like they are actively serving God (this is the key to encouraging their involvement in the church). Martinez points out that I Corinthians 1:10 is a fundamental text for their congregation because it highlights the goal of the church, which is to be united.

In response to my questions about their understanding of Luke 4:18-19, Aguila mentioned that, almost always, when the ICIRMAR Church has evangelistic services, they also have a section for divine healing. Once the person receives healing, the person also accepts the Lord and passes from being a sinner to the knowledge of the light of Christ. In this respect, Aguila continues, "we work with people's social issues during these services."

Analyzing Luke 4:18-19 Peña (Vive Church) states that, "the work we do today, is the same work Jesus began in the past. The same power that was in Jesus is the power we have today. We are the instruments of Jesus in this world."

According to Obispo (*Independent Pentecost* Church), Luke 4:18-19 reaffirms that there is spiritual warfare in this world. It also shows that the church needs to be reinforced with the power of the Holy Spirit.

Martinez, *El Centro de Fe, Esperanza y Amor*, states that Luke 4:18-19 is one of the basic teaching texts that describes Jesus' reason to come to earth. "All that we do, in terms of outreach or projects outside of our church, is based on this text; for us this is a practical text," said Martinez.

Regarding their understanding of the first chapter of Acts, Aguila from the ICIRMAR Church affirms that Acts 1:8 and 2 are key texts for the church, especially their emphasis on spiritual growth. After reflecting on these texts Aguila said, "We as a church do not emphasize prosperity, the only true prosperity is found when Jesus comes to the people's heart."

For Peña, *Vive* Church, "some of the Acts texts are for us today and others just describe the church of Jerusalem." Peña interprets the section "to be my witnesses in Jerusalem, Judea, Samaria and to the end of the earth" as the priorities in a church's ministry. By this he means that. they first target the person, second the family, third the congregation, fourth the society and finally the ends of the earth.

According to Martinez from *El Centro de Fe, Esperanza y Amor*, the description of the Jerusalem church having 'all things in common' was only for that particular church and does not apply to us today. However, "We agree that the church needs to be concerned with the needs of others. Our teachings, our focus is to win the hearts of the people so that they will believe what the church said and thereby experience what the church of Jerusalem experienced, but in a new way," said Martinez. The Holy Spirit plays a key role in the development and projection of the church.

In sum, most of the pastors interviewed agree that the Spirit plays a key role in the vitality of the church and its mission. Some of the pastors, however, reduce the role of the Spirit to external manifestations. The Pentecostal pastors interviewed do not have a unified view of the gospel: some of them spiritualize the text by applying anything supernatural to the church today, but discard any social or cultural references. These pastors claim that that priority of the church is to win souls for Christ and therefore most of this group's pastoral task is focused on evangelistic efforts. On the other hand, there are those who believe that the gospel not only is involved in the spiritual matters but also in the social areas, thereby imitating Jesus' ministry. Some of the pastors take the Scriptures very literally.

Theological Issues

According to Aguila, ICIRMAR Church, "Our goal is classic Pentecostal: we let only the Holy Spirit direct us. The emphasis of our doctrine is: Salvation, Holy Spirit and Sanctification."

Martinez says that the fundamental vision of *El Centro de Fe, Esperanza y Amor* is the numerical growth, not only internal (as a church) but also external (creating new congregations). In the last six years the church has established six new congregations in the Mexico City area. He says that prayer and fulfilling the great commission of sharing the good news are the key elements that made this numeric growth possible.

In his final statements Martinez said that he feels that time is running short and that Jesus is coming soon. The prophecies about the end of the world are being fulfilled and our time as a church is limited. Therefore, he said, "we need to do our work as soon as possible. Again we need to fulfill the Great Commission by the empowerment of the Holy Spirit."

It seems that there is generally an overemphasis on numerical growth among Pentecostal churches in Mexico. Some of the interviewees seem to equate spiritual vitality with numerical growth. For some, the motivation for wining souls is based on an eschatological view of the gospel that, in one way or another, blinds the churches to the present socio-economic, political and environmental realities in the society. Because the church is unable to see the reality in which it exists, the church is limited in its ability to be a true agent of change in Mexico.

General Statements

Talking about the role of the Christian church in the Mexican society, Aguila of the ICIRMAR Church points out that before the year 2000, he was pleased with the growth of the Protestant church in Mexico. However, since 2000, there has been a change in the Mexican social and the economic situation (increasing violence, more people living below the poverty level, and increasing immorality) and the question has changed to this: if the churches are growing, then is the movement not making an impact on the general society? "This is our dilemma today," says Aguila. He claims that the main problem of the Mexican Pentecostal church is the lack of a solid doctrine among their people. "This is why we have in Mexico a large quantity of poor quality Christians. It is something I admire of Mainline groups that they have a solid doctrinal commitment," Aguila continues, "Sadly these churches do not grow because they are *conformistas,* 'conformists;' having lost their desire to gain more souls."

According to Aguila, "the key point that makes the Pentecostal church grow is prayer. These people pray a lot and, without foreign help, we develop our own evangelistic campaigns. However, when the people accept the Lord in our campaigns, we lack a stable follow-up program. Therefore, many of the people who once made a decision for Christ end up leaving our groups and sometimes go to non-Christian groups, like Mormons and Jehovah Witnesses."

Peña, *Vive* Church, disagrees with Aguila when he says, "Thousands and thousands of people have moved from the Mainline Protestant churches to the more spiritually-oriented Pentecostal churches." He says there is a mosaic of churches in Mexico, churches are very segregated from each other and often the pastors do not have good relationships.

Peña also points out three major problems that are affecting the Mexican people: (1) the lack of knowledge, (2) poverty that is the result of ignorance, and (3) idolatry that began during the colonization.

Aguila from the ICIRMAR Church points out that there is no unity among the Mexican Protestant churches. Every day there are more and more groups that, because they lack a solid doctrinal foundation, split and form new groups when any disagreement arises. "The church in Mexico is diverse and in some ways segregated," continues Aguila. "The hope of the Christian churches in Mexico is based on the new (2006) elections. We have several Protestant candidates that perhaps can be elected. We, as a church, need to have good Christian officials on the local and national level or else there will be no change in the society."

Peña of the *Vive* Church concludes similarly, pointing out that, although the church in Mexico is growing today, it is a segregated church. "We have all kinds of churches in Mexico from conservatives to liberals and from legalists to those with free wills." Peña believes that the future of the Protestant church in Mexico is uncertain. "We will soon arrive to a point of confusion for the lack of solid doctrine and theological foundation. There are many new groups coming from Brazil that bring with them a wrong doctrinal belief, such as *Pare de Sufrir,* "Stop Suffering," group which emphasizes the theology of prosperity." Peña claims that even Protestants and Roman Catholics are leaving to join groups such as this.

Martinez from *El Centro de Fe, Esperanza y Amor* agrees with Aguila and Peña regarding the segregation of the Mexican church. He says, "We are isolated from each other; each one working on our own." Yet, Martinez sees a positive side of this segregation saying that it has allowed the church in Mexico to reach several areas of the society. Martinez said that, in general, the Christian church is doing a good work. The fact that people are moving from one place to another shows the spiritual needs people are facing. Martinez sees this reality not as a problem but, as a good opportunity.

For Martinez, the key to changing the Mexican situation is the conversion of people, which should be the church's primary target. "If God does not change people's hearts, we can have excellent programs without good results. Thus, the main goal of the church in Mexico should be to point people in the direction of knowing Jesus and being transformed by his message."

Talking about the increasing growth of the Neo-Pentecostal churches in Mexico and in Latin America, Martinez says that the statistics do not lie. These churches are, in fact, more prosperous (numerically and economically) demonstrating that the Holy Spirit is working there. "It is true that there are many different kinds of biblical interpretations among them, but if the Bible is the foundation for their work, then it is fine," he said.

Talking about the role of the women among Pentecostal groups, Aguila of the ICIRMAR Church points out that "except for the fact that they are not allowed to use the pulpit, women work in many areas of the church and they are respected." Peña of the *Vive* Church points out that, women have a place in the ministry but never in leadership above their husbands.

Conclusion

It seems that each Pentecostal Protestant church in Mexico has its own pastoral plan that in one way or another is determined by its denominational affiliation. A common pastoral goal among Pentecostals in Mexico is numerical growth.

It seems that, in general, the Pentecostal Protestant churches in Mexico do not have an established program of social involvement. All the interviewees agree that the church's main focus is evangelistic rather than social but there are some groups that are working in isolated social programs. All agree that this is not a ministry priority.

Although Mexico City is facing serious environmental issues such as air and water pollution, insufficient water supplies, and insufficient sewage systems, etc., none of the Pentecostal Protestant churches have a commitment to addressing environment issues. The consensus among the Pentecostal pastors interviewed is that this is a new area that the church has not begun to analyze.

Experience, awareness of the social situation, evangelistic focus, and spiritual warfare are some of the main concerns that have encouraged the Pentecostal Protestant pastors in Mexico to do their work.

Interviewees agree that Protestant churches in Mexico are segregated in small self-centered groups and that members are transient among these churches caused by a lack of profound biblical and doctrinal foundation. Pastors agree that every day there are more and more Christian groups (caused by divisions) and new missionaries in the Mexican society making the Christian witness more difficult. They also agree that the church has lost its vitality as an agent of change in an increasingly violent and insecure society.

It seems that numerical growth is the major priority, and growth is thought to be proof of healthy spirituality among Pentecostal Protestant churches in Mexico. Therefore most of the churches' missiological and ecclesiological goals are focused on evangelistic efforts. Theologically speaking, the churches are saying in effect that the church is growing because the Holy Spirit is working.

Pentecostal Protestant Churches in Colombia

In Bucaramanga, Colombia, I interviewed four pastors from Pentecostal Protestant circles. Table 13 summarizes the general information about each pastor and their corresponding church.

Table 13. Pentecostal Protestant Pastors/Churches Interviewed in Colombia				
Name	Juan Bautista DAZA	José Alberto VARGAS	Aristobulo GARCIA	Luis Alfredo MORENO
Experience/ Position	He is a gynecologist/ Associate Pastor	33 years/Pastor	Pastor	Pastor
Nationality	Colombian	Colombian	Colombian	Colombian
Age	Early forties	Early sixties	Late forties	Late forties
Church	*Centro Familiar de Adoración (CFA)*	*Centro de Adoración y Fe*	*Movimiento Misionero Mundial*	*Cuadrangular, La Cumbre*
Denomination	A branch of Assemblies of God	Assemblies of God Independent	World Missionary Movement[3]	Foursquare Gospel Church
Social Background	Middle-high	Middle-low	Middle-Low	Low
Average Attendance	2,500 people	250 members	250 members	

Like the church in Mexico, it seems that each Pentecostal Protestant church in Colombia has its own pastoral plan that in one way or another is determined by its denominational affiliation. Something that is common among the Pentecostal Protestant churches in Colombia is that their pastoral plan has evangelistic purposes. For instance, The *CFA* Church led by Daza utilizes a basic evangelistic program that consists of cell groups that meet throughout the city of Bucaramanga. According to Daza, the main goal of this cell groups is numerical growth. The *CFA* Church targets several groups in the city such as businessmen, professional men and women, women's group, and family groups. According to Daza the *CFA* Church's successful growth is based on: (1) a solid growing vision on the part of the leadership; (2) an economic investment that has supported this growth since the beginning (this economic support comes from other mega churches in Colombia and Brazil where this mission originated); (3) having an international speaker (prophets and evangelists) every month to help spiritually feed the people; (4) having cell groups to help people relate with each other and through which they can invite more people to the church events; and (5) having prayer support for part of another mega- church in another Colombian city, Cucutá, which is led by Do Santos' father.

The *El Centro de Adoración y Fe* Church led by Vargas also has an established evangelistic program that consists of a group of church members who go out and preach on the streets of Bucaramanga. They also have cell groups that are used as an evangelist strategy. Once in a while the church has special evangelistic events in the temple and each member of the church is requested to bring a new friend. Vargas points out that every member of the church is encouraged to be a carrier of the gospel; in doing that, they are fulfilling the Great Commission to "Go and preach the gospel."

The *Movimiento* Church led by Garcia is also working with cell groups, again with a primary goal of evangelism. These services take place on Fridays and Saturdays. The church has had a radio program for 15 years through which they share and motivate their members. According to Garcia, "the church is the accomplishment of people from the community with little help from the exterior. We feel proud that the building and the programs the church has in this moment are fruit of our own work and dedication." The *Movimiento* Church began in Cuba by a Puerto Rican missionary, Luis M. Ortiz, and today is spread around the world. According to Garcia, in Colombia alone there are approximately 1,300 such churches.

Pastor Moreno, *Cuadrangular, La Cumbre* Church, points out that in the last six years the church has discovered that the social areas of the community are also part of the gospel. This change, according to Moreno, came after a prayer time and a serious study of the Scripture, especially the Gospels. The main goal of the church is evangelism, but this is accomplished through social work. Since 1998, the church has been following a multiplication growth program called *Pastoreo por Excelencia*, "Excellence in Leadership."[4] This project has encouraged the church to be more involved in the community; according to Moreno, this has helped the Christian witness of the church in the community.

Moreno points out, "we are instructing our members to be sent." In doing that the church follows four main areas: (1) discipleship: this is for new people, what the church is looking to do is instill a foundation about what the gospel of Jesus means; (2) deaconate: this is to show believers areas where they can serve inside the church; (3) leadership: developing the ministry that the person has discovered; and (4) Preaching schools: training in basic hermeneutics principles.

Social Involvement

In contrast to the church in Mexico, it seems that the Pentecostal Protestant churches in Colombia have a more established social program. There are some Pentecostal Protestant churches in Colombia that once-in-a-while are participating in the social arena and one has a well-established program. For instance, at the time of the interview, the CFA Church led by Daza did not have any established social program but through the CFA women's association, the church sporadically provides groceries to church members who are in need. Daza said that the church is planning to begin a medical project to provide support to the area of the community in which they serve.

The social involvement of *El Centro de Adoración y Fe* Church led by Vargas is limited to helping the members of the church with groceries and providing economic assistance. The church also offers counseling to its members.

Garcia's *Movimiento* Church occasionally provides some medical support and distributes clothing and food in some of the marginalized areas of the city. The church is also supporting a drug rehabilitation program that is part of the greater denomination.

Cuadrangular, La Cumbre Church led by Moreno has a children's ministry program called *Fuente de Vida*, "Fountain of Life." The last activity the church did was the distribution of Christmas gifts to more than 750 children of the neighborhood. The church is planning to start a feeding program for children as well.

Environmental Involvement

When I asked about their involvement in environmental issues, all of the pastors responded that their churches do not have any program or involvement in this area. Thus, like the church in Mexico, none of the Pentecostal Protestant churches in Colombia have a commitment to environmental issues.

Biblical Basis for Their Work

The bases for the programs that the Pentecostal protestant churches provide are varied. For instance, the *CFA* Church led by Daza, cites the needs of the Colombian country (people who have been displaced and in need) as the main motivation for their work. According to Vargas, *El Centro de Adoración y Fe* Church, his church programs are motivated by the biblical principles to minister to people in, *una forma integral*, "an integral way." For Garcia of the *Movimiento* Church, the love of God for their people without forgetting the human needs is the major incentive for their involvement. According to Moreno, *Cuadrangular, La Cumbre* Church, "there are many churches to preach the gospel, but few churches that feed the people and work with the human part of the person. This is what God has put in our hearts."

The biblical foundations that encourage each Pentecostal Protestant church interviewed in Colombia for their social and pastoral involvement are also varied. Vargas (*El Centro de Adoración y Fe* Church) states that the main text that describes the church is found in Jesus' words to the Samaritan woman, implying that "God is looking for worshipers that worship him in spirit and truth. Our main goal is that people know the Lord Jesus Christ." On the other hand, the slogan text that the *Movimiento* Church led by Garcia uses as a basis for its pastoral and social work is located in Matthew 28:19 (this text is interpreted through evangelistic lenses). Just as the name of the church is "World Mission," this text provides the basis of preaching the gospel around the world. The *Cuadrangular, La Cumbre* Church led by Moreno uses Hebrews 13:8 as its foundational text and biblical basis. They say: "Jesus is the same, yesterday, today and forever: The same Jesus who healed the sick and loves the segregated and the sinner is the same Jesus that has encouraged us to do the same."

Regarding their understanding of Luke 4:18-19, Daza, *CFA* Church said, "We identify ourselves with this text. We have churches in Colombia, Argentina, Venezuela, and Chile." It seems that they reduce the interpretation of the text to numerical growth and proclamation rather than integral involvement. It appears that they measure the spiritual vitality of their churches with numerical growth; "God's presence is shown through the church's size."

According to Vargas, *El Centro de Adoración y Fe* Church, Luke 4:18-19 shows the importance of the fullness (baptism) of the Holy Spirit in order to do God's work in the world. Jesus received the Spirit in order to propagate the Kingdom of God. We need the experience of the Holy Spirit in order to share the gospel: that includes setting the people free from the slavery of Satan.

For Garcia, *Movimiento* Church, Luke 4:18-19 summarizes the gospel that we preach in our mission. "We bring the gospel to the captives and healing to the sick; we believe that Jesus still makes miracles today." Hebrews 13:8 has some relationship with the Luke text he said because Jesus is the same yesterday, today and tomorrow. It seems that their hermeneutics link to the spirit, power, and miracles, which is contrary to the social justice view of the text.

According to Moreno, of the *Cuadrangular, La Cumbre* Church, many preachers take Luke 4:18-19 as a word of God for them. "However, I think the call of God is general and God's spirit is open and available to all who are willing and open to serve the Lord." It seems that he rejects the text by generalizing it to the rest of the New Testament.

Talking about his understanding of the first chapters of Acts; Daza of the *CFA* Church, points out that the church fulfills these chapters through their senior pastor's missional experience, meaning, perhaps, that it does not apply to the whole church. The senior pastor, Do Santos, is frequently traveling and speaking to other churches to several places in Colombia, Latin America and the World. Again, it seems they interpret Luke and Acts with an evangelistic focus that applies to the pastor of the church but not necessarily to the whole church.

For Vargas, *El Centro de Adoración y Fe* Church, Acts shows the implications that mark the flourishing church such as (1) being obedient to the Word of God, (2) having faith to receive what Jesus was promising, and (3) after receiving the experience of the Holy Spirit, the church is responsible to go and proclaim the gospel.

According to Garcia, *Movimiento* Church, the first chapters of Acts describe the philosophy of the denomination. "Our goal is to share the gospel throughout the world. We do not have many resources but he has given us the power through his Holy Spirit to do his work," Garcia said.

For Moreno, at the *Cuadrangular, La Cumbre* Church, Acts 1:8 points out that we need to worry first about our own town, later for the town next to us and finally our focus should be the world. "We believe God has us for great things. For now we are applying the text of being a witness to the world but this begins with being a light inside of the church," he said.

In sum, although it seems that the biblical understanding among Pentecostal pastors varies according to their denominational affiliation and theological preparation, most of the pastors agree that the gospel has an evangelistic purpose. The hermeneutics used for some leads to the spirit, power and miracles.

As we saw in Mexico, many of Colombian Pentecostal pastors have a dualistic view of salvation, reducing the interpretation of the text to numerical growth and proclamation rather than integral involvement. For them, it appears that they measure the spiritual vitality of their churches with numerical growth. God's presence is shown through the church's size. On the other hand, there are some pastors that see salvation in a more integral way and most include a social justice ministry.

Theological Issues

According to Daza, *CFA* Church, "there is a great need for peace in the Colombian people. A prophecy was given 25 years ago to Do Santos' father that Colombia is a happy country. Therefore, every time a prophet comes to the *CFA* Church and prophesies peace and prosperity, we are encouraged and renewed; we feel that God is caring for us." Daza points out that the difference between the *CFA* Church and other churches, including the Roman Catholic Church, is that they preach a true gospel that can save people's lives. This is a gospel of power that really changes people's lives.

Vargas, *El Centro de Adoración y Fe* Church, said that the church sees humanity as Genesis sees it, a humanity that was made in God's image. "Therefore, humans are spiritual beings covered with human nature. Thus, when we minister to humans we minister to their spiritual areas that can be only filled with the Holy Spirit." This dualistic view of the person sees the physical body as evil and inner spirit as good.

Moreno, *Cuadrangular, La Cumbre* Church, argues that the social involvement of the church has helped their spiritual growth. For instance, the commitment to prayer is a deeper reality of the church every day. During the worship time there is a real expression of joy and thanksgiving for what God has done and is doing in the community.

In general, it seems that, in their desire to find comfort and answers to the socio-political and economic crisis Colombia is facing, some of the Pentecostal Protestant churches are open to listen to new prophecies that are not necessarily biblically supported. While some Pentecostal pastors are starting to see a more integral dimension of the gospel, others still focus on a more dualistic view.

General Statements

It appears that women play a key social and ministerial role in the Pentecostal Protestant church in Colombia. For instance, according to Daza, although the *CFA* only has around 10 dedicated women, they play a key role in the *CFA* Church: visiting the sick and helping those who are in need. Garcia also says that women play a key role in the ministerial work of the *Movimiento* Church as well.

According to Daza, *CFA* Church, there are jealousies among other Protestant churches because the *CFA* has grown very fast. Daza points out that the Roman Catholic Church has lost strength while the Pentecostal Protestants have gained it, producing some friction among the churches. Daza thinks that the Roman Catholic Church as well as other Protestant churches believe that his church is stealing their members and their ministerial space. "Although there is sometimes friction between us and other churches, we should not worry about these kinds of issues," Daza said.

Despite the fact that, according to Daza, there is no dialogue or understanding between them, the Protestant churches in Colombia are growing. He thinks that this growth is perhaps motivated by the people's need for peace, security and a new alternatives to life that are opposite to the ways that Colombian people are living.

Vargas, *El Centro de Adoración y Fe* Church, once a Colombian candidate for the senate, says that his experience has pointed out that "we need to have a better intellectual, spiritual, social and biblical preparation and have a deeper Christian responsibility, in order to be effective."

Talking about the relationship of his church with Roman Catholic Church, Garcia of the *Movimiento* Church, points out that it is distant because, "the Roman Catholic Church still has the protection of the government." In fact, in some parts of Latin America, Protestant churches have to pay taxes but the Roman Catholic Church does not. Garcia mentioned that there are still isolated incidents when Protestants are persecuted by the Roman Catholic Church, especially during evangelistic campaigns.

Analyzing the situation of the *Cuadrangular* Church as a whole, Moreno points out that the church is a content church that has not understood its commitment to look out. "There is too much apathy of the church in regard to missions," Moreno states. Despite this, he said that the *Cuadrangular, La Cumbre* Church has implemented some carpentry workshops, and shoe and clothing making workshops last year but none of the participants got involved in the church. According to Moreno, "The main error was that we as pastors never touched the spiritual life of the people through a devotional time or something similar."

Conclusion

Like the church in Mexico, it seems that each Pentecostal Protestant church in Colombia has its own pastoral plan. Something that is common among the Pentecostal Protestant churches in Colombia is that their pastoral plan has evangelistic purposes.

Unlike the church in Mexico, it seems that in general the Pentecostal Protestant churches in Colombia are more involved in social issues. There are some churches that are working in isolated social programs and one church that has an established social program. Like the church in Mexico, the Pentecostal Protestant churches in Colombia do not have a commitment to environmental issues.

For the social ministering that the churches are doing, it is their awareness of the social situation, evangelistic focus, and the negligence of other churches in the area that encourages the work.

Like the church in Mexico, pastors interviewed agree that Protestant churches in Colombia are segregated into small self-centered groups and that membership is transient as church goers move from one church to another.

It seems that some of the bigger Pentecostal Protestant churches determine their evangelistic success by the following measures: (1) leadership vision; (2) economic investment; (3) international speakers (prophets and evangelists); (4) cell groups; and (5) prayer. It seems that, although Pentecostal churches are growing, the members' commitment and spiritual growth are questionable. Success is reduced to numerical growth that in one way or the other is achieved by the money invested and the charisma of the leader. Most of the guest speakers employ sensational, manipulative strategies that are non-biblical to produce faster yet superficial growth.

Pentecostal Protestant Churches in Peru

In Lima, Peru, I interviewed four pastors from Pentecostal Protestant circles. Table 14, on the following page, summarizes the general information about each pastor and their corresponding church.

Like the church in Mexico and Colombia, it seems that each Pentecostal Protestant church in Peru has its own pastoral plan that in one way or another is determined by its denominational affiliation.

Talking about the pastoral plan that shapes the *La Luz del Mundo* Church, Ruiz points out that there is a *nueva unción*, "new anointment," of the spirit in Lima and that they are recipients of this new anointment which they call the *nuevos soles*, "new suns," or *vino nuevo*, "new wine." This means there is a church with new revelation and a new word for the people today. It seems that

Table 14. Pentecostal Protestant Pastors/Churches Interviewed in Peru

Name	Rony RUIZ	Pedro Jorge VELIZAROFF	Oscar UGARTE	Florencio LIÑAN
Experience/ Position	Apostle[5]	Pastor	Pastor	Pastor
Nationality	Peruvian	Peruvian	Peruvian	Peruvian
Age	Late forties	Middle-sixties	Late fifties	Early sixties
Church	La Misión Cristiana La Luz del Mundo: Restauración, Avivamiento y Prosperidad	La Iglesia Cristiana Tú y Tú Casa	Jesucristo es el Camino	El Rebaño de Dios
Denomination	Independent	Independent Pentecostal	Independent	Assemblies of God
Social Background	Middle	Middle-low	Middle-low	Low
Average Attendance		300 members	200 members	60 members

this extra-biblical revelation is evaluated by them in the regular basis. What they feel applies to them, they receive graciously and what does not, they just reject.

Tú y Tú Casa Church, led by Velizaroff, has education programs that include Sunday school classes, married couples, teenagers and youth groups, and adult's classes; a radio program every Thursday and theological classes. The strongest ministry the church has is the ministry of healing and miracles where God manifests himself through many signs. The church itself develops the theological and biblical material used in these classes.

According to Ugarte, the vision of the *Jesucristo es el Camino* Church points in three principal directions, (1) looking toward heaven: focusing on a church that worships God and prays (every day the church has a prayer service at 6:00 a.m.). (2) looking inside through a discipleship plan that is helping build the foundation of the church. This discipleship plan is formed by basic Bible studies and a Biblical Institute (this church has an agreement with Rio Grande Bible Institute[6] that provides the theological and biblical preparation). According to Ugarte, in order to be a church elder one must have a diploma in theology. (3) looking outside: this has consisted in supporting other churches in the area through programs of evangelism. The *Jesucristo es el Camino* Church has evangelistic equipment (speakers, stands, microphones, materials, etc.) that they loan to other churches from different denominations. Last year the churches helped 30 churches with their evangelistic campaigns. "Our goal is to extend the kingdom of God rather than make a religious proselytism," said Ugarte.

The *Jesucristo es el Camino* Church also has an evangelistic team of approximately 50 people who go door-to-door sharing the message. They have divided the area where they live by zones in order to cover the area. Once a month the church has a harvest celebration program where the church extends the invitation to the new converts and has a musical concert to welcome them to the church's community.

El Rebaño de Dios Church led by Liñan has the traditional Assemblies of God programs such as evangelism, Bible school, counseling, teenager's class, and parenting schools. The material used for these classes are produced by the denomination of the Assemblies of God.

Social Involvement

Only one of the four Pentecostal Protestant churches interviewed in Peru has an established social program. The rest of the churches, like the churches in Mexico do not have a solid established social program.

Since the beginning of the church seven years ago, *Tú y Tú Casa* Church, led by Velizaroff, has been involved in: (1) Supporting street children (this has been reduced due to lack of economic support); (2) Visiting sick people in hospitals of the city (not only do they visit them but they also provide economic help for medicine); (3) Making health brigades in men's and women's prisons (the church has a staff of medics who are not Christians but who agree to share with the church's projects); (4) Supporting, help, and receive people who have been released from prison for a period of six months. Most of those that they have served in this way have been foreigners that need some kind of support (for instance, the church has helped some United States citizens, Canadians, Germans, etc); (5) The church also receives drug addicts who are in recovery and help them through that process (approximately 50 people had passed through the church and who are still leading drug-free Christian-lives); (6) Counseling for marriage, both Christians and non-Christians; (7) Praying, Velizaroff has prayer meeting every week with the mayor of the province of Magdalena (this is the area where the church is located) where he shares the Scripture and sometimes they discuss social improvements for the community; (8) Caring. The church also uses the Micah Project[7] that has specific involvement with social justice (especially caring for the poor and needy).

While they do not have an established program, like the churches of Mexico and Colombia, there are some Pentecostal Protestant churches in Peru that once in a while participate in social issues. For instance, *La Luz del Mundo* Church, led by Ruiz, does not have established social programs but occasionally the church helps children who are in need with some food and Bible studies.

The *Jesucristo es el Camino* Church, led by Ugarte, does not have any social programs that target the community where it ministers, but occasionally the church provides food to some members of the church who are in need.

El Rebaño de Dios Church, led by Liñan, also does not have any established social programs, but the church does help with social issues in the community where they live. For example: last year they began *un projecto maxivo de casamiento*, "a massive marriage project," for many people in the community who were single couples.

Environmental Involvement

Although the city of Lima is facing a deep environmental crisis, such us the accumulation garbage, pig farming that contaminates the neighborhoods, polluted rivers, and more, like the churches in Mexico and Colombia, none of the Pentecostal Protestant churches interviewed in Peru have a commitment to address environment issues.

Biblical Basis for Their Work

It seems that each church interviewed in Peru has its own programs and is motivated by several factors. Most of these factors come from a biblical perspective. For instance, *Tú y Tú Casa* Church, led by Velizaroff, bases its pastoral work on the teaching of Act 16:31 which recounts the salvation of persons and his/her whole household. "This promise is fulfilled in this church, a person comes here and, after a few more visits, the whole house is converted. The key evangelistic tool is the testimony of transformation of the Christian member, plus the visitation and follow-up our church offers the new believer," said Velizaroff. He said that the families of every single person who has accepted the Lord at this church have also become believers after a few months.

According to Ugarte, *Jesucristo es el Camino* Church, people are perishing for lack of the knowledge of God and therefore knowledge of the Scriptures is fundamental in his church. "Isaiah 54 is the story of our church," said Ugarte. When he joined the church it was also a barren lady. The key to the success today of the *Jesucristo es el Camino* church is linked to the Word of God. For instance, the church never has fundraising campaigns to pay the church's debts; all of this comes through people's tithes and offerings. "Our people have learned that it is a privilege to give for the extension of the kingdom of God," said Ugarte.

The main biblical motivation for *El Rebaño de Dios* Church, led by Liñan, is found in the teaching of the Great Commission, that "encourages us as a church to Go and preach the gospel to the whole world," said Liñan. It seems he provides a narrow and spiritualistic interpretation of the Great Commission because there is no evidence of outreach involvement in this church.

Responding to my questions about their understanding of Luke 4:18-19, Ruiz, the *La Luz del Mundo* Church, points out that the mention of the Holy Spirit's anointment in the text means the fresh anointment (the revelation of God to us). He said that this needs to be applied within the church. It seems that some churches interpret the Luke text focusing on the external manifestation of the Spirit and missing the social implications of the text.

According to Velizaroff, Luke 4:18-19 had been and is fulfilled in *Tú y Tú Casa* Church. "We are fulfilling this passage faithfully and we are announcing the year of the Lord's favor," he says. He goes on to say that the gift of healing is manifested faithfully in the church's services.

Talking about his understanding of Luke 4:18-19, Ugarte points out that there are three main areas that the *Jesucristo es el Camino* Church stands on: the vision, the dreams, and the prophecy. Ugarte points out that they see these main areas not in a mystical sense but in the practical way. (1) The vision: it is God's plan for us as church; (2) the dreams: they are the desires and goals we have as church; (3) the prophecy: this is the confirmation of this reality that is based on the Word of God that has already been spoken to us.

Responding my questions about their understanding of the first chapters of Acts, Ruiz, *La Luz del Mundo* Church, points out that *poder*, "power" is the key word in the text. "This means that God changes, by the power of the Holy Spirit, my character first and in this way the power of God will change others," said Ruiz.

For Velizaroff, *Tú y Tú Casa* Church, the book of Acts is a reminder of his own experiences; the miracle healing of his father's and his wife's cancer. He met the Lord through these experiences and since then he has served Him faithfully. "The Lord has treated me in such a way that I do not have another way than serve Him," said Velizaroff. "How do I understand the book of Acts? Through *actos reales*, "real acts," of God in my life and in the community's life."

For Ugarte, *Jesucristo es el Camino* Church, Acts provides some evangelistic strategy, focused more precisely on a geographic understanding: first Jerusalem, second Judea, third Samaria, and finally the end of the earth. This understanding provides a working model for the church; meaning that the priority of their church at this moment is to focus on the community (in the spiritual sense: gain souls for Christ) where they are ministering. Once they finish this they will move on to the rest of the city. This inwardly focused missiological view has reduced the effectiveness of most of the churches in Peru to impact the society at large.

In conclusion, it seems that most of the Pentecostal Protestant Peruvian pastors interviewed have found through the reading of Scriptures a living reality that they are experiencing in their own life and community through signs, miracle healings, and a perceptive presence of the Holy Spirit in their services. Thus, most of the pastors interviewed have found that the Word of God is a living reality in their lives. It seems that the understanding of the Scriptures has shaped their ecclesiology and missiological understanding. Apart from Velizaroff, *Tú y Tú Casa* Church, it seems that the Pentecostal pastors interviewed have a narrow understanding of the Scriptures that moves them to only focus on the spiritual dimensions of the person, lacking a more integral missiological and ecclesiological approach.

Theological Issues

According to Ruiz, *La Luz del Mundo* Church, what the Christian church in Lima needs is to be constantly in renewal, receiving the "new wine," the "new suns" of God for His church. He says that the first love is something we need to always conserve in our life and remember that God's will for society will be fulfilled through us. "The Word of God is powerful if we only summit ourselves to Him and believe that what He says is true."

Ruiz points out that physical and mental sickness in society are the result of spiritual oppressions that come from the mother's womb. Therefore, as a church we need to minister in terms of liberation and healing to those who are in these conditions in order to set them free.

Ruiz states that *La Luz del Mundo* Church is a fertile church. "Everyone who sows in our church receives a double pay. This is a blessed church because we have taught the people how to plant," he says. "We have taught the people to give their offerings, tithes and offerings of thanksgiving, and based on that, the church has prospered," Ruiz continues. "This is a year of the harvest and even the wealth of the pagans will come to us. We have prophets in our church that have told us all these things." This is clearly an example of prosperity gospel that is strongly spread throughout Latin America.

According to Ruiz, the best evangelistic tool is when God begins to prosper you economically. When the non-Christian sees your economic life begin to be prospered, they want to know how to prosper as well. "We are teaching the church that Jesus Christ was not a poor person, as the Hollywood movies lead us to think; we are teaching people that Jesus was *un hombre rico*, "a wealthy man." Ruiz claims that, according to theologians, Jesus' clothing cost 3,000 dollars and his shoes cost 1,000 dollars and Jesus' disciples were wealthy men as well. For instance, Judas was a wealthy businessman. "Thus, we are called to be wealthy as well. God wants us to be prosperous too because He is the owner of all the gold and silver," Ruiz said. Throughout Latin America one can find many wealthy mega churches that originated from Brazil and follow the prosperity gospel's understanding leaving thousands and thousands of people disappointed with God and these churches after their own promises of prosperity go unfulfilled.

According to Velizaroff, *Tú y Tú Casa* Church, condemnation is the evangelistic strategy that most of the Protestant churches use in Peru; meaning that if one does not accept Jesus as a savior, he/she will go to hell. Velizaroff does not agree with this evangelistic strategy; his approach is more of welcoming the sinner and providing them a new alternative life in Jesus.

Velizaroff points out that what is crucial for the *Tú y Tú Casa* Church is feeling God's presence. He said that the church feels God's presence often in their services. In Velizaroff's life as well as in the church's life, signs (miraculous healings, showing God's presence, and comforting joy) play a crucial role. These things in one way or another have confirmed God's power and care for them.

For the *Jesucristo es el Camino* Church and Ugarte a key ministerial principle is "we cannot teach what we do not know; we cannot give what we do not have." By this he means that everyone in the church should have the same preparation and should get to the same level as the pastor in order to spread the gospel.

In sum, theologically speaking, it seems that the Pentecostal Protestant pastors interviewed in Peru have different understandings that have influenced their biblical formation. For instance, Ruiz's theological view is influenced by a prosperity gospel (some of this teaching has been achieved through a poor hermeneutics and sometimes manipulation of the text). He has a narrow monetary understanding of the gospel where those who give would receive double. This view of the gospel measures the spirituality of the church by the economic level, health, and prosperity it enjoys. This theological understanding is widely accepted and preached throughout Latin America, especially in many mega churches. Although many Pentecostal churches in Latin America are open and follow this prosperity gospel, there are many churches that do not agree with this; such is the case of Velizaroff, Ugarte and Liñan.

General Statements

After regularly attending the Peruvian pastoral meetings for several years, Velizaroff points out that the Protestant church in Peru consists of a divided people; a people who do not want unity; a people who steal members; and in the last years with the ministry of the G-12, churches are evangelizing those who are already evangelized. He said, "most of the mega churches that offer ministerial conferences to other churches end up with 80 percent of those who attended the conference joining the mega church rather than the sponsoring church. The reality in Peru is that most of the new churches are composed of members from other churches who have been persuaded to join the church in exchange for leadership positions." Mexico and Colombia are facing a similar situation that Velizaroff describes. It seems that there is not an ethical attitude among churches and pastors. Again it seems that the church with the most money and programs controls the spiritual flow and numerical growth.

According to Velizaroff, *Tú y Tú Casa* Church does not work with people from other churches. "If somebody from another church comes to our church, we restore them and later we send them back to their churches," said Velizaroff. It seems that Velizaroff provides a good ethical model for other churches.

Velizaroff says that only a few Protestant churches in Peru are implementing the Micah project because, "Peru is a church of beggars. They are used to receiving help from outside and they do not want to support programs like Micah because this implies a local economic investment." It seems that the topic of dependence and independence plays a key role in the churches in Peru and Latin America. Sadly many churches and mission organizations think that money is the only solution to meet people's needs and it is the only thing they offer.

Talking about the Christian situation in Peru, Ugarte from *Jesucristo es el Camino* Church points out that they are lost; lost in the sense that they do not know where they come from and where they are going. He says that the Peruvian Protestant church has lost its sense of direction and focus. "The church needs to know its reason and purpose for existence in order to be effective in the community where the Lord has placed it," Ugarte claims. Of course, churches should look to the Scripture for their identity, purpose and sense of direction. He thinks the growing number of new, segregated denominations breeds the confusion. Likewise, Liñan from *El Rebaño de Dios* Church says that there is no unity among the Protestant churches in Peru; each one has its own programs and activities. This is not a good testimony for the church nor, he emphasized, is it a message of salvation. It seems that the topic of disunity and conflict among churches is a reality throughout most of Latin America.

Conclusion

Like the church in Mexico and Colombia, it seems that each Pentecostal Protestant church in Peru has its own pastoral plan that in one way or another is determined by its denominational affiliation.

Apart from *Tú y Tú Casa* Church, like the church in Mexico, it seems that in general the Pentecostal Protestant churches in Peru do not have any established and ongoing social involvement plans. Although Lima is facing a critical environmental situation such as the accumulation of garbage, environmentally unsafe pig farming, polluted waterways and more, like the church in Mexico and Colombia, the Pentecostal Protestant churches in Peru are not committed to environmental issues.

It seems that most of the Pentecostal pastors interviewed in Peru have found a living reality through the reading of the Scriptures. This understanding of the Scriptures shapes their ecclesiology and missiological understanding. However, apart from Velizaroff (*Tú y Tú Casa* Church), it seems that the Pentecostal pastors interviewed have a narrow understanding of the Scriptures that moves them to only focus on the spiritual dimension of the person lacking a more integral missiological and ecclesiological dimension of the gospel. In many cases spiritual blessing is equal to economic prosperity.

Like the church in Mexico and Colombia, pastors interviewed agree that Protestant churches in Peru are segregated into small self-centered groups and that there is an exodus of members among them. They also point out that the disunity among the Protestant people has affected the church's witness and social impact within the Peruvian society.

Pentecostal Protestant Churches in Argentina

In Buenos Aires, Argentina, I interviewed four pastors from Pentecostal Protestant circles. Table 15 on the following page summarizes the general information about each pastor and their corresponding church.

Table 15. Pentecostal Protestant Pastors/Churches Interviewed in Argentina				
Name	Roberto **PRIETO**	Pablo **VIVIAN**	Manuel **CORREA**	Gilberto **JORGUERA**
Experience/ Position	12 years as Director for South America and currently President of the mission in Argentina/Pastor	President of the Association of Pentecostal Protestant Pastors of Buenos Aires/Pastor	Pastor	Pastor
Nationality	Argentinean	Argentinean	Argentinean	Argentinean
Age	Mid-sixties	Early fifties	Mid-fifties	Late forties
Church	*Cuadrangular, Buenos Aires*	*Iglesia Independiente Pentecostes*	*La Casa de Todos*	*Alianza Cristiana y Misionera*
Denomination	Foursquare Gospel Church	Independent Pentecost	Independent	Christian Missionary Alliance[8]
Social Background	Middle-high	Low	Low	Low
Average Attendance	150 people	200 members	40 members	100 members

It seems that each Pentecostal Protestant church in Argentina has its own pastoral plan that in one way or another is determined by its denominational affiliation. For instance, the main pastoral focus of the *Cuadrangular, Buenos Aires* Gospel Church led by Prieto is evangelization. To accomplish this, the church, as a denomination, has several radio programs and they are looking for some spaces in the TV stations. As a local church they offer general programs for youths, adults and children and they have an evangelism team.

There are two key ministerial programs that the *Independiente Pentecostes* Church led by Vivian focus on: restoration and evangelism. The church also has a program for children and cell groups that meet once a week. These cell groups do not follow any structure; there are about 6 cell groups that meet and they range in size between 12 and 40 people.

La Casa de Todos Pentecostal Church's, led by Correa, main pastoral program is also evangelistic. They have regular services on Sunday and hold a Wednesday prayer meeting.

The *Alianza Cristiana y Misionera* Church led by Jorguera has a prayer walk group that covers the streets of the neighborhood in prayer every Wednesday morning. They also offer Christian education, youth and adult groups, classes for children and, on Wednesdays, the church has cell group meetings in people's homes.

Social Involvement

Unlike the churches in Mexico, Colombia, and Peru, three of the four Pentecostal Protestant churches interviewed in Argentina have some sort of formalized social involvement strategy.

According to Prieto, *Cuadrangular, Buenos Aires* Church, "Saint James reminds us that if we see our brother or sister hungry or cold and we only say, 'God bless you,' then we are not helping their hunger or cold." Therefore, as an Argentinean denomination they are actively working in the social area as well. For the past 15 years the Argentinean *Cuadrangular* church has had 22 drug rehabilitation homes. These homes do not charge the people being served. Actually, the program provides training workshops and it pays those who work. The church also runs a program that feeds children from Monday through Sunday and they also help cloth those who are more needy.
Through the support of wealthy (Pentecostal and Mainline) churches in the area,

La Casa de Todos Church, led by Correa, acquired clothing, groceries and medicine to support families of the church and the community. The church also provides a space for women from the community so that they can learn a skill such as hair-cutting or shoe making. The church also works with after school programs for children.

The *Alianza Cristiana y Misionera* Church led by Jorguera has been involved in social areas such as: skills workshops (making clothing and shoes) and aerobics and other exercises for its neighbors. There is an adult night school and they distribute clothing that is sold at a low cost.

Environmental Involvement

Although Buenos Aires is facing severe environmental issues, such as river and channel pollution, the lack of proper sewage systems, and air pollution, like the church in Mexico, Colombia, and Peru, none of the Pentecostal Protestant churches interviewed in Argentina have a commitment to addressing environmental issues.

Biblical Basis for Their Work

It seems that the needs of the people are the main motivation that encourages the churches interviewed in Argentina to do their pastoral work. For instance, for Prieto, *Cuadrangular, Buenos Aires* Church, the main motivation for their work is the overwhelming needs of the people and their commitment to love the people. "When God loved, he gave; God gave his son because he loves us. We love our people; therefore, we show our love by giving ourselves to them," said Prieto.

According to Prieto there are two main biblical texts that describe the *Cuadrangular, Buenos Aires* Church: Hebrews 13:8 which is the slogan of the church and Ezekiel 1:10 that shows the philosophy of mission of the *Cuadrangular, Buenos Aires* Church. Prieto points out that the four faces

Ezekiel sees in a vision are interpreted as the four faces of Jesus' ministry: (1) Jesus is the savior of the soul (Man's Face); (2) Jesus is who baptizes with the Holy Spirit (Lion's Face); (3) Jesus carried over him our sickness (Ox' Face); and (4) Jesus is the king who will come again to find the church (Eagle's Face). It is from these four faces and their meanings that the *Cuadrangular, Buenos Aires* Church's mission is derived. Prieto's interpretation of these texts comes from Aimee Semple McPherson (1890-1944) who was the founder of the International Church of the Foursquare Gospel.

Correa, *La Casa de Todos* Church, says that he began understanding more about the social injustice in the Argentinean society, the people's daily struggle to survive, and what the gospel's response to these social issues is when he began attending meetings of the CLAI, *Consejo Latinoamericano de Iglesias*, "Latin American Council of Churches."

Responding to my questions about their understanding of Luke 4:18-19, Prieto points out that in order for the church to do its task, it needs the anointment of the Holy Spirit. Just as *la unción del espiritu vino sobre Jesús*, "the anointment of the Spirit came over Jesus," the head of the church, the church that is the body of Christ needs the same anointment. The mission that is exposed in Luke 4:18-19 has to do with the proclamation of the Gospel and this is the mission the church needs to fulfill. He said that there are three main reasons that the church has been anointed. Prieto points out, (1) As in the past, those anointed were the kings; in the same way, we as believers are anointed as kings to go to war. Thus, our function as a church is to battle evil. (2) The second persons anointed were the prophets; the prophets had words of authority. The church has a prophetic role as those who give words of authority. (3) The third persons anointed were the priests; the main function of the priest is to worship God. In the same way the church has the authority to worship God in the way God wants and not in the way I want. Thus, Luke's passage points out the authority the church has to proclaim God's power and his anointment. The Word of God is what made the miracles possible. We as a church are a miracle of the Word of God. The main emphasis of this text is the announcement of the salvation, we need to be clear that salvation is not only for eternal life but we need to note that salvation starts here on earth.

In response to my questions regarding their understanding of the first chapters of Acts, Prieto points out that the church receives power to be a witness. He also points out that the Jerusalem church made some mistakes; for instance, rather than selling all their possessions the church should have been a better administrator. "In the late chapters of Acts we see that Paul is collecting offerings for the Jerusalem church because they where in need. Despite these mistakes, there is a clear principle that we need to take into consideration; it is to care for the needs of our neighbor. If we do this, we will defeat the hunger of the world. If the church really cares for those who are in need in its surroundings (believers and unbelievers), we could finish with the problem of hunger in the world," said Prieto. It seems that Prieto's hermeneutics mentions only some mistakes the church made and leaves out others.

For Vivian, *Independiente Pentecostes* Church, "Acts makes emphasis on the anointment of the Holy Spirit not as an act in the past but for us today. We need to be filled with the Holy Spirit. Time after time this text reminds us that theology without anointment is nothing."

In sum, it seems that for the Pentecostal Protestant pastors interviewed in Argentina, the anointment of the Holy Spirit plays a key role in today's church and ministry. With the emphasis on the Spirit the churches are not necessarily looking at it as a mystical experience but as an empowerment to do God's work in the world. It seems that the study of the Scripture has challenged the church in Argentina to be more involved in social issues and act as an agent of change.

Theological Issues

According to Vivian, *Independiente Pentecostes* Church, the Spirit of God is reserved for only a few people. In other words only a few can feel its presence. The presence of the Spirit is reduced to external feelings.

According to Jorguera, *Alianza Cristiana y Misionera* Church, there are many organizations that are helping people with their social needs; this support, after a period of time, creates an unhealthy dependence. He says that in order to avoid this unhealthy behavior, the church needs to help the people by empowering the people to discover their own abilities and, in this way, find their role in society and in the kingdom of God.

In sum, it seems that theologically speaking the Pentecostal Protestant church in Argentina is influenced by their doctrinal and biblical understanding. For instance, while some churches see the role of the Spirit as a crucial agent that encourages the church to do its work, other churches reduce the presence of the Spirit to a simple emotion that only a few enjoy. In regard to the issue of financial dependence and independence it seems that the churches' opinions are divided. While some churches expect economic or material support, other churches work on their own to accomplish their pastoral plan. It seems that this attitude is linked to their biblical and doctrinal formation as well.

General Statements

According to Prieto, the *Cuadrangular, Buenos Aires* Church never asks its members for tithe or give offerings. They believe giving is a voluntary act and, "in doing that we are telling our people that they are more important to us than what they give. There are too many people who are hurt because of money issues, so the church wants to be careful in this area."

Talking about the Pentecostal Protestant church in Latin America, Prieto points out that in the past the church committed the error of looking inside. The church thought that once people became Christians, they were different and therefore they separated themselves from the reality of this world. In John 17 Jesus prayed that God does not take us out the world but rather to protect us from its evil. Prieto points out that *legalismo extremo*, "extreme legalism," disconnected the Pentecostal Protestant church from the reality the continent was and is facing, putting the church years and years behind. Prieto thinks that God surprised the Pentecostal church in Latin America with a numerical explosion and neither the church nor the leadership of that time were prepared and ready for it. Therefore they tried to maintain the holiness of the church without knowing how to do it. They thought that making laws would be a solution and the legalism was total. They completely missed the text in which Jesus reminds us that we are the light and the salt of the earth yet, Prieto thinks that the church is changing in Latin America and the unity, although not perfect, that reigns among the Protestant people is helping to break the legalism of the church enabling it to impact the society.

Prieto also believes that in order for the church to be effective it needs to have several congregations rather than mega churches. The general rule should be that the church *vaya*, "goes," where the people are and not expect the people *venga*, "to come," where the church is.

Prieto emphasized that he is against the theology of prosperity but that he in favor of the God who is prosperous. The theology of prosperity promises things that God never promised. It says give first in order for God to give to you, when examples in the Bible show that God is the owner of everything. "God first gives to me and, as response to what He has given me, I give him ten percent. I do not pay God for what He has done for me; I give freely in obedience to him." Prieto continues saying, "The theology of prosperity is a big lie; many people are hurt because apparently God did not fulfill what he promised." According to Prieto, the Universal Church in Argentina has this kind of theology. These groups are called Neo-Pentecostals and are the fastest growing and the wealthiest groups in Argentina.

Talking about the relationship between the Roman Catholic Church and the Protestant churches, Prieto points out that there are more things that unify the churches than those which divided them. In other words, he is sympathetic to ecumenical participation. In fact, he is part of an ecumenical group in the Buenos Aires metropolitan area.

Talking about the situation of the Protestant churches in Argentina, Vivian, *Independiente Pentecostes* Church, points out that there are many people who have been hurt by other members of the church and also by the leadership. There are many pastors whose main focus is more on money and popularity than really sharing the gospel of Jesus Christ. Vivian again links church growth with spiritual vitality, which in reality is not necessarily a good link. It is possible to see large but unhealthy churches throughout the region.

According to Vivian the lack of church growth in Argentina is based on the lack of anointment by the Holy Spirit. He said, "There are evil spirits that are taking possession of the cities of our countries; so, we need to discern where these spirits are and go proclaim freedom and liberation."

According to Correa, *La Casa de Todos* Church, because many women in the community are living in free union, or are single mothers without a stable partner, many of the Pentecostal churches in the area marginalized them. In other words these churches do not allow the women be part of the church. These churches require them to be married or living without a partner in order to accept them as a members in the church. Correa points out that other Pentecostal churches look down on *La Casa de Todos* Church because they are trying to do a more integral work with the members of the community. When he says "an integral work," Correa means that *La Casa de Todos* Church is helping people not only in the spiritual part of their life but also in their social, economic, and personal lives. *La Casa de Todos* Church is receiving those women that are considered sinners by other Pentecostal churches of the area. "If a sick person goes to a Pentecostal pastor in the area, the only thing they do is pour oil over them and pray. We not only pray for them, we also provide them medicine and food," Correa said.

Jorguera, *Alianza Cristiana y Misionera* Church, believes that the church is involved in the social areas of the community and that has allowed them to demonstrate another kind of gospel; a gospel that not only cares for the soul of the person but also cares for their physical needs. It has helped the members of the church to put their gifts into the service of the kingdom of God. Jorguera says, "People do not only come to the church to worship but they also find a place where they can serve their neighbors."

According to Jorguera, his call to ministry took place through a biblical study of the second coming of Jesus. He feels the need to go and preach the gospel to the people. On his way home one cold night in southern Argentina Jorguera saw two children trying to protect themselves from the cold in a supermarket heating system. He picked up the children and brought them home. The next day he took them to their home and he realized the extreme poverty in which they lived. Since that day Jorguera has had a conversion experience to care for people's physical needs.

Jorguera observed that there are many new and growing Neo-Pentecostal churches with a primary emphasis on economic factors. These churches are preaching a prosperity gospel and these churches have several meetings during the week in order to increase their profit.

Talking about the role of the Roman Catholic Church in Argentina, Jorguera argues that they have a strong social program because they have the economic funds needed to do so. Still, he thinks that the impact of the church is minimal because there is no change of life of the people who receive these benefits.

Conclusion

Unlike the church in Mexico, Colombia, and Peru, it seems that three of the four Pentecostal churches interviewed in Argentina have an established social involvement program. Although Buenos Aires is facing a critical environmental situation, like the church in Mexico, Colombia, and Peru, the Pentecostal Protestant churches in Argentina do not have a commitment to environmental issues.

It seems that the needs of the people and the study of Scriptures have challenged the Pentecostal Protestants interviewed in Argentina to be more involved in social issues. It seems that, for the Pentecostal Protestant pastors interviewed in Argentina, the anointment of the Holy Spirit plays a key role in today's church and ministry. Although, this was also the claim in other Latin American countries, it seems in Argentina that they minister more integrally. This anointment is the empowerment of the Spirit to do God's work in the world.

Apparently the doctrinal and biblical understanding of those interviewed influences their missiological enterprise. For instance, while some churches see the role of the Spirit as a crucial agent that encourages the church to do its work, other churches reduce the presence of the Spirit to a simple emotion that only a few enjoy.

It seems that there is more unity among Pentecostal Protestant churches in Argentina than in the past. Pastors agree that the extreme legalism in the past and the theology of prosperity in the present are the two of the main obstacles preventing the Pentecostal Protestant churches from being more effective in the Argentinean society. Pastors interviewed in Argentina question the growth of the Neo-Pentecostal churches because of their close connection to the prosperity gospel in their services and doctrine.

Summary

The Pentecostal Protestant churches in Latin America follow their own pastoral plans that, in one way or another, are determined by their denominational affiliation. It seems that a common pastoral theme among Pentecostal Protestant churches in Latin America is the focus on evangelism.

It seems also that, in general, the Pentecostal Protestant churches in Latin America do not have established social involvement programs. Most of the interviewees agree that the church's main focus is evangelistic rather than social. While there are some groups that are working on isolated social projects, with the exception of Argentina, the general consensus is that this is not an area of ministerial priority.

Although most of Latin America is facing serious environmental issues, none of the Pentecostal Protestant churches interviewed have a commitment to address environmental issues. Here there is general agreement among the pastors interviewed that this is a new area that the church has not begun to analyze.

Pentecostal Protestant pastors in Latin America are encouraged to do their work based on experience, awareness of the social situation, evangelistic focus, and spiritual warfare.

Interviewees agree that Protestant churches in Latin America are segregated into small self-centered groups and that members are shifting between churches due to a lack of profound biblical and doctrinal foundations. The pastors interviewed agree that every day there are more and more Christian groups (caused by divisions) in the Latin American society making the Christian witness more difficult. They also agree that the church has lost its vitality as an agent of change in a society of growing violence and insecurity.

Pastors agree that the past extreme legalism and the present theology of prosperity are two of the main obstacles for the Pentecostal Protestant churches to be more effective agents of change in the Latin American society. Although many of the Latin American Pentecostal pastors interviewed agree that numerical growth is the church's major priority and in some sense is proof of a healthy spirituality, they are suspicious of the growth of the Neo-Pentecostal churches because of their close connection to the prosperity gospel and their million-dollar building acquisitions.

With a fairly extensive overview of the actual situation in Latin America based on field research discoveries, a historical overview of Latin America, and a Lukan understanding of God's mission, the next chapter will attempt to respond to the overall questions of this investigation. What kind of initiative can be developed within the Latin American context that will help develop the Roman Catholic and Protestant theology of mission in order to result in a healthier ecclesiology and prepare and energize the church for its integral missiological task?

Notes

1. Just as I did in Chapters 4 and 5, I collected data through an interview process in order to accomplish my research goal,. I selected four pastors from four Pentecostal Protestant churches from major cities within four main countries in Latin America. I purposely interviewed pastors belonging to churches of different socioeconomic backgrounds in order to achieve a better representation of the actual reality that describes each city and country. I will follow the same pattern and categories I used in chapters 4 and 5.

2. This is an evangelistic cell group model that was developed by the Colombian pastor Cesar Castellanos. According to Castellanos, "The model of ministry based on 12 is the most effective means of obeying the Great Commission of Jesus Christ to win disciples and of growing the Church" (Mitchell 2006). The main focus of this program is based on the belief, according to Castellanos that, "every Christian has a purpose. That purpose is to win the lost for Jesus. If you don't fulfill that purpose, then you will never be fulfilled. The purpose is best fulfilled within the G12 cellular vision. If you don't fulfill your purpose today, you may never fulfill it at all" (Mitchell 2006).

3. For more information about this denomination see: http://www.mmm-usa-siteoficial.org/

4. It is a combination on both evangelistic and discipleship programs that originated in Bogotá, Colombia by a Cuadrangular Gospel pastor. Its main focus is on how to follow up and empower new members to become active in the church. Its roots are based on both Scripture and personal pastoral experience.

5. There are several Pentecostal groups in Latin America that call their ministers apostle rather than pastor. This understanding is based on 1 Corinthians 12:28 which says, " God has appointed in the church first apostles, second prophets, third teachers, then workers of miracles, then healers, helpers, administrators, speakers in various kinds of tongues."

6. The Rio Grande Bible Institute (also known as RGBI) is a nondenominational school located in Edinburg, Texas, which has two main purposes: to serve as a seminary to students from Mexico, Central America, and South America, and to serve as a Spanish-language institute for non-Spanish-speaking North Americans who will serve as missionaries in Spanish-speaking Latin America.

7. Micah Projects Inc originated in the United States and its mission is a worldwide project to respond to people who experience exclusion, poverty, injustice and social isolation so that they may experience inclusion, economic well-being, justice and connection within their community of choice. They seek to work collaboratively and respectfully with the indigenous community. They embrace their responsibility to redress the dispossession of indigenous people from their land (Micah Project Inc. 2006).

8. I classified this *Alianza Cristiana y Misionera* church in Buenos Aires as part of the Pentecostal churches because, according to Jorguera, this church identifies itself as a Pentecostal congregation.

Chapter 7

Redefining the Theology and Practice of the Church in Latin America

The researchable problem of this project was threefold: (1) I wanted to briefly explore the historical development of Latin America, specifically surveying the social, political, economic, environmental and religious factors that have contributed in some way to what Latin America is today. This provided a context for understanding the churches. (2) I wanted to investigate the current practice and theology of some of the Roman Catholic and Protestant churches in five main cities of four Latin American countries in order to understand their current theological views and their involvement in mission. (3) I intended to evaluate how Luke 4:16-30; 5:27-32; 19:1-10; Acts 2:42-47; and 4:32-37 could provide a paradigm for integral mission in Latin America. In this way, the church may be able to address the social, political, economic, environmental, and spiritual questions the continent is raising.

The Lukan perspective supports this investigation in three ways: a). Luke-Acts provides an evaluation of the Latin American churches' theology of mission; b). Luke-Acts provides a model of mission for the Latin American churches; and c). Luke-Acts questions and challenges the actual Latin American churches' missional practices. In one way Luke-Acts evaluates how the church is doing mission and in another way, the church in Latin America's method of doing mission provides new lenses through which to read Luke-Acts. The following table suggests some of the synergies between Luke-Acts and the church in Latin America based on this research project (see Figure 5).

The key questions I have sought to answer and that became the driving questions of this project are: (1) How have the Roman Catholic and Protestant churches in Latin America arrived at their present understandings of mission, their present structures for ministry, and their current practices of mission? (2) What are some of the current biblical bases and missiological practices of the Roman Catholic and Protestant churches in Latin America? How does the churches' biblical understanding position them with respect to their cultural, social, and political context? (3) What significant missiological implications could Luke 4:16-30; 5:27-32; 19:1-10; Acts 2:42-47; and 4:32-37 provide about the local church's part in God's salvific mission in Latin America? (4) Based on field research, a historical overview, and a Lukan understanding of God's mission, what kind of initiative can be developed in the Latin American context that would help develop Roman Catholic and Protestant theology of mission that could result in a healthier ecclesiology and that would prepare and energize the church for its integral missiological task?

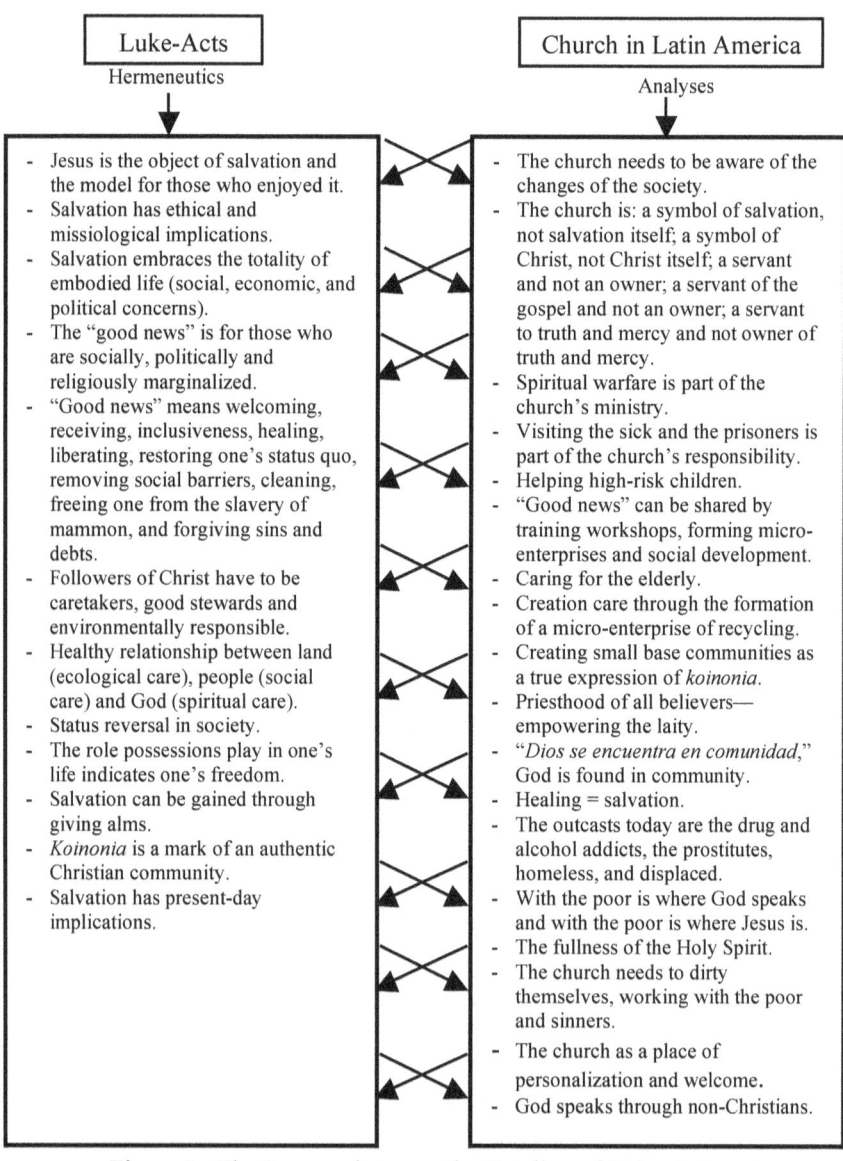

Figure 5. The Synergy between the Reading of Luke-Acts and the Analyses of the Latin American Church

In order to answer these questions, I began with an overview of colonization and Christian influence in Latin America (Chapter 2) and studied Luke-Acts theology and mission for the Latin American context (Chapter 3). As I explained in the first chapter, I chose four main countries in Latin America: Mexico, Colombia, Peru, and Argentina and in each of these countries I interviewed four Roman Catholic priests, four Mainline Protestant pastors, and four Pentecostal Protestant pastors (Chapters 4, 5, and 6). The main goal with these interviews was to analyze the theology and praxis present in these three main groups. The following overall conclusions are drawn from the entire study. To see a graphical overview of the field research in each country, refer to Appendix C, D, E, and F.

Overall Conclusions

The conquest of Latin America began 500 years ago and continues today with the current forces of neo-colonization and a brutal global capitalistic system, resulting in increasing poverty, inequality and exploitation of Latin America's natural resources and society. The contemporary forces of urbanization and globalization are challenging the socio-economic, political, religious and familial structures completely altering where people live, how they live and make decisions and how they relate to one another and their surroundings. The conquest of Latin America and the forces of globalization and urbanization have resulted in new cultural realities that the church must address.

This study has revealed six significant and interrelated issues that challenge the traditional views of the Latin American church and provide new theological, ecclesiological and missiological insights for its integral ministry throughout the region while at the same time addressing the driving questions of the investigation. These issues are: (1) People are still being forced into poverty; (2) The church in Latin America is still struggling with contextualization of the gospel; (3) Creation care needs to be recovered as a responsibility of the church; (4) The hope of renewal is alive in the Roman Catholic Church; (5) All churches experience barriers to and opportunities for building a biblical community; and (6) There are seeds of a theology propagating an integral mission consistent with the Luke-Acts view of salvation.

1. People are Still Being Forced into Poverty

Based on this research, external and internal forces have shaped the Latin American reality of today in terms of the social, political, economic, and environmental situation. In addition to the deteriorated Christologies described in Chapter 2, the external factors include the colonization forces of foreign invasions and the neo-colonization forces of globalization, capitalism and neoliberal government systems. In some ways these external forces have altered the sociological, anthropological, and psychological landscape of the region thereby producing internal forces that also affect the overall situation.

The internal forces include government corruption, segregation, discrimination, violence, popular religiosity and rural-urban migration. Mexico City is a clear example of the problem of rapid urbanization that is seen throughout Latin America. The people moving from rural to urban settings, as specifically seen in Mexico City, need food, shelter, and employment. They use more water, create more sewage, and contribute to more air contamination. As millions of people compete for the same space, the same jobs, and the same resources violence increases and the socio-political, environmental, economic and spiritual systems are stressed, challenging the governmental policies and ultimately challenging both the Roman Catholic and Protestant churches and their ministry.

The situation in Colombia is no better than in Mexico. Colombia has suffered years of Civil War, Guerilla War and Drug Cartel War that are, in some ways, inter-related and have resulted in urban migration as families, widows and orphans are displaced by the violence. The exploding population in the cities faces the same challenges as those seen in Mexico City. Those who have been displaced by war are competing for the same food, water, jobs, health care, and justice and cardboard neighborhoods have become the reality in all major cities. Further escalating the already desperate situation is the governmental corruption. Likewise the Roman Catholic Church has been closely aligned to the power in Colombia and therefore had been involved in the oppression until the last four decades. Additionally, Fundamental Pentecostal groups (the fastest growing faction of the Protestant church) have blinded the church to social issues making its witness virtually ineffective to integrally impacting the general society.

The study of Peru highlights the effects of political corruption on the nation. Throughout history Peru has played a crucial role in the Latin American society due to its central location on the continent. Remnants of the highly civilized Incan nation from the country's days of pre-colonization are still evident today and the Roman Catholic Church's involvement since the time of colonization continues in its strong presence there. Like Mexico and Colombia, Peru is also suffering from human rights violations, the gap between the rich and poor is widening daily, and it is experiencing drastic environmental challenges in addition to the problem of political corruption previously mentioned.

Argentina in the South has not escaped the problems facing Mexico, Colombia and Peru. It too has experienced its share of dictatorships and governmental corruption and violence. Here the economic struggles have been very evident throughout the country's history. Argentines suffer the same maladies of the other countries' residents like poverty, pollution, human rights violations, and urban explosion. One clear example of that is seen in Buenos Aires with more than 14 million residents. In addition, throughout Argentina as well as Latin America, multinational companies force the land to be used in ways that are not environmentally responsible and the crops that are produced are exported; for example, soybeans are grown where cattle were once raised. Not only do soybeans not feed the country's population but also the wages they produce for the farmers are not sufficient for survival.

This investigation focused specifically on the environmental issues Mexico is facing, the religious history in Colombia, the political influences in Peru and the aggregate economic situation in Argentina. Each individual case study reflects the reality of the others and as a result there are great masses of people in Latin America who live in extremely difficult circumstances. Unemployment, lack of housing, malnutrition, extreme indigence, exploitation, environmental crises, socio-economic polarization, and displacement due to violence are some of the realities describing most of Latin America today. In some of the Latin American countries this situation is caused by governmental corruption and decisions that are in favor of the entrance of multinational corporations on the pretext that this will foster industrial development.

Clearly the economies of the Latin American countries are dependent on foreign nations; these outsiders see Latin America as a source of raw materials and cheap labor.

Looking at the Latin America situation, one cannot see poverty as a virtue, or a description of "just the way things are," or the fruit of the laziness of the people as proponents of the "Culture of Poverty" concept would argue. Instead, poverty is caused by oppression at the national and international levels and at the individual and collective levels.

Although most of the Bible translations in both English and Spanish use the terminology "poor" and *pobre* to describe the recipients of the "good news" in the Lukan literature, clearly these words are inadequate to describe the reality of the Latin American region and of the Two-Thirds World countries. The standpoint of the poor in Latin America will not allow for the narrow definition of *pobre* in terms of only economic factors. Of course *pobre* has financial connotations as 40 percent of the region's wealth is owned by a mere ten percent of the population but the *pobre* in Latin America also includes those who are socially and spatially marginalized, pushed to the boundaries of society where they are segregated from it and in some cases discriminated against. Influenced by global capitalism, most Latin American countries are adopting the neoliberal system, which continues to benefit the rich minority and leads the poor majority into deeper poverty thereby contributing to the fragmentation of the civil society. Finally, religious marginality also contributes to the definition of *pobre* in Latin America as those who profess to be Roman Catholic experience greater freedom, opportunity and privilege within the society than those who do not.

In the original text Luke used three different words to indicate "poor" but the primary word used was πτωχός which comes from the social classification presented in the Roman tradition. To understand the meaning of the Greek words, one has to understand the context from which these words developed. The Holiness Code and Deuteronomy provide standards that share two main principles: wholeness/completeness and separateness. Beginning with dietary rules to learn what was clean and pure, the Jews also learned to distinguish between people according to their occupation, gender, physical conditions and nationality thereby developing a conscious system of discrimination. Examples of outcasts by the time of the Second Temple were (1) those who experienced discrimination because of their occupation, (2) those who experienced discrimination because of sickness, and (3) those who experienced discrimination because they were sojourners or resident aliens. These classifications were received via ascription just as many of the marginalities described in Latin America are also ascribed. In other words, people do not choose their categories but they are born into them. It can be said, therefore, that people are forced into poverty, just as this investigation has demonstrated.

The hope for Latin America also comes from the Lukan literature. Luke carefully chose his words and strategically placed the word πτωχός within the text to emphasize who is now being included in Jesus' missional task. Luke 4:16-30 is a key text of the Lukan literature because it describes the opening of Jesus' public ministry, especially verses 18 and 19 where Jesus is citing Isaiah 61:1-2 and 58:9. Jesus' mission statement was to preach, to send and to proclaim. When Jesus offered release he was offering the restoration of one's social status and "freedom from the binding power of Satan." Luke's intention was to share the truth that those who are marginalized, oppressed, and cast out from society are the "poor" and as such they are precisely the recipients of the "good news." The rationality for this is that God is the God of justice and because poverty is injustice God chooses the side of the poor.

Again, Luke does not ascribe the terminology *pobre* only to those with financial difficulties. This is clearly demonstrated in Luke 5:27-32 and 19:1-10 when Jesus embraced the πτωχός, tax collectors Levi and Zacchaeus, who according to the religiosity of the time were considered sinners because of their occupation despite their economic wealth. Jesus challenged the social structure of his time by welcoming and dining with them, reaffirming their social status. The rich ruler (Luke 18:18-29) in comparison to Zacchaeus reveals the truth that the role possessions play in a person's life determines their self-identity, their world-view and their salvation.

Similarly, is the church in Latin America choosing the side of the poor? According to this study, despite all of its negative influence throughout history, the Roman Catholics have tended to some of Colombia's social needs through their support of welfare institutions and the creation of schools. Colombian Mainline Protestants have also participated in caring for people's needs through the formation of hospitals and by making the Bible more available to the people.

Unfortunately, most of the Neo-Pentecostals and some of the Pentecostal Protestant churches have missed the message of the Lukan literature and throughout Latin America they preach a prosperity gospel. Those who do not espouse the prosperity gospel often tend to preach separation from society. In addition to not addressing the reality of poverty in their midst, one problem with the prosperity gospel teaching is that the possessions often become the god. One such church in Peru goes so far as to teach that Jesus was wealthy, claiming that this teaching is based on Scripture and is a valid goal for humanity. Yet, it was the rich man in the Gospel of Luke who was unable to give up his possessions and therefore excluded himself from salvation.

At churches such as the one in Peru, members are taught to give tithes and offerings to prosper the church. The church prophesies indicate that even pagan wealth will come to them. Prosperity teachings promise financial security through the manipulation of the Scriptures. In fact a Mexican Pentecostal pastor says that as long as the Scriptures are used, any interpretation of them is acceptable. This creates false expectations and leaves thousands of people disillusioned by the pastor, the church and God when their expectations go unfilled. Often these people leave the church in a worse situation than when they joined and they believe in a God who does not care for their needs. They have been taught that God's blessings are only financial in nature.

Churches that subscribe to the prosperity teaching generally emphasize numbers and prosperity as indicators of spiritual health. This emphasis reduces the complex problems of poverty in Latin America to being only monetary. Yet, as Peter reminded Simon the Sorcerer in Acts 8:20, it is not possible to purchase souls. "May your money parish with you, because you thought you could buy the gift of God with money!" These Neo-Pentecostal churches also have a narrow eschatological view of salvation, which blinds them to the present reality of the society and limits their opportunities for integral service as Luke-Acts challenges.

While one of the Charismatic Roman Catholic priests in Colombia is quick to point out that social involvement is not a solution to the needs of the society, another priest emphasizes that the poor "have dignity and the potential to succeed if we give them the opportunity." This type of thinking also challenges the "Culture of Poverty" ideology.

Velizaroff of the Pentecostal *Tú y Tú Casa* Church says that "Peru is a church of beggars." He claims that people want to receive, not give. A Roman Catholic priest in Argentina echoes this opinion saying that too often people have a "mentality of dependence" which is why some of their social programs have failed. An example of this was also seen in Colombia when a church basically had to rebuild after World Vision left.

It is for this reason that a Roman Catholic priest in Peru emphasizes the importance of teaching and empowering the poor rather than giving. The Free Lutheran church in Peru agrees that it is not money that people need; instead it is to be empowered to find their own destiny. One of the Pentecostal pastors in Argentina emphasizes the importance of empowering the people to find their role in society and, indeed, in the Kingdom of God to avoid creating an unhealthy dependence. Luke-Acts teaches to give, not for the sake of receiving, but give for sake of the poor, the outcasts, the segregated, and the marginalized.

Clearly the best way to serve the *pobre* is not simply to throw money at them, or even attempt to extract it from them. While the concept of integral service will be covered more completely in another section, one of the Pentecostal Protestant churches in Peru (*Tú y Tú Casa*) is addressing new dimensions of ministering to the *pobre*. Among the social programs offered is a specific ministry for prisoners, which directly speaks to Luke's emphasis on Jesus' ministry "to proclaim freedom to the prisoners." This ministry includes health brigades for prisoners thereby offering "recovery of sight to the blind." (Similarly, they also provide financial assistance and support for the sick in hospitals). This same church also helps prisoners who have been released, many of them foreigners, just as the Lukan literature challenges the church to receive and welcome the foreigners and outcasts. The welcoming environment and assistance through rehabilitation provide a new lens through which to read and live out the teachings found in the Lukan literature.

Finally, although in most of the Latin American countries the Roman Catholic Church and the State are officially separated, the Roman Catholics still enjoy certain government privileges such as tax benefits and certain influence in social decisions. This creates tension between Protestants and Catholics and fuels the desire for many Protestants to reject anything that is "Catholic." In addition, there are still instances of isolated persecution against Protestantism in some rural areas of Latin America. This tension is another contributing factor to the poverty that the region is experiencing.

2. The Church in Latin America is Still Struggling with Contextualization of the Gospel

The Gospel of Luke and the book of Acts were chosen for this study because they provide an integral view of salvation that involves spiritual and social action, including the whole community of believers which, in one way or another, challenges the Latin American context. Green emphasizes that salvation addresses individuals' social, economic and political concerns in addition to the spiritual dimension. Most scholars agree that Luke and Acts should be read as a single unit because Acts answers some of the questions raised in Luke; these books demonstrate the reality that Jesus' mission was the same as the mission of the early church. The books have ecclesiological, missiological and evangelistic purposes and therefore provide a good framework for the ministry of the Latin American churches today.

The church is in fact a vital part of Latin America's history but its effectiveness as a Christian witness in the region is in question as it faces the challenges of yesterday and today. Throughout the continent's modern history Latin America has been subjugated to foreign powers that have, in many ways, forced upon it not only a distorted image of Christ but also the framework in which religion should be lived out.

As the investigation has indicated, since the time of colonization the Roman Catholic Church and the state have been closely linked resulting in the abuse of power and improper evangelistic techniques that were concerned only for the conquest of people and not for the people themselves. Deteriorated Christology, paganism and syncretism became the religious reality throughout the continent. As Figure 7 points out, beginning with the Vatican II in 1962 and in consequent leadership gatherings designed to discuss evangelization and the church's commitment to Latin America, a new paradigm has been emerging as the theology and praxis of mission of the Roman Catholic Church is redefined and the church's eyes are opened to the reality of the society it serves and the role of the church within that society. Although it is not yet united in its efforts, the Roman Catholic Church is increasingly more involved in the social, economic and religious (evangelism and discipling) realms of the Latin American society.

Although they represent the minority on the continent, since their arrival in the past two centuries, Protestants have played an important role in the society as well. They introduced a different image of Christ, a living Christ with whom a relationship is possible, but this only represents one part of the gospel. As a result, the Christological understanding of many of the Protestant churches is distorted throughout Latin America and is shaped by those who brought the gospel. The Christ presented is more interested in individual souls than the overall needs of the people and therefore the Protestant church has been less effective in dealing with the suffering, the excluded and the powerlessness of the majority.

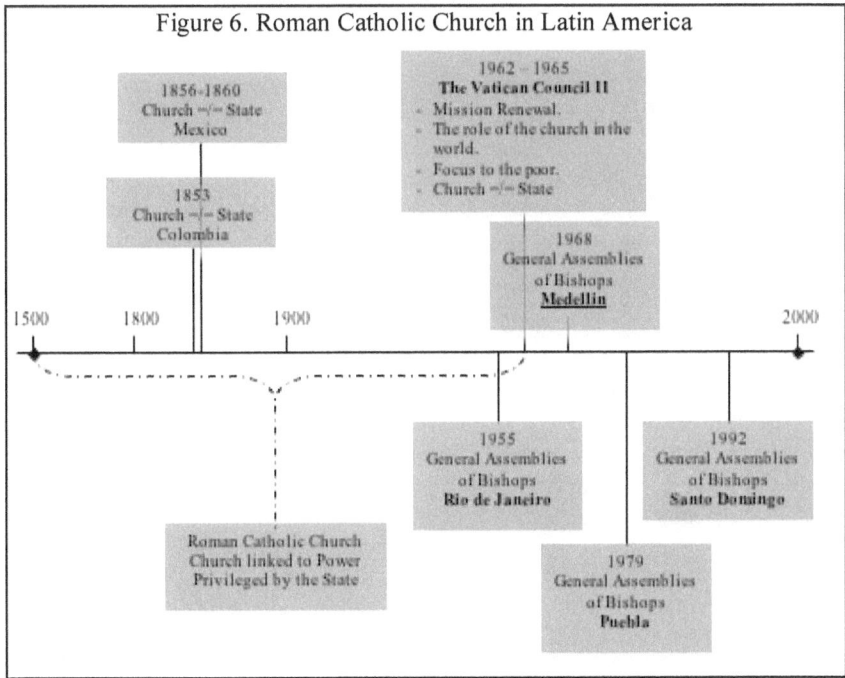

Figure 6. Roman Catholic Church in Latin America

As demonstrated in the last section by the prosperity gospel teachings throughout Latin America, some of the churches in the region continue to be either not aware of or apathetic toward the reality of the society in which they minister. One of the Argentinean Roman Catholic priests interviewed says that because poverty (in all of its forms) is the reality in Latin America and Jesus' example was to be with the poor, the church also needs to "dirty themselves" by working with the poor and being among them. Just as the Lukan literature had to be evaluated in its context, so must the current Latin American context be understood for effective ministry to take place in the region.

Some of the Mexican mainline Protestant pastors are concerned about the present and future of the church for this very reason. One of their specific concerns is that the Mexican church tends to be too fundamental or legalistic thereby isolating itself from society. This is dangerous because, as one of the

Mexican Roman Catholic Priests pointed out, understanding the context in which one serves is essential for completing the missiological task.

Contextualization issues can be as complex as the issues raised by poverty or globalization (as will be discussed next) or as simple as speaking the same language. Here, Argentina provides an excellent example. The Argentinean immigrants were more diverse than in the other countries studied. Those immigrants brought with them their own religions, making the religious landscape of Argentina a bit more diverse and complex than in the other countries. The fact that services were held in the native languages until recent times indicates that the churches struggled to become contextualized, or incarnate, in the new society where they ministered.

In fact many churches utilize literal English to Spanish translations of Christian materials and music without considering the social context in which it is being presented. One pastor in Peru expressed concern over the implementation of the G-12 strategy throughout all of Latin America. His point is that this program was developed in Colombia for Colombians and therefore does not necessarily work within other contexts where the church is serving. A Roman Catholic priest in Colombia echoes this concern saying that theology must address the questions that are being raised by the people within a given society.

As discussed in the research, the forces of globalization have particularly affected the younger generation. The research shows that children of very religious people live with virtually no religion. Perhaps this generation gap is also a result of the extreme legalism of the church. Clearly, the church is a few years behind the times and is not talking the same language as the youthful society nor addressing the questions they are asking. Mexican and Colombian pastors from all of the Christian categories emphasize the importance of reaching and ministering to the younger generation. Now it must find ways to reconnect with and involve this segment of the population.

Churches in Peru and Argentina are, in a sense, "dirtying themselves" to address this very concern rather than just talking about it or wishing for a change. The Free Lutheran Church in Peru, aware of the violence in society due to gang friction, embraced the situation. The church welcomed gang members and actually curbed violence in the area by implementing a soccer tournament. This is a creative ministry idea from God that was spoken through a non-Christian conduit. The pastor of this church says that it is the talented people in society who tend to cause problems due to the lack of challenge. The soccer tournaments and the music classes offered at his church directly addresses these needs within society and "release the oppressed," as mentioned in Luke 4:18.

The Mennonite Church in Argentina offers similar programs involving sports and music activities in an attempt to attract youth and children. Clearly, the need to reach the younger generations is a recurrent theme throughout Latin America. The fact that churches are incorporating sports into their programs speaks to the understanding that these generations cannot be reached in the same way as their parents were reached.

As Baspineiro, a Baptist pastor in Argentina, points out, the goal is to establish relationship and dialogue with people and to be incarnational. In fact he says that "Incarnation is the price every church needs to pay if it wants to be Christ-like in the world." While another conclusion from this study will address social involvement in more depth in regard to integral mission, one of the Pentecostal pastors in Argentina says that social involvement is helping church members as they come to church not only to worship God but also to serve their neighbors. Perhaps this is another new lens through which Latin America is reading Luke-Acts but, of course, being incarnational is not easy. Pastors appear to be cautious about the ways in which social assistance are administered in order to prevent unhealthy dependency, as seen in the previous section.

Even so, the gospel is based on action. It takes embracing the situation, as has been the example of the church in Peru, to affect change within society. Through the church's involvement in the community, the people now have a place to turn in times of trouble. Perhaps the people are seeking refuge from society but the pastor of this church emphasizes that his goal is to help people face their problems, not escape from them. In a sense this church reminds the society that true peace and security do not come from the absence of violence but from the presence of Jesus. This church is a living example of Christ's presence in its society; this church is incarnational.

Another recurring theme throughout all of the interviews in all of the countries has been the church's place in society. Most of the churches are incorporating cell groups into their program of ministry and there seems to be a growing emphasis on the church going to the people rather than the people going to the church, as stated by one of the Pentecostal Pastors in Argentina. In fact, it is the goal of one of the mainline Protestant churches in Argentina to be where the people are and, for this reason, they only use their church building on Sundays; the rest of their work is done in the neighborhoods. This form of contextualization is also bringing renewal to the Roman Catholic Church and will be discussed in a later section of this evaluation. It should be noted that one of the keys to the success of this movement toward the people in all of the churches will be based upon the unity exemplified within each church and between churches, as will be discussed in another overall conclusion.

Clearly, the Latin American church's lack of contextualization in the past and its move toward becoming more contextualized, with the exception of some of the Pentecostal churches, has missiological implications and is affected by the theology and ecclesiology of each individual church.

3. Creation Care Needs to be Recovered as a Responsibility of the Church

An important part of the context in which the Latin American Church operates is the environment. Research indicates that the environmental situation throughout Latin America is grave, particularly within the cities where rapid overpopulation has become the everyday reality. Air and water pollution are obvious results, which leads to the spread of diseases. As the population grows, the problems will become more amplified, endangering both human and environmental health. There are also issues related to deforestation and barren soil resulting from improper farming techniques, just to name a few.

As studied in Chapter 3, when Luke proclaims the year of the Lord's favor (4:19) he is actually referring to the Law of Jubilee addressed in Leviticus 25 and Deuteronomy 15. In addition to releasing economic and social oppression, the Law of Jubilee has direct environmental implications because it implies rest for the land to prevent or recover from improper or over use. This serves as a reminder that the church, as the extension of Jesus' mission, is the steward and caretaker of creation.

Despite this challenge from scripture and the environmental struggles seen throughout Latin America, the church remains virtually silent. Of the 48 priests and pastors interviewed less than ten percent have any involvement at all in addressing environmental issues and only two churches, both of them Roman Catholic, have incorporated creation care into official programs of the church.

Most of the adopted projects are socially motivated and, with the exception of tree planting and recycling, many of the projects simply involve applying pressure to the government or society and do not require the church to actually get its "hands dirty." The projects are, however, important to the overall well-being of society and the environment and include a micro-enterprise recycling program, installation of a sewage system, preventing garbage burning and contamination from pig farming for health reasons, protesting abuse of public beaches and reforestation.

The fact that there is at least a little bit of environmental involvement brings a little bit of hope to the region. However, the consensus from the pastors and priests is that this is not an area that the church is addressing. It should be noted that none of the Pentecostal churches interviewed believe that environmental issues are within the scope of their ministry, despite the fact that they serve the fastest growing churches in the region and the environment is an ever-present reality in the lives of all of their members. Clearly, the church in Latin America has a long way to go in its efforts to fulfill the commands of the Scriptures in terms of creation care.

4. The Hope of Renewal in the Roman Catholic Church

Almost all of the Roman Catholic priests interviewed mentioned Vatican II as being important to some aspect of their local ministry. As discussed previously, this council (1962-65) and other similar councils served to open the church's eyes to its need for contextualization to properly fulfill the church's mission.

One example of renewal is found in the SINE (Integral System of New Evangelization) program. This program is an evangelistic strategy that decentralizes the power of the church, by bringing the church to the people. Implementation involves the use of cell groups, which empowers local leadership. Although SINE is only specifically mentioned in Mexico its concepts are mirrored in other countries. For example, in Colombia the priests discussed the PDRE (Project Diocesan of Renovation and Evangelism), which also decentralizes the power of the church by creating small communities that move from a conglomeration to a real representation of God's people. In so doing, not only does the Roman Catholic Church become more contextualized but it transfers leadership responsibilities from the priest to the people. Realizing that the job of ministry is too big for one person, a Roman Catholic priest in Peru has implemented a program of training lay pastors. This concept is perhaps a sign of renewal in the Catholic Church, reminiscent of the lesson taught in Acts Chapter 6 where the responsibilities were divided to enhance the ministry.

As one of the Argentinean priests pointed out, the Church in Rome and the Church in Latin America are two different entities. As the Roman Catholic Church moves toward the people, it also becomes more contextualized thereby seeing and understanding the society through new lenses. Unfortunately though, much of the biblical basis for the Roman Catholic Churches is still stipulated by Rome but there is evidence that this is changing. A prime example of this can be seen in one of the Mexican priests, Father Herrera's, interpretation of Acts. He said that this text has implications not only for the priests but also for all believers. He believes in the "priesthood of all believers" as agents of change within society. It appears that some of his colleagues agree, both in Mexico and throughout Latin America, as many of the priests interviewed talked about empowering the laity to be active participants in not only their own faith but also that of the parish and in their society as well. Again, the move toward empowering the laity is clearly seen. In fact, one only needs to review the charts for each country that are found in Appendixes C, D, E, and F to see that empowering the laity is an underlying theme in all four countries.

Another benefit of this decentralization, the empowering of laity and the emphasis on cell groups and base communities within the Roman Catholic Church is the role that these play in personal discipleship. Some priests emphasize reading the Bible for oneself and they point out that individual change leads to societal change. In Mexico a priest emphasizes the importance of living an exemplary Christian life as a key evangelistic tool. He also said that conversion is a process, clearly indicating that the individual must be involved in working out his/her faith. Another priest in Colombia talks about personal encounters with Jesus and faith. This emphasis on discipleship and living out ones own faith is a new theme that is emerging in the Roman Catholic Church.

The field research highlighted many other areas that offer the promise of renewal for the Roman Catholic Church. One that might possibly bring about change (and may not be so obvious) is the changing relationship between the church and state. Although officially the ties have been cut between the two entities after nearly 400 years of partnership, the reality is that it has been an unraveling process. The relationship still exists, in some places stronger than others, as previously discussed. But the church is struggling to define the relationship or separation further. For example, in Mexico the Roman Catholic Churches attempt to differentiate themselves from the government by defining what areas each institution handles; claiming that social issues are the responsibility of the government. Likewise the Argentineans say that their social involvement addresses the areas that the government is neglecting. Perhaps the most interesting comment comes from Monsignor Thorndike in Peru who claims that the spiritual situation is better now than when Roman Catholicism was the state religion. "Since there is freedom of religion in Peru [and Latin America], people willing choose to go to the services and live a deeper life with the church and with the sacraments."

Of course, there are more theological, ecclesiological and missiological whispers of renewal within the Roman Catholic Church in Latin America. In Argentina the priests openly expressed their concern with the overall structure of the church but one expressed hope that the structure will change, bringing with it renewal to the Roman Catholic Church. As previously mentioned there is more emphasis on relationship, on community and even trinitarian theology. While 16 priests only represent a very small sample of the reality of the Roman Catholic Church in Latin America, the comments from the Argentinean priests in particular bring with them a breath of fresh air. One of the Roman Catholic priests in Colombia defined the world as his parish. This sounds very much like some of John Wesley's reflections in the eighteenth century that brought renewal to the Anglican Church and perhaps may be evidence of renewal coming to the Catholic Church in Colombia and Latin America.

A personal reflection

I grew up in the Roman Catholic Church in Colombia and many of these topics that are suggesting renewal in the church were not present in my experience. However, of all concepts uncovered during my field research, the most significant one is the emphasis on community that was a recurrent theme throughout the interviews. One Argentinean priest talked about the importance of the church being welcoming and personal. When I was growing up there was no relationship in the Catholic Church, neither between the priest and his parish nor between parishioners. One of the key factors of my family's conversion was the community that we found in the Protestant church. In the Protestant church we found that religion was no longer a cold ritual but we were able to personally find Christ through the embrace of the congregation. In my experience, unity was a key to the expansion of the gospel, just as it is today. This topic will be covered more completely in the next section.

5. Barriers to and Opportunities for Building a Biblical Community

The early church described in Acts embraced the poor and needy in an integral manner in Acts 2:42-47 and 4:32-37, becoming a community of spiritual, emotional and physical support and therein continuing Jesus' missiological task that began in Luke 4:18-19. This investigation has already discussed the reality of poverty within the Latin American society and the following section will address the concept of integral mission more fully, but the exposition of these ideas would not be complete without also dealing with the need to establish biblical community. The Christian church in the book of Acts assumed the *koinonia* practice as part of it's ecclesiological identity demonstrating the spiritual unity among believers and showing authentic Jubilee community. This good news has both eschatological and present day implications.

Just as internal and external forces cause poverty, true unity happens from the inside out. In other words, a church must first achieve unity within its own congregation before ecumenical unity can be successfully achieved. Why is this important? Because, according to one of the Roman Catholic priests in Argentina, John 17:21 reminds believers that unity is the key to evangelism.

Individualism is one of the key barriers to unity within the church and among churches. Green maintained that no culture has been able to escape individualism as a result of urbanization. Latin America is no exception, both within the society and within the church. Added to the influence of urbanization is the influence of the religion itself. Both a Peruvian and an Argentinean mainline Protestant pastor expressed concern that too much is copied from the United States and European churches. Because those who bring it often shape the religion and because the USA and Europe represent individualistic societies, the gospel that has emerged is also individualistic and salvation has been reduced to an individual decision. In contrast, *Tú y Tú Casa* Pentecostal Church in Peru, abiding by the promise of Acts 16:31 which speaks of salvation coming to an entire household, follows up with new believers in such a way that in every case the entire family has also accepted the gift of salvation. After all, the Roman Catholic priest in Argentina points out, it is through community that God is revealed and found. This reflects God's nature; God is community and reveals himself into community (God the Father with God the Son with God the Holy Spirit).

As demonstrated in the Roman Catholic Church and indeed among most of the churches interviewed, the trend toward combating individualism is growing as churches throughout Latin America incorporate cell groups and small groups into their programs of ministry. Some commented that this was an attempt to imitate the early church but the Mennonite pastor in Colombia says that unity is a key to the survival of his church, particularly because they have |no church building. Traditionally, unity and fellowship have been a weakness of the Roman Catholic Church but, as discussed earlier, it seems that the SINE and the PDRE projects may be changing that. Now the emphasis is on knowing the parishioners, on becoming a family, and growing in faith to become a true representation of God's people.

In Colombia the Roman Catholics and the mainline Protestants emphasize the importance of fellowship as both a program of the church and as an important part of the theology of the church. The Mennonite pastor points out that unity within the church is a key evangelistic tool, "we have unity…for the world to believe in Jesus." However, for the Pentecostal Protestants the purpose of cell groups and fellowship is strictly for the numeric growth of the church.

While unity and fellowship within the church are important, the Presbyterian pastor in Colombia says that the church's egocentrism is a mistake. "When the church spends too much time looking at itself it immediately loses focus on the true commitment and goal of the gospel." Admittedly, some of the pastors interviewed during my field research believe that the references to the early church in Acts are strictly informational and not applicable to the church today.

If this is truly the case, perhaps it does not matter if the general consensus of the pastors is that the church throughout Latin America is divided, segregated and at times even competitive. Some of the tension is between Protestants and Catholics to the extreme of religious persecution or segregation, as already discussed. However, most of the tension is not quite so overt.

According to a pastor in Colombia, mainline Protestants have strong doctrine but their voice is weak due to the size of their congregations. In addition, there is ongoing friction between Protestants and Catholics; in fact one of the Pentecostal Protestants says that the Pentecostals are gaining strength at the expense of the Roman Catholics. The mainline Protestant pastors claim that the Pentecostals are "costing" them in terms of membership as well. While this example comes specifically from Colombia, I received similar information in each country. Clearly, the Latin American church is still seeking for true unity among all believers that is exemplified in the book of Acts, chapters 2 and 4 and one of the key sources of friction between churches is transient membership.

The problem of transient membership was repeated in interview after interview. Perhaps this is a sign of the times, as people living in a globalized world tend to be more mobile. Transient members are those people who go from church to church, in many cases seeking to satisfy their own emotional needs and desires. As Pastor Cruz in Mexico says, they want to "feel good without any commitment." While this is good news perhaps to the Neo-Pentecostal churches whose primary focus is on growth, it is a source of concern for Roman Catholics and Protestants alike particularly because it demonstrates a lack of commitment among Christians, the superficiality of discipleship, and self-centeredness. One of the Pentecostal pastors in Peru, however, does his part in trying to combat this saying that his church will not accept members from other churches. Instead, they receive them, restore them, and send them back to their original church.

Once community is restored within the individual churches, how is biblical community achieved between the churches in this segregated and competitive climate, or is it even possible? Believing that the individual churches are in some cases too small to affect societal change, the Mennonites in Colombia join with other churches in their denomination for social involvement projects. Yet Verdegal, an Argentinean priest, claims that between denominations, "ecumenism [generally] is reduced only to meetings of good education." His colleague, Father Arsaine, says that dialogue with Protestants is difficult because many of those churches do not yet know their own identity; perhaps this is reflected in their struggle to be contextualized, as previously discussed. Some of the interviews revealed similar sentiments or cited the fundamentalism or legalism on the part of some Protestants as a barrier to communication and therefore unity.

In Peru, the mainline Protestants agree that there is division among the churches, even going as far as to use the terms "conflict," "envy," and "condemnation." One of the mainline pastors there cautioned that this division could lead to confusion and, as is the case in Europe, people will become apathetic, believing in nobody in only 40 to 50 years. In contrast, a Mexican mainline Protestant Pastor believes this segregation is good because it allows the church access to parts of the society it could not otherwise reach.

Based upon my field research, it would appear that there are murmurs of ecumenism emerging from this region of the world. In Argentina a Baptist congregation met in a Catholic Cathedral and a Presbyterian Church after it's own building was burned. In addition, a Pentecostal church in Colombia loans its evangelistic equipment to other churches to use during their own evangelistic campaigns. The pastor emphasizes that anyone who is reached through these campaigns goes to the church that borrowed the equipment, not to his church as is more often the case with this type of partnership.

In most cases, however, the cooperation between churches is happening in response to societal needs and the depth of the relationship is varied. For example: in Colombia, one of the social programs of a Protestant church is supported in part by a Roman Catholic Church. While this partnership seems ecumenical there is no other relationship or dialogue between the two entities. In Peru, a mainline Protestant church is working in partnership with an independent church to provide meals and after school support for children in a very poor neighborhood. Finally, in Argentina there is evidence of mainline and Pentecostal Protestants working together to assist abused children and the homeless. The ecumenical relationship began in 1982 when the churches came together to pray about the Falklands War facing Argentineans.

Of the four countries, the church in Argentina seemed to be the most open to Christian partnership. Here one of the Pentecostal pastors says that it is through his involvement in an ecumenical group that he realized the social needs of the society and the gospel's response to them. The pastor of the Mennonite Church said it best when he said, "Listening to each other is one of the most constructive learning experiences we as leaders and church members can have." A Pentecostal pastor says, in reference to the relationship between Protestants and Roman Catholics, that there are more things that unify than divide the churches. Perhaps this is the beginning of the type of unity described in Acts.

Just as one of the Roman Catholic priests in Argentina emphasized, it should be noted that ecumenism is dependant upon the head of each individual church. Still, perhaps there is hope for renewal in the church through an improved sense of ecumenism. Prieto of the Foursquare church in Argentina believes that this unity is beginning to break the legalism of the church and impact society, though not all pastors agree about the extent of the church's overall impact on society. Mainline Protestants in Mexico are concerned that church membership among evangelicals, particularly Pentecostals, is growing but the effect of this is not evident in the society. This concern is echoed by one of the Pentecostal pastors who says that the church has lost its vitality as an agent of change in a growing violent and insecure society. As mentioned earlier this is the result of transient membership, demonstrating poor commitment, discipleship and the lack of establishing a strong biblical community. In some ways, it seems that the church in Latin America is a mile wide and an inch deep.

As exemplified in Jesus' life in the Gospel of Luke and later in the life of the church as demonstrated in Acts, one of the Roman Catholic churches in Colombia emphasizes that living out one's faith in community is more effective than doctrinal exposition. This challenges the Western view of rationalizing the presentation of the faith through strategies such as the Four Spiritual Laws that has been propagated throughout Latin America.

Finally, ecumenism clearly has implications for social involvement, which will be covered in the following section. Perhaps the most effective way to meet the needs of society in an integral way is by working together or establishing networks to allow the strengths of one member or one congregation to compliment the weaknesses of another.

It would be simplistic to assume that the issues expressed above are the only issues contributing to disunity or that the examples and suggestions for unity covered above provide the only solutions. However, this discussion demonstrates that the unity of believers has both ecclesiological and missiological implications that is affected by one's theology. Actually, it is within the community of believers where one establishes his/her theology, comes to terms with his/her ecclesiology, and lives out his/her missiology.

6. Propagating an Integral Mission Consistent with the Luke-Acts View of Salvation

The Lukan literature challenges the traditional, narrow understanding of salvation that is just seen as forgiveness of sins. While it is that, specific examples demonstrate that salvation means much more in Luke and Acts; salvation also means healing, it also means welcoming the outsiders and reversal of status, it also means liberation from oppression, it also means acceptance into community without changing cultural and religious boundaries, and it also means cleanliness. Clearly, salvation has purpose; people are not only saved from but are also saved for what usually has missiological implications.

Drawing from I and II Kings, Luke 4:16-30 refers to the stories of Elijah and Elisha alluding to Jesus' prophetic role and his inclusion of those who have been segregated and discriminated against, in other words the *pobre*, and highlights that the plan of salvation is inclusive for all.

Throughout his ministry Jesus broke down social barriers as he welcomed the outcasts to his table, and in so doing welcomed them into the kingdom. Theologically, this shows that salvation embraces the outcasts; ecclesiologically, it demonstrates that it is in the body of Christ where the salvific plan of redemption takes place; and missiologically it calls the universal church to welcome the outcast. By sharing meals Jesus demonstrated that he cares for the whole person in an integral way, meaning that, from a dualistic perspective he cared not only for the spiritual needs but also for the physical and social needs. Jesus always saw humans as whole, not in part, yet many churches attempt to address one or the other.

Stereo-typically speaking, one would expect Roman Catholics and mainline Protestants to focus their ministry more on the social areas and Pentecostal Protestants to focus on the spiritual. In fact, my hypothesis is that the overall church in Latin America tends to have a dualist view of the world, of salvation, and of the church's own part in the mission of God in the world. Some of the Pentecostal Protestants interviewed confirm my hypothesis; for example, all of the Pentecostal pastors in Mexico agreed that their emphasis was evangelistic and not social. In addition, there were a few Roman Catholic Churches who choose to only address spiritual issues, leaving the social areas to the care of the government. The danger of this type of thinking is that, as Baspineiro, a Baptist pastor in Argentina put it, evangelization without social involvement only "targets the spiritual needs that any religion can satisfy." Similarly, the Lukan literature challenges this view by teaching that Jesus Christ came not only as a savior but to demonstrate the way to live out God's mission within a given context, thereby emphasizing that salvation is an ongoing process and is integral rather than simply a spiritual status

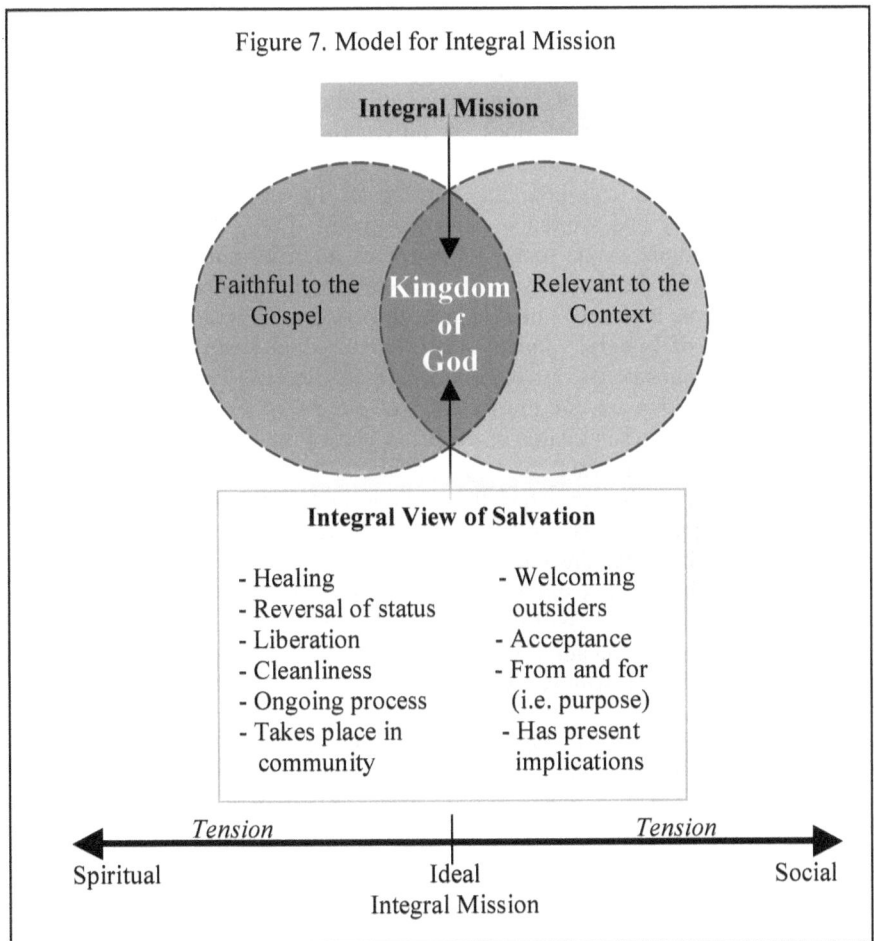

Figure 7. Model for Integral Mission

As demonstrated, the Pentecostals and more specifically the Neo-Pentecostals do tend to be more spirit-focused, but the field research does not support the mainline Protestant and Roman Catholic stereotype and therefore tends to refute my hypothesis. This, of course, is good because it demonstrates a more balanced approach. As demonstrated in Figure 8 on the preceding page, churches that put proper and balanced emphasis on both the gospel and the context in which they serve achieve a more integral mission, as exemplified in Christ's life.

To see what integral mission looks like in Latin America one needs only to look at the many examples of specific ministries that have already been covered in this Chapter and indeed more can be found by reading Chapters 4, 5, and 6 or reviewing the tables in Appendixes C, D, E and F. Churches are ministering integrally by feeding the hungry, welcoming the outcasts, caring for the sick, releasing the prisoners, providing income to the poor, protection for the vulnerable and more, as first demonstrated in the Lukan literature. Clearly Christ's example offers exciting challenges for the church in the Latin American region. His ministry to the *pobre*, in their own context and through the community of his deity was a task that was later passed on to the Christian church both in the days of Acts and today. In Peru *La Casa de Él* Church does not minister to outcasts, it is composed of outcasts. In this way the church reemphasizes that the gospel does not differentiate between the social and the spiritual realms.

As previously mentioned, the Pentecostal Protestant churches in Latin America typically had limited social involvement. Those Pentecostal churches that do incorporate some social involvement in their ministry are generally motivated only by the desire to assist the members of the individual church or as a tool to promote their own numeric growth. Perhaps this is changing as some of the examples of integral ministry that were used previously in this chapter describe the ministry of *Tú y Tú Casa*, a Pentecostal Protestant church in Mexico. In addition one of the Pentecostal pastors in Argentina has recently discovered that "the social area of people is part of the gospel." As the church has changed to incorporate social participation, they have learned that in fact social involvement has enriched the worship and spiritual growth because it helps people appreciate what God is actively doing in the society and those who are giving realize that they are active participants in God's kingdom. Their ministry is no longer to a small parish and even their prayers are bigger as they now pray for others outside of their own fellowship. A Roman Catholic priest in Peru mirrors this experience saying that it is in caring for other's needs that the youth find their own identity. As exemplified in Zacchaeus' life, it is through giving that one receives.

Of course popular religiosity is still alive and, in some places quite strong, in Latin America. One example of this is the veneration of Mary, the Virgin of Guadalupe (in Mexico) and hundreds more saints. This represents a strong challenge for discipleship within the church, contributes to the poverty, and creates further division. Another challenge for the Latin American church comes from foreign missionaries. One of the Protestant leaders in Argentina expressed concern over missionaries, particularly from the United States, who due to financial ties to home, are forced to make political decisions and focus on numeric results rather than focus on the needs of the people.

Still, there is hope. The good news of the gospel is being preached through the example of living community in Latin America and if people continue to follow the example of Christ, the prospects are promising. When reviewing Luke 4:18-19, Prieto, a Foursquare Pentecostal pastor in Argentina said that the anointment of the Holy Spirit enables the church to battle evil, fulfill its prophetic role, and worship God. He continued by emphasizing that the church is to proclaim salvation, not a salvation that starts in eternity but salvation that begins here on earth. It is an integral salvation.

Conclusion

All of the areas covered above are interrelated, as they should be. Integral mission implies the whole community. We cannot make a dichotomy between spiritual and material based upon the Lukan view of salvation. The Lukan view introduces us to a gospel that integrates all of these areas, integrates the whole person as well as God's creation as a unit. Caring for the poor, healing the sick, welcoming the outsider, setting free the captive and being a good steward of God's creation are part of saving souls. In the same way, we are all part of creation and God's plan and one part cannot be completely extracted from another part.

Except for the Roman Catholic Church, whose biblical basis is determined by Rome, it seems that the biblical understanding is varied between churches and tends to support the individual church's programs and social involvement. The encouraging points are that: 1) Roman Catholic and mainline Protestant churches seem to desire to serve more integrally than in the past and are attempting to address social concerns; 2) the Latin American church seems to be striving toward the biblical teaching regarding the unity of believers, if not between churches at least within individual churches; 3) there seems to be hope of genuine renewal within the Roman Catholic church; and 4) some Latin American churches are awakening to their responsibility to care for God's creation. Looking at the biblical basis for their work generally reaffirms my hypothesis, be it good or bad, that theology, ecclesiology and missiology are interrelated, determined one by another, as demonstrated in Figure 9.

Implications for Ministry in Latin America

History is a good teacher; either one can learn from the mistakes and successes of the past or one can ignore them, taking the risk of repeating the same mistakes the past generations made. The truth is that the Latin American church does not live in a vacuum, it stands on the shoulders of previous generations that, bad or good, have left a legacy on which the present and future generations must build.

As this study shows, the Latin America situation is very complex. It would be simplistic to provide simple solutions for the continent and simply wish for the situation to change and therefore I do not want to make the mistake of offering a simple list of solutions to make the situation better. Purposely, I want to let the investigation speak for itself demonstrating that the solution requires an ongoing process, understanding and commitment. The fact is that the church in Latin America has a great responsibility and a great opportunity to be agents of God in a changing world. This can be possible if the church continues ministering integrally and following Jesus' example.

Figure 8. Demonstrates the Interrelatedness of the Topics Being Studied.

Based upon the conclusions of this investigation, the following are a few practical implications that hopefully will provide some theological, ecclesiological and missiological insights to help the Latin American church spread the kingdom of God.

Addressing the Latin American Situation Integrally

The Latin American situation is very complex; it is suffering from socio-economic, political, environmental and spiritual struggles that require a serious and committed participation from government and non-government organizations as well as national and international partnerships. The church in Latin America cannot continue to be indifferent to the social and spiritual realities the region is facing, wish for things to miraculously change, or maintain a narrow view of the church's role in society. One Colombian Pentecostal pastor sees the church as only a place of refuge. He says that church growth is stimulated by people's need for peace, security and a new alternative to the life they are living. Every month international prophets are welcomed at this church, many of them bringing new prophesies that deal with symptoms but not the root of the problem. People are looking for good news in the midst of their present suffering, violence and oppression. While the pastor claims that they worship in "spirit and truth," the truth is that the good news of the gospel offered in Luke-Acts is not based only on words and wishes; it assumes the prophetic role of the church that proclaims the good news and denounces the injustice of the oppressors. Good does not come from desires; the Gospel teaches us that we must become involved and embrace the outcasts, the widows, the prostitutes, the *pobre*.

Good examples of embracing the Latin American situation can be seen in the examples of the Free Lutheran Church in Peru that actually curtailed gang activity by offering the youth another avenue for expression, namely sports. Contrary to the situation in Colombia, the Free Lutheran pastor has learned that the Gospel is not based on wishes. Wishing did not stop the violence but embracing the situation did. This church along with *Tú y Tú Casa* in Peru (prisoners, drug addicts, sick, street children, governmental officials, etc.), *La Casa de Él* in Mexico (alcoholics, drug addicts, prostitutes, homosexuals, etc.), *Nuestra Señora de Aranzaso* in Argentina (food, medical assistance, clothing, showers, etc.) and many others, is a living example of Christ's presence in its society and it is a good role model for the whole Latin American church. When churches are willing to get their hands dirty, just as Jesus did, they can affect real and lasting change in society.

Hugo Magallanes in his book *Introdución a la Vida y Teología de Juan Wesley*, "Introduction to the Life and Theology of John Wesley," provides a good historical example of how life and theology can be combined to work integrally to the benefit of the society. Wesley's first sermon outside of the Church of England took place in Bristol on April 1739, and on that day Wesley used Luke 4:18-19 as his main text. The use of this text shows Wesley's intention of serving the common people and caring for the people's social, physical and spiritual needs. Wesley was following the same desire that motivated Jesus' ministry, meaning the longing to preach "the good news" to those who where in the margins of the society and the religious spheres (2005:66-67). Just as Wesley's legacy transformed the church in England, it is still influencing the present generation. Wesley's example of integral mission might provide a good blueprint for ministry throughout Latin America.

Networking among Churches to Approach the *Pobre*

Although there are many gifts among the Christian church in Latin America, the reality is that the Latin American church is divided, segregated and at times there is animosity among pastors and congregations. This reality has crippled the Latin American's efforts to be salt, light and a true agent of change in a society that suffers. Throughout this study one can see small and isolated sparkles of light trying to shine in the region but sadly these are not strong enough to produce a light capable to direct the path of the general society of Latin America. Therefore, I think that the best alternative to the Latin America church is to try and unify these segregated lights and to work together as a true community of koinonia, as modeled in Acts 2:42-47; and Acts 4:32-37, through the establishment of Christian networks.

Perhaps as a result of this research one such Christian network has already been established. My contact in Peru was the Free Methodist Pastor there and he accompanied me to every interview. In so doing his eyes were opened to what other churches were doing and he began making contacts with them. He said that in the early life of his church all of the conflicts had come from other churches. Now he sees a new alternative to work in partnership with other churches, hopefully allowing the strengths of one church to complete the weaknesses in his own and vice versa. Just as one of the mainline Protestant pastors pointed out that God speaks through other people, sometimes non-Christians, and a Pentecostal pastor pointed out that God's power works through other people, perhaps the churches in Latin America can begin to see God at work in and through other churches for the benefit of all and the extension of the kingdom of God. The concept of unity suggested here and earlier in this chapter is the same as the *koinonia* present in the church of Acts; an ecclesiological identity that demonstrates the spiritual unity among believers and authentic Jubilee community. This good news has both eschatological and present day implications.

Another example of a networking partnership among churches is found in the Argentinean church. According to a Baptist pastor in Argentina, in order for the Christian church to impact the society, the church needs to be more involved in ecumenical relationships. As this study pointed out, after the Baptist church was burned by vandals in 2005, a Roman Catholic church called the pastor to express sympathy and offered its building for service. The Baptist church met at the Roman Catholic building for a while as well as at the Presbyterian building that also made a similar invitation. It is important to note that this ecumenical partnership has been in place for almost 24 years and has produced social impact in the area where these churches operate. This example shows that networking is possible in Latin America and it has benefits for the Christian community as well as the general society.

New Lenses to See the Roman Catholic Church

In many Protestant circles the Roman Catholic Church has been considered a pagan and syncretistic Christian organization. From personal experience I know that many Latin American Protestants do not consider Roman Catholics to truly be Christian and therefore they are identified as evangelistic targets. My perception of the Roman Catholic Church as a child and young adult was that it espoused a distant and unfriendly environment. However, the church I found while conducting the field research is a very different Catholic Church: I saw a church that cares for the needy, the poor and the segregated in society. In many places the Roman Catholic Church is a friendly place, a welcoming church that, through small communities, is opening the Bible for its members to study and learn, and it is a church that is empowering the laity to participate in the life of the church and in their own relationship with Jesus.

Although in some countries the Roman Catholic Church is still too tied to its hierarchy, in some places it supports popular and syncretistic religiosity, and it still enjoys some unofficial links to the government; the fact is that there is a renewal in the Roman Catholic Church in Latin America. As this study reveals, Vatican II (1962-1965) opened a new missiological dimension for the church that has allowed it to care for the social and spiritual needs of people. The empowering of the laity has also opened the door of the church to be in touch with socio-economic, and spiritual realities the region is facing. The *comunidades de base*, "Bases Communities," have recovered a sense of the Roman Catholic Christian community and koinonia that it has lost in the past. *Comunidades de base* is empowering the priesthood of all believers and has brought a sense of renewal into the church.

Because about 87% of the population in Latin America considers themselves to be Roman Catholic, it is important for anyone ministering in the region to understand the role of the church in both the past and the present tense. Even though one of the Mexican priests said that thousands are baptized but only a few are practicing, the traditions, ideologies and even identities are linked to the Roman Catholic Church. Therefore it is my belief that understanding the church, in particular, recognizing its positive impact on society will enrich any ministry in the region.

Creation Care as a Ministerial Focus

Clearly this is an area that is lacking in the Latin American Church. As the rich get richer and poor get poorer, the dirty get dirtier. The impact of globalization (i.e. industrialization) and urbanization is having a devastating affect on the environment. In many places, the water is unsafe to drink and the air is unsafe to breathe contributing to grave health concerns. Even when coupled with ruined farmland and deforestation only a small fraction of the problem is visible. The sad fact is that only a small fraction of the church in Latin America is even addressing this escalating situation.

As pointed out in this investigation, the church is called to care for creation. Humans were put in dominion over creation, not to destroy it but to manage it and care for it. By making reference to the Jubilee Law in the gospel of Luke, Jesus is demonstrating that creation care was part of his missional task. Likewise it is part of the missional task of the church today.

Suggestions for Further Research Study

Throughout the investigation process of this research, I have had the opportunity to think about areas of further study that perhaps will help to continue the process of analyzing and understanding the socio-political, economic, environmental and spiritual situation of Latin America and the Two-Thirds World. With the idea of integral mission as a missiological model, the following are some areas that perhaps will provide scholarly insights to intercultural studies.

Creation Care

Although the environment has been one of the most neglected areas of ministry for the Latin America church, it is an area of great opportunity. Nature is one area that has received the direct consequences of poor decisions of national and international policies that have thrown the Latin American region into a profound and difficult crisis. The Lukan literature challenges the church to be involved as care takers of the creation as part of its missiological task. Thus, a study that targets the environmental situation in Latin America and its implications for present and future generations and biblical basis to support a more integral and deep involvement of the church would be beneficial.

Following the Same Approach by Targeting the Laity

All of the interviews for my field research were conducted with Catholic priests and Protestant pastors who provided their insights based upon their ministerial experience. However, I wonder what the laity's views would be about the same issues? A study focusing on the laity would perhaps provide a broader view of the socio-political, economic, environmental and spiritual reality in Latin America.

Neo-Pentecostal Focus

During my field research I discovered that the Neo-Pentecostal churches are the fastest growing and wealthiest churches in Latin America. Due to time limitations and the difficulty in gaining access to them, it was impossible for me to interview any of those leaders. All the information collected about these groups comes from close experiences of other Protestant and Catholic ministers that were interviewed. Because this portion of the Christian church is experiencing such significant growth, a further study targeting these Neo-Pentecostal groups would provide additional insight to help understand the Latin American church.

Narrowing the Study to a Region or a Single Country

As I explained in Chapter 1, I focused my field research primarily in four Latin America countries where I made a total of 48 interviews, 12 interviews for each country. Although the information gathered provides a quite extensive view of the Latin America situation, at times I felt that the information gathered was too broad. Therefore, a closer focus on a single country or region of the country would perhaps provide a more precise view of the situation.

Spiritual Warfare

Finally, one of the topics that came up during several interviews was the topic is Spiritual warfare. This is a topic primarily addressed by Pentecostal Protestants and Charismatic Catholics. Spiritual warfare has a very real presence in Latin America and cannot be ignored in order to have effective ministry in the region. While it is dangerous to over-emphasize this area, it is a topic that the

Lukan literature addresses as part of Jesus' ministry. Further study on this topic would benefit Christians ministering in Latin America and would contribute to a better understanding of the region.

Appendix A

Interview Schedule

The following are the set of questions, and the Spanish translation, that was used in the grounded investigation.

1. What programs does this church have?
   ¿Cuáles programas tiene esta iglesia?

2. What outreach ministry does this church do?
   ¿Cuáles programas de ayuda social tiene esta iglesia?

3. Could you tell me about these programs?
   ¿Puede contarme acerca de estos programas y ministerios?

4. How long have you been doing this work or activity?
   ¿Hace cuanto tiempo estan haciendo o teniendo estos programas?

5. Could you give a short overview of the history of your congregation?
   ¿Puede darme una pequeña reseña historica de esta congregación?

6. What are the reasons that led you or your congregation to have the programs that you have?
   ¿Cuáles son las razones que motivaron a esta congregación a tener los programas que tienen?

7. Is the church or any member of the church involved in the government? If so, what kind of involvement?
   ¿Esta la iglesia o algún miembro de la iglesia envolucrado en el gobierno local? Si sí, ¿qué clase de envolucramiento?

8. Is the church involved in any kind of environmental program or activity? If yes, what kind of program, for how long, and what influence does it have in the society at large?
   ¿Esta la iglesia envolucrada en algún programa o actividad relacionada con la preservación del medio ambiente? Si sí, ¿cuál(es) programa(s), por cuanto tiempo, y qué influencia esto ha tenido en la sociedad en donde ustedes viven?

9. Is the church involved in any activity regarding social justice in the community, in the city, or in the country? If yes, what kind of programs and for how long? What are some reasons that led you to be involved in these programs?
   ¿Esta la iglesia involucrada en alguna actividad relacionada con justicia social en la comunidad, en el barrio, en la ciudad, o en el pais? Si sí, ¿cuál(es) programa(s), por cuánto tiempo? ¿Cuáles son las razones que motivo a esta congregación a estar envolucrados en estos programas?

10. Is there any Scripture that closely relates to you and your church and the philosophy of work to which you ascribe?
    ¿Hay alguna parte de la Biblia (verso o capítulo) que es considerada como parte fundamental de esta congregación y que describe su filosofía de trabajo?

11. Luke 4:18-19 provides an understanding of a way of doing mission. What do you think about this text? What implications do you think this has in the way your church does missions?
    Lucas 4:18-19 provee una forma de hacer misiones. ¿Qué piensas acerca de este texto? ¿Qué implicaciones piensa usted que este texto tiene en la forma que su iglesia hace misiones?

12. Acts 1 is used by many churches to describe their philosophy of mission. What is your understanding of this passage? What implications do you think this has in the way your church does missions?
    Hechos 1 es usado por muchas iglesias para resumir su filosofía de ministerio. ¿Qué piensas acerca de este texto? ¿Qué implicaciones piensa usted que este texto tiene en la forma que su iglesia hace

Appendix B

Theology and Praxis of Mission in Mexico

Table 16.	Roman Catholic	Mainline Protestant	Pentecostal Protestant
Programs	• SINE – decentralized power of church with use of cell groups. • Spiritual retreats • In-home visitation • Evangelistic programs • Empowerment of the laity. • Small cell groups and discipleship. • Ministry to younger generation and families.	• Discipleship • Focus on the Poor. • Youth • Children • Evangelization • Discipleship • Compassion. • Focus on drug addicts, homosexuals, prostitutes, and alcoholics.	• Spiritual Warfare. • Evangelistic Programs. • Children • Youth • Men • Women • Doctrinal training. • Restoration. • Liberation. • Cell groups.
Social Involvement	• Tension between government's and the church's responsibility. • Fear of being misinterpreted. • Medical work. • Promoting self-improvement. • Fighting injustice.	• Ministry plan for single women: spiritual, emotional, intellectual, and skills support. • Economic fund for savings and emergency. • Micro-enterprise programs. • Home for elderly. • Relief for natural disasters. • English and computer classes. • Provide food, shelter and basic needs for outcast.	• Church's main focus is evangelistic, not social. • Occasionally support single mothers & children. • Occasionally support drug and alcohol rehabilitation programs. • Occasionally offer adult education programs. • Occasionally provide food and clothing to their own mission.

	Roman Catholic	Mainline Protestant	Pentecostal Protestant
Environmental Involvement	None.	Sporadic participation. • Tree planting	None.
Biblical Basis for Work	• Stipulated by Rome. Luke: • Poor are seen as economic, religious and cultural disadvantaged. Acts: • Mission understood in terms of Priesthood of believers. • Giving without creating dependence. • Ideal for today. • Individual change leads to social change • Love is key.	Matt 5-7: • Live out the beatitudes. Acts 1:8: • Evangelism. 1 Peter 3:15: • Producing fruit as an identity. Luke: • Integral liberation. • Imperative for church today – no choice. • Church goes to the people not people to the church. Acts: • Purpose is to expand Kingdom of God. • Holy Spirit motivates for God's work. • Do not reduce the Spirit's presence to simply emotions.	Acts 2: • Emphasis on Holy Spirit, Sanctification and Church growth. 1 Tim. 3:15: • Church is the foundation of truth. Deuteronomy 22:5: • Women cannot wear pants. 1 Corinthians 1:10: • Unity of the church. Luke: • Emphasizes healing. Acts: • Spiritual growth. • Applies only to the Jerusalem church. • Acts 1:8: Determines priority in ministry. • Narrow view of gospel: only to win souls.
Theological Issues	• Introducing a new understanding of God (Love, Mercy, and Forgiveness). • Conversion is a process. • Exemplifying a Christian life as an evangelistic tool. • Understanding the context leads to effective ministry. • Focus on finding Jesus in community.	• Kingdom of God fills all dimensions. • Mission is extension of Kingdom of God in the world. • Ministry should be integral. • Sharing God's unconditional love, especially to the outcasts.	• Only the Holy Spirit directs us. • Internal and external numerical growth. • Prayer. • Fulfilling the Great Commission. • Eschatological view motivates evangelism. • Spiritual vitality equals numerical growth.

	Roman Catholic	Mainline Protestant	Pentecostal Protestant
General Statements	<ul><li>Structurally tied to hierarchy.</li><li>Millions baptized but few practicing.</li><li>Fear of liberation theology's revolutionary connotations.</li><li>Vatican II provide renewal to church.</li><li>Devotion to Mary highlights importance of women.</li><li>Focus on evangelization of the younger generations.</li></ul>	<ul><li>Mexican Protestant's mindset is too fundamentalist.</li><li>Commercialization of churches.</li><li>Superficial discipleship.</li><li>Lack of ethical pastoral behavior.</li><li>Transient membership.</li><li>Neo-charasmatic churches fastest growing: prosperity gospel, high class, mega churches, focus on feelings not commitment.</li><li>Evangelicals have forgotten social responsibility.</li><li>Church desires recognition and power</li><li>Protestants competing for members, money and power.</li><li>Isolated Catholic to Protestant persecution.</li><li>Women play important role in the church.</li></ul>	<ul><li>Church's growth is not impacting general society.</li><li>Pentecostal churches lack a solid doctrine.</li><li>Segregation and division between churches resulting in self-centered groups.</li><li>Bad relations between pastors.</li><li>Place hope in governmental candidates to affect change in society.</li><li>Influence of prosperity theology is growing.</li><li>As long as scripture is used, any biblical interpretation is allowed.</li><li>Women's ministry is restricted.</li><li>Transient membership.</li></ul>

Appendix C

Theology and Praxis of Mission in Colombia

Table 17	Roman Catholic	Mainline Protestant	Pentecostal Protestant
Programs	<ul><li>PDRE philosophy of work.</li><li>Sociological analysis of the area.</li><li>Fellowship.</li><li>Small communities.</li><li>Empowering lay leadership.</li><li>Pastoral visits.</li><li>Prayer and healing ministry. Charismatic.</li><li>Combating Spiritual Warfare Charismatic.</li><li>Liberation Charismatic.</li><li>Manifestations of the Spirit Charismatic.</li></ul>	<ul><li>One-on-one discipleship.</li><li>Bible study groups.</li><li>Fellowship dinners.</li><li>Cell groups.</li><li>Leadership training.</li><li>Preaching training.</li><li>Outreach programs.</li><li>Youth.</li><li>Children.</li><li>Women.</li><li>Fasting.</li><li>Prayer.</li><li>Watch-night services.</li></ul>	<ul><li>Radio program.</li><li>Evangelism.</li><li>Cell groups for purpose of numeric growth.</li><li>Street preaching.</li><li>Evangelistic services.</li><li>Social work for evangelism.</li><li>Discipleship.</li><li>Discover areas of service for new believers.</li><li>Leadership development.</li><li>Preaching training.</li></ul>
Environmental Involvement	1 of 4 interviewed has an established program.<ul><li>Recycling</li></ul>	<ul><li>None.</li></ul>	<ul><li>None.</li></ul>

	Roman Catholic	Mainline Protestant	Pentecostal Protestant
Social Involvement	<ul><li>Visit the sick.</li><li>Economic support.</li><li>Home for high-risk children.</li><li>Assistance to the needy.</li><li>Micro-enterprise.</li><li>Skills workshops.</li><li>Elder home.</li><li>Feeding the homeless Charismatic</li></ul>	<ul><li>Education and food scholarships for poor children.</li><li>Support missionaries in 6 other countries.</li><li>Participation in denominational social organizations.</li><li>Education for marginalized children.</li><li>Parenting workshops.</li><li>Feeding programs for children displaced by war.</li></ul>	No established social programs.<ul><li>Occasionally provide groceries for needy members.</li><li>Economic assistance for members.</li><li>Counseling for members.</li><li>Occasionally provide medical support and food and clothing distribution to poor.</li><li>Support denomination's drug rehabilitation program.</li><li>Distribute Christmas gifts to children.</li></ul>
Theological Issues	<ul><li>Encounter with Jesus, with faith, and with the Word of God.</li><li>The world is the parish.</li><li>Living out doctrine through the community.</li><li>Seeing humanity and ministering to it in an integral way.</li><li>Theology must address society's questions.</li><li>Living participation of the congregation. Charismatic</li></ul>	<ul><li>Loving others is non-negotiable.</li><li>Jesus is the direction and means to get to the Father.</li><li>Fellowship is key theological, ecclesiological and missiological factor.</li><li>Church is instrument to make disciples.</li></ul>	<ul><li>New prophecies about countries' happiness determine theology.</li><li>International prophets speak monthly.</li><li>True gospel equals power.</li><li>People are Spiritual beings covered with human nature.</li><li>Social involvement helps Spiritual growth.</li></ul>

	Roman Catholic	Mainline Protestant	Pentecostal Protestant
Biblical Basis for Work	- Tradition and history of Saint Jeronimo. - Vatican II. Luke: - Focus on serving the poor. - Provides mission and the strategy. Acts: - Justice, Love, Equal opportunity. - Giving alms.	- Practical, biblical and theological motivation. - Love others. - Be involved in society. - Resolve conflicts. - Non-violent resistance. - Work for peace. - Integral ministry as church identity. Gospels: - Goal is to imitate Jesus. John 17:21: - Unity as evangelism. Luke: - Spirit's presence evident through action. - Jesus' and the church's agenda based on word of God. - Build Kingdom of God not church's kingdom. - Liberation focus. Acts: - Witnessing implies sacrifice. - Presence of the spirit equals social and spiritual action.	- Worship in spirit and truth. Matt 28:19: - World evangelism. Hebrews 13:8 Luke: - Seen as church expansion. - Focus on the role of the Spirit for spiritual warfare. - Jesus performs miracles today. - Anointment of the Spirit is for all. Acts: - Fulfilled through pastor's international preaching. - Obedience to the Word, fullness of the Spirit, and going and proclaiming. Acts 1:8 - Missiological strategy.
General Statements	- Liberation theology helps church minister to the poor. - Garage churches causing division and confusion among people. - Women play a key role in life of church.	- Liberation theology puts the Gospels in practice but extreme can be dangerous. - Competition between churches. - Transient membership. - Pentecostal churches growing at expense of Mainline churches.	- Women provide social outreach. - No dialogue or understanding between churches. - Church is an escape from reality. - Roman Catholic still has social, economic and political privileges. - Church is content.

Appendix D

Theology and Praxis of Mission in Peru

Table 18	Roman Catholic	Mainline Protestant	Pentecostal Protestant
Programs	<ul><li>Children.</li><li>Young people.</li><li>Families.</li><li>Pre-Marital classes.</li><li>Fist communion and Confirmation.</li><li>Visiting and assisting the poor.</li><li>Biblical formation.</li><li>Base communities.</li><li>Empowering the laity.</li><li>Individual Bible study.</li></ul>	<ul><li>Children</li><li>Teenagers and Youth.</li><li>Women.</li><li>Music ministry.</li><li>Prayer ministry.</li><li>Discipleship.</li><li>Door-to-door evangelism.</li><li>Integral ministry.</li></ul>	<ul><li>Holy Communion at every service.</li><li>New revelation for the people today.</li><li>Weekly radio program.</li><li>Sunday school classes.</li><li>Theological classes.</li><li>Miracles and healing ministry.</li><li>Daily Prayer ministry.</li><li>Discipleship in Bible Studies and Biblical Institute.</li><li>Supporting other churches through evangelism programs.</li><li>Door-to-door evangelism.</li><li>Monthly celebration for new converts.</li><li>Counseling</li><li>Youth classes.</li><li>Parenting schools.</li></ul>

	Roman Catholic	Mainline Protestant	Pentecostal Protestant
Social Involvement	- Remar Mar Adentro – socio-religious census to better meet needs. - Food services. - Support for elderly. - Environmental work. - Seminars on hygiene, health, parenthood, family relationships, respect and the dignity of life/human rights. - Nursing home and homeless shelter visits. - Annual clothing collection for the needy.	Only 2 of 4 have established program. - Lunch and after school support to needy children. - Soccer tournaments among gang groups. - Program for poor children for the spiritual, social, emotional, and physical development. - Musical Instrument classes for adults and children. - Christmas gift, clothing and grocery distribution to the poor.	Only 1 of 4 have an established program. - Supporting street children. - Visiting the sick and offering financial assistance for medicine. - Health brigades in prisons. - Help prisoners (many foreigners) who have been released. - Assist drug addicts through recovery. - Marriage counseling. - Weekly mayoral prayer meeting. - Micah Project to care for poor and needy. - Occasional food and Bible Studies for needy children. - Occasional food for needy church members. - Once established marriage project for single couples.
Environmental Involvement	- Prevent garbage burning. - Preventing pig farming. - Reforestation projects. - Protest to prevent abuse of public space on the beach.	1 of 4 churches had minimal involvement. - Combating deforestation.	- None.

	Roman Catholic	Mainline Protestant	Pentecostal Protestant
Biblical Basis for Work	- Social needs of society. - Tradition of Saint Rosa. John 17:21: - Unity as the key to evangelization. Luke: - Jesus exemplifies the mission for the church. - Jubilee is grace and extending salvation to the whole person. - Revelation to Jews and us today. Acts: - Identity is found in community.	Matt 5-7: - Beatitudes are the core ministry values. Matt 11:28: - Rest in Jesus. Matt 28:19: - Go and make disciples. Luke: - Material and Spiritual poor. - Being empowered to do God's work. Acts: - Christian life is practical and priesthood of all believers. - Holy Spirit empowers the church in good times and bad.	Acts 16:31: - Salvation to the person and their household. Isaiah 54 - It is a privilege to give. - The Great Commission. Luke: - Anointment of Holy Spirit is God's anointment of church. - God's power changes individual character which then changes others. - Revealed through real acts of God. - Geographic evangelistic strategy.
Theological Issues	- Care for social and spiritual needs. - Involvement in social issues brings youth close to God. - God is community. - Humanity finds God in community. - Church has prophetic role against injustice.	- God speaks through people, both Christian and non-Christians. - Church has prophetic role to denounce injustice. - Social involvement and evangelism go together.	- Christian church needs constant renewal. - Spiritual oppression brings physical and mental sickness. - Tithes and offerings prosper the church. - Prosperity is an evangelistic tool. - Jesus was a wealthy man. - Evangelism through condemnation. - Evangelism as welcoming. - Miracles and signs are spiritual reality. - We cannot teach what we do not know.

	Roman Catholic	**Mainline Protestant**	**Pentecostal Protestant**
General Statements	<ul><li>Freedom of religion allows voluntary participation.</li><li>Relativism in the Peruvian society.</li><li>Lack of biblical conscience.</li><li>Church and politics should be separate.</li><li>Liberation theology has good points but is Marxist.</li><li>Vatican II: helped put the Bible in people's hand and it provided renewal to the church.</li><li>Women play a key role in the church.</li></ul>	<ul><li>Women play key role in church.</li><li>Liberation theology encourages us to live in the society and addresses sin and the system.</li><li>Belief that spiritual level is determined by membership levels.</li><li>Two kinds of spiritual involvement: diaconal and political.</li><li>Peruvian church copies too much from USA and Europe.</li><li>Competition, envy and condemnation among Protestants.</li></ul>	<ul><li>Divided church.</li><li>Transient membership.</li><li>No desire for unity.</li><li>Members from other churches are restored and sent back to original church.</li><li>Peru is a church of beggars.</li><li>Church has lost its sense of direction and focus.</li></ul>

Appendix E

Theology and Praxis of Mission in Argentina

Table 19.	Roman Catholic	Mainline Protestant	Pentecostal Protestant
Programs	<ul><li>Liturgy.</li><li>Biblical formation.</li><li>Teaching of confirmation and first communion.</li><li>Ministry to the family, elderly, single parents, children, young people and sick people.</li><li>Radio Station.</li><li>Elementary, middle and high School.</li><li>The Sacraments.</li></ul>	<ul><li>Integral ministry.</li><li>Small groups for discipleship.</li><li>Acts as community center.</li><li>Gym for community welcome.</li><li>Monthly new members retreat.</li><li>Liturgy.</li><li>Spiritual retreats.</li></ul>	<ul><li>Door-to-door evangelism.</li><li>Radio and television programs.</li><li>Youth.</li><li>Adults.</li><li>Children.</li><li>Restoration programs.</li><li>Cell groups.</li><li>Wednesday morning prayer walk.</li><li>Christian Education.</li></ul>
Environmental Involvement	None.	No established plan.<ul><li>Encouraged government to install sewage system.</li><li>Cleaned up the streets and the neighborhood.</li></ul>	None.

	Roman Catholic	Mainline Protestant	Pentecostal Protestant
Social Involvement	<ul><li>Caritas.</li><li>After school program for at-risk children.</li><li>Pre-school in high-risk area.</li><li>Special skills workshops.</li><li>Medicine distribution.</li><li>Church is expected to provide what the government neglects.</li><li>Several projects discontinued.</li><li>Bank of the Poor.</li><li>Bi-weekly meals at half-price or no price depending on need.</li><li>Feeds school children.</li><li>Clothing distribution.</li><li>Dental office.</li><li>Breakfast and showers for the homeless everyday.</li><li>Visiting the sick.</li><li>Program for young people.</li><li>Family and penal lawyer consultations.</li><li>Alcoholic's Anonymous and *Gordos* Anonymous.</li></ul>	<ul><li>Hosts community discussions on social issues.</li><li>Houses instruments for community musical groups.</li><li>Women's programs for exercise, dancing, fokelore.</li><li>Christian Sport Center.</li><li>Fellowship Sundays to share with non-believers.</li><li>Economic support for a Pentecostal home for abused children.</li><li>Elementary and high school programs for adults.</li><li>Micro-enterprise.</li><li>Feeding programs for children.</li><li>Office to help job search and with legal documents.</li><li>Drug rehabilitation.</li><li>After school program for at-risk children.</li><li>Meals for the homeless.</li><li>Homeless shelter.</li><li>Campaigns to protect the voiceless.</li></ul>	3 of 4 have established program.<ul><li>Drug rehabilitation homes.</li><li>Feeding program for children.</li><li>Clothing distribution.</li><li>Offers food, clothing and medicine to needy families.</li><li>Skills workshops.</li><li>After school programs.</li><li>Exercise programs.</li><li>Night school for adults.</li></ul>
Theological Issues	<ul><li>Trinitarian view.</li><li>According to Books of Ruth and Nehemiah, church must be personal and welcoming.</li></ul>	<ul><li>Integral ministry requires hard work and commitment to God and the society.</li><li>Main goal of the church is to be where the people are.</li></ul>	<ul><li>The Holy Spirit is only available to a few.</li><li>Church needs to empower people to discover their own abilities.</li></ul>

	Roman Catholic	Mainline Protestant	Pentecostal Protestant
Biblical Basis for Work	• Argentinean Roman Catholic church bases on scriptures as whole. John 13: • Service. 1 Cor. 12: • Community and diversity. Phil 2:1-11: • Jesus' identification with humanity. Acts 2:42-44: • Unity and sharing. • Joseph: Second stage person serving the Lord. • Devotion to Mary. Luke: • Heal and save are the same verb. • Treat others with respect and dignity. • Everybody is poor. Acts: • Community demonstrates Jesus' presence. • Shows the influence of the Holy Spirit.	Duet. 8:11a: • Love God and your neighbor. Luke 4:18-19: • Church's mission. Hab 3:2: • Church's spirituality. 2 Tim 2:2: • Church's formation. Acts 5:42: • Church's strategy. Mark 12:30-31: • Worship and communion, mission, and service. Luke: • Disciples of Christ must have his vision. • Social/human and spiritual dimension. • Holy Spirit plays key role in missiological task. Acts: • Practicing love and justice. • Live a daily testimony. • Fundamental to the direction of the church and should be reviewed regularly. • Shows how God worked in history.	• Imitating God's love. Heb. 13:8 Eze 1:10: • Philosophy of mission. Luke: • Church needs anointment of the Holy Spirit to proclaim salvation that begins on earth. Acts: • Church receives power to witness and needs to care for its neighbor's needs today. • Theology without anointment is nothing.

	Roman Catholic	Mainline Protestant	Pentecostal Protestant
General Statements	<ul><li>People have dependence mentality.</li><li>During dictatorship, church became advocate of human rights and social justice.</li><li>Vatican II transformed the ecclesiology and missiology the Church.</li><li>Ecumenism only happens occasionally on local levels and only with Mainline Protestants.</li><li>Ecumenism is difficult because of Protestant's fundamentalism and lack of identity.</li><li>Overall views about hierarchy of Roman Catholic Church are changing.</li><li>Roman Catholic Church is too tied to tradition, decisions makers lack contact with reality, needs more democratic structure, celibacy makes ministry ineffective, need to revise segregation of divorced rules.</li><li>Roman Catholic Church in Latin America is completely different than that of Rome.</li><li>Women's role is important.</li><li>Parishes are mostly women.</li><li>Church structure will change to allow for renewal.</li></ul>	<ul><li>Ecumenical groups to address social issues.</li><li>Protestants influenced by United States missions avoid social involvement to avoid being seen as Marxist.</li><li>Numerical results equal superficial results.</li><li>Division and segregation in the church results in infectivity and loss of prophetic voice.</li><li>Too much reflection and not enough action on social issues.</li><li>Individual salvation, lacking concern for other's needs.</li><li>Targeted middle class, forgetting the poor.</li><li>Prosperity theology has damaged the reputation of the Protestant church in Argentina.</li><li>Neo-Pentecostals are targeting feelings and emotion for good results.</li><li>Mainline are targeting rational brains with little result.</li><li>Individualism is obstacle to ecumenism.</li><li>Liberation theology challenges that of the First World.</li></ul>	<ul><li>People are more important than what they give.</li><li>Church looks inside and separates itself from the world.</li><li>Church's legalism has hurt its effectiveness.</li><li>Leaders didn't know how to deal with rapid church growth.</li><li>Church should go to the people.</li><li>Theology of prosperity has hurt many people.</li><li>Neo-Pentecostals are fastest growing and wealthiest in Argentina.</li><li>More things unify than divide churches.</li><li>Many pastors focus on self rather than gospel.</li><li>Evil spirits taking possession of cities.</li><li>Single women in free union relationships are outcast by many churches.</li><li>People come to church to worship and serve.</li><li>Roman Catholics have economic support for social programs but societal impact is low due to lack of life change.</li></ul>

Persons Interviewed

Aguila Basurdo, Armando
    2006   Personal interview made by the author on February 8.

Andrade, Luis Sarmiento
    2006   Personal interview made by the author on January 19.

Aragon, Pablo Ignacio
    2006   Personal interview made by the author on January 22.

Arenas Bolivar, Oswaldo
    2006   Personal interview made by the author on January 15.

Arsaine, Jorge Eduardo
    2006   Personal interview made by the author on January 24.

Baspineiro, Arturo Humberto
    2006   Personal interview made by the author on February 2.

Barajas Carrillo, Eduardo
    2006   Personal interview made by the author on January 15.

Barrios C., Wilson
    2006   Personal interview made by the author on January 17.

Correa, Manuel
    2006   Personal interview made by the author on January 29.

Cruz, Victor Pedroza
   2006   Personal interview made by the author on February 10.

Daza, Fredys Samanca
   2006   Personal interview made by the author on January 14.

Daza Gonzalez, Juan Bautista
   2006   Personal interview made by the author on January 11.

Ferrer, Manuel
   2006   Personal interview made by author on February 5.

Gali, Jorge
   2006   Personal interview made by the author on January 30.

Garcia, Aristobulo
   2006   Personal interview made by the author on January 11.

Garcia Pinilla, Cesar Arturo
   2006   Personal interview made by the author on January 7.

Guarillo, Jorge
   2006   Personal interview made by the author on February 11.

Gutierrez, Juan Angel
   2006   Personal interview made by the author on January 27.

Herrera, Benjamin
   2006   Personal interview made by the author on February 5.

Jorguera, Gilberto
   2006   Personal interview made by the author on January 27.

Juliecer, Fernando
   2006   Personal interview made the author on January 29.

Liñan Romero, Florencio
   2006   Personal interview made by the author on January 13.

Loli, Marco Antonio
   2006   Personal interview made by the author on January 18.

Lopez, José Luis
   2006   Personal interview made by the author on January 19.

Martinez, Noé
    2006   Personal interview made by the author on February 10.

Martinez, Sergio Oliba
    2006   Personal Interview made by the author on February 7.

Miuler, Klaus
    2006   Personal interview made by the author on January 18.

Moreno, Luis Alfredo
    2006   Personal interview made by the author on January 14.

Obispo Ramirez, Cutberto
    2006   Personal interview made by the author on February 12.

Pabón, Nelson Javier
    2006   Personal interview made by the author on January 10.

Peña Careon, Benjamin
    2006   Personal interview made by author on February 7.

Perez, Eli Gamas
    2006   Personal interview made by the author on February 12.

Perez, Luis Maria Carreño
    2006   Personal interview made by the author on January 15.

Prada, José Manuel
    2006   Personal interview made by the author on January 20.

Prieto, Roberto
    2006   Personal interview made by the author on January 31.

Puell, Roque Felix
    2006   Personal interview made by the author on January 25.

Ramirez, José Antonio
    2006   Personal interview made by author on February 4.

Ramirez, Luis Alfonso
    2006   Personal interview made by the author on 12.

Robles, Mercelo
    2006   Personal interview made by the author on January 30.

Ruiz Sintia, Rony
    2006   Personal interview made by the author on January 25.

Thorndike, Ricardo Wiesse
    2006   Personal interview made by the author on January 19.

Toxtle, Samuel Fernandez
    2006   Personal interview made by the author on February 10.

Ugarte Mejia, Oscar
    2006   Personal interview made by the author on January 20.

Vargas Games, José Alberto
    2006   Personal interview made by the author on January 12.

Villavona, Herbert Monsalve
    2006   Personal interview made by the author on January 8.

Vivian, Pablo
    2006   Personal interview made by the author on January 31.

Velizaroff, Pedro Jorge
    2006   Personal interview made by the author on January 22.

Verdegal, Pablo
    2006   Personal interview made by the author on January 27.

References Cited

Arlandson, James Malcolm
    1997   Women, Class, and Society in Early Christianity. Peabody, MA: Hendrickson Publishers.

Barrett, David B., ed.
    1982   World Christian Encyclopedia: A Comparative Study of Churches, and Religions in the Modern World AD 1900-2000. Nairobi: Oxford University Press.

Barrett, David B., George T. Kurian, Todd M. Johnson, eds.
    2000   World Christian Encyclopedia: A Comparative Survey of Churches and Religions AD 30-2000. New York: Oxford University Press.

Blumer, Herbert
    1995   Social Movements and Social Order. In Social Movements: Critiques, concepts, case studies. ed. S. M. Lyman. London: MacMillan Press Ltd.

Boff, Leonardo
    1984   When Theology Listens to the Poor. Maryknoll, N.Y.: Orbis Books.

Bonino, Jose Miguez
    1984   Faces of Jesus: Latin American Christology. N.Y.: Orbis Books.

Chomsky, Noam
1999   Latin America: From Colonization to Globalization. Melbourne, N.Y.: Ocean Press.

2000   Rogue States: The Rule of Force in World Affairs. Cambridge, MA: South End Press.

CIA World FactBook
2006   "Peru." Internet accessed on March 15, 2006. http://www.cia.gov/cia/publications/factbook/geos/pe.html

Cities in a Globalizing World
2002   Global Report on Human Settlements 2001. London and Sterling, VA: Earthscan Publications.

Collins, Michael, Matthew A. Price.
1999   The Story of Christianity: A Celebration of 2,000 Years of Faith. Oxford: University Press.

Costas, Orlando E.
1979   "Contextualization and Incarnation," *Journal of Theology for Southern Africa*, No. 29 (December): 23-30.

Country Analysis Briefs
2006   "Mexico-Environmental." Internet accessed on August 12, 2006. http://www.converger.com/eiacab/contents.htm

Creswell, John W.
2003   Research Design: Qualitative, Quantitative and Mixed Methods Approaches. 2nd edition. Thousand Oaks, London: Sage Publications.

Crockett, Larrimore C.
1969   "Luke 4:25-27 and Jewish-Gentile Relations in Luke-Acts," *Journal of Biblical Literature*, No. 88 (January): 177-83.

Crow, John A.
1992   The Epic of Latin America. Berkeley, CA: University of California Press.

Diamond, Jared M.
1998   Guns, Germs, and Steel: The Fates of Human Societies. N.Y.:W.W. Norton & Co.

Douglas, Mary
1966   Purity and Danger: An Analysis of Concepts of Pollution and Taboo. New York: Routledge.

1973 "A Critique and Commentary," in The Idea of Purity in Ancient Judaism. By Jacob Neusner. Leiden: E. J. Brill.

1975 "Deciphering Meal," in Implicit Meaning: Essays in Anthropology. London and Boston: Routledge & Kegan Paul.

1999 Leviticus as Literature. Oxford: Oxford University Press.

Dumont, Louis
1980 Home Hierarchies: The Caste System and Its Implications. Chicago, IL: The University of Chicago Press.

Dunn, J. D. G.
1988 "Pharisees, Sinners, and Jesus," in The Social of Formative Christianity and Judaism: Essays in Tribute to Howard Clark Kee. ed. J. Neusner et al. Philadelphia: Fortress.

Eilberg-Schwartz, Howard
1990 The Savage in Judaism: An Anthropology of Israelite Religion and Ancient Judaism. Bloomington and Indianapolis, IN: Indiana University Press.

El Tiempo (The Time)
2006 Economics. "Uribe quiere ser 'buen componedor' en las peleas con E.U. en la region." Internet accessed on March 16, 2006. http://eltiempo.terra.com.co/hist_imp/HISTORICO_IMPRESO/econ_hist/2006-03-15/ARTICULO-WEB-NOTA_INTERIOR_HIST-2792720.html

Ellis, Joseph A.
1975 Latin America: Its peoples and Institutions. 2ed. Beverly Hills, CA: Benziger Bruce and Glencoe, Inc.

Ember, Melvin and Carol R. Ember, eds.
2002 Encyclopedia of Urban Cultures, Cities and Cultural Around the World. vols. 1, 3. Danbury, Connecticut: A Scholastic Company.

Fahlbusch, Erwin...[et. Al.]
1999 Encyclopedia of Christianity. vol. 1. Grand Rapids, MI and Cambridge, UK: William B. Eerdmans Publishing Company.

2003 Encyclopedia of Christianity. vol. 3. Grand Rapids, MI and Cambridge, UK: William B. Eerdmans Publishing Company.

2005 Encyclopedia of Christianity. vol. 4. Grand Rapids, MI and Cambridge, UK: William B. Eerdmans Publishing Company.

Fox, Arturo A.
2003 Latinoamérica: Presente y Pasado. Upper Saddle River, NJ: Person Education.

Frank, Andre Gunder
1969 "Sociology of Development and Underdevelopment of Sociology" in Latin America: Underdevelopment or Revolution.

Galeano, Eduardo
1973 Open Veins of Latin America: Five Centuries of the Pillage of a Continent. N.Y. and London: Monthly Review Press.

Gilbert, Alan and Josef Gugler
1992 Cities, Poverty and Development: Urbanization in the Third World. New York: Oxford University Press.

González, Justo L.
1984 The Story of the Christianity: The Early Church to the Dawn of the Reformation. vol. 1. New York, NY: Harper Collins.

Green, Bill
2000 "Is there a Need for Reformed Fellowship?" Internet accessed on March 8, 2006. http://www.reformedmissions.org/fellowship.htm

Green, Joel B.
1994 "Good News to Whom? Jesus and the "poor" in the Gospel of Luke," in Jesus of Nazareth Lord and Christ. Joel B. Green and Max Turner eds. Grand Rapids, MI: William B. Eerdmans.

1995 New Testament Theology: The Theology of the Gospel of Luke. Cambridge: Cambridge University Press.

1997 The New International Commentary of the New Testament: The Gospel of Luke. Grand Rapids, MI: William B. Eerdmans Publishing Company.

Gutierrez, Gustavo
1986 A Theology of Liberation: History, Politics and Salvation. Trans. and ed. Sister Caridad Inda and John Eagleson. Maryknoll, N.Y.: Orbis.

Hoppe, Leslie J.
    2004   There Shall Be No Poor Among You: Poverty in The Bible. Nashville, TN: Abingdon Press.

Howell, Martha, and Walter Prevenir
    2001   From Reliable Sources: An Introduction to Historical Methods. Ithaca and London: Cornell University Press.

Infoplease
    2006   "History of Argentina." Internet accessed on March 15, 2006. http://www.infoplease.com/ce6/world/A0856692.html.

Jedin, Hubert
    1981   History of the Church: The Church in the Modern Age. vol. 10. New York: Crossroad.

John Paul II
    2006   *Ecclesia in America,* the Post-Synodal Apostolic Exhortation of the Holy Father John Paul II: *Encounter with the Living Jesus Christ: the Way to Conversion, Communion and Solidarity in America.* Internet accessed on May 29, 2006. http://www.ewtn.com/new_evangelization/america/synod/exhortation.htm

Johnson, Luke T.
    1981   Sharing Possessions: Mandate and Symbol of Faith. Philadelphia, PA: Fortress Press.

    1997   The Literary Function of Possessions in Luke-Acts. Missoula, MO: Scholars Press.

Klaiber, Jeffrey
    1998   The Church, Dictatorships, and Democracy in Latin America. Maryknoll, New York: Orbis Books.

Latourette, Kenneth Scott
    1943   A History of the Expansion of Christianity: The Great Century. vol. 5. New York and London: Harper & Brothers Publishers.

Lenski, G. E.
    1966   Power and Prestige: A Theory of Social Stratification. New York: McGraw-Hill.

Libânio, Joâo Batista
    1979   "A Community with a New Image." *International Review of Mission*, 68 (July):272:243-265.

Lynch, John
    1986   "The Catholic Church in Latin America, 1830-1930," in <u>The Cambridge History of Latin America</u>. Leslie Bethell, ed. vol. IV. New York: Cambridge University Press.

Mackay, John A.
    2001 [1933]   <u>The Other Spanish Christ: A Study in The Spiritual History of Spain and South America.</u> Eugene, Oregon: Wipf and Stock Publisher.

Magallanes, Hugo
    2005   <u>Introdución a la Vida y Teología de Juan Wesley.</u> Nashville, TN: Abingdon Press.

Marshall, I. Howard
    1970   <u>Luke: Historian and Theologian.</u> Grand Rapids, MI: Zondervan Publishing House.

    1983   "Luke and His 'Gospel'. In *Das Evangelium und die Evangelien: Vorträge vom Tübingen Symposium 1982,* edited by Peter Stuhlmacher, 298-308. WUNT 28. Tübingen: J. C. B. Mohr (Paul Siebeck).

McGee, Gary B.
    2006   "Tongues, the Bible Evidence: the Revival Legacy of Charles F. Parham," in *A Journal for Pentecostal Ministry: Enrichment Journal.* Assemblies of God. Internet accessed on August 29, 2006. http://www.ag.org/enrichmentjournal/199903/068_tongues.cfm

Micah Projects Inc.
    2006   "Breaking Social Isolation, Building Community," internet accessed on September 5, 2006. http://www.merivale.org.au/

Milgrom, Jacob
    1990   "Ethics and Rituals: The Foundations of the Biblical Dietary Laws," in <u>Religion and Laws: Biblical-Judaic and Islamic Perspective.</u> ed. By E. B. Firmage et. al. Winona Lake: Eisenbrauns.

Mitchell, Steven
    2006   "Glancing at the G12 Movement." Let us Reason. Internet Accessed on August 31, 2006. http://www.letusreason.org/Latrain24.htm

Newton, Rae R., and Kjell Erik Rudestam
   2001   Surviving Your Dissertation: A Comprehensive Guide to Content and Process. 2nd Edition. Thousand Oaks, London: Sage Publications.

Nuñez, C. Emilio A., and William D. Taylor
   1989   Crisis in Latin America: An Evangelical Perspective. Chicago, IL: Moody Press.

O'Toole S.J., Robert F.
   1983   "Luke's Position on Politics and Society in Luke-Acts," in Politics Issues in Luke Acts. eds. Richard J. Cassidy and Phillip J. Scharper. Maryknoll, NY: Orbis Books.

   1984   The Unity of Luke's Theology: An Analysis of Luke-Acts. Wilmington, DE: Michael Glazier.

Padilla, C. René. ed.
   1976   The New Face of Evangelicalism: An International Symposium on the Lausanne Covenant. Downers Grove: InterVarsity.

Padilla, C. Rene
   1985   Mission Between the Times: Essays on the Kingdom. Grand Rapids: Wm. B. Eerdmans Publishing Co.

   1996   "The Relevance of the Jubilee in Today's World (Leviticus 25)." *Mission Studies* 13 no. 1-2. World Wide Libraries: 131.

   2004   Transforming Church and Mission. Thailand: 2004 Forum for World Evangelization.

Palma, Marta
   2004   "A Pentecostal Church in the Ecumenical Movement." *Ecumenical Review* 37:85:223-229.

Palmer, D. James and Teresa
   1995   "Mexico City." Internet accesses on April 26, 2005. http://www.macalester.edu/courses/geog61/jpalmer/index.html

Pilgrim, Walter E.
   1981   Good News to the Poor: Wealth and Poverty in Luke-Acts. Minneapolis: Augsburg.

Pohl, Christine D.
   1999   Making Room: Recovering Hospitality as a Christian Tradition. Grand Rapids, MI and Cambridge, U.K.: William B. Eerdmans.

Political Constitution of Peru
    1993   "Article 50." Internet accessed on March 15, 2006. http://pdba.georgetown.edu/Constitutions/Peru/per93.html

Powell, Mark Allan
    1991   What Are They Saying About Acts. Mahwah, NJ: Paulist Press.

    1998   Fortress Introduction to The Gospels. Minneapolis, MN: Fortress Press.

Ringe, Sharon H.
    1985   Jesus, Liberation, and Biblical Jubilee: Images for Ethics and Christology. Philadelphia, PA: Fortress.

Romero, Catalina
    2001   "Globalization, Civil Society and Religion from a Latin America Standpoint," in *Sociology of Religion*. 62:4. Winter.

Rynkiewich, Michael
    2001   "Strangers in a Strange Land: Theologies of Land," in Land and Churches in Melanesia: Issues and Contexts. ed. Michael Rynkiewich. Papua New Guinea: The Melanesian Institute.

Sanders, J. A.
    1974   "The Ethics of Election in Luke's Great Banquet Parable," in Essays in Old Testament Ethics: J. Phillip Hyatt, In Memoriam. ed. J. L. Crenshaw and J. T. Willis. New York: Ktav.

Schmitt, Karl
    1971   The Roman Catholic Church in Modern Latin America. New York: Alfred A. Knopf.

Sendek, Elizabeth
    1993   "The Christ We Worship," (a Master of Arts Biblical Studies thesis, New College for Advance Christian Studies). Berkeley, CA.

Sklair, Leslie
    2002   Globalization: Capitalism and Its Alternatives. Oxford: University Press.

Sloan, Robert B.
    1992   "Jubilee," in Dictionary of Jesus and the Gospels. eds. Green, S. Mcknight, I. H. Marshall. Downers Grove: InterVarsity.

Snyder, Howard A.
 1995 Earth Currents: The Struggle for the World's Soul. Nashville, TN: Abington Press.

 2005 "Salvation Means Creation Healed: Creation, Cross, Kingdom, and Mission." Wilmore, KY: E. Stanley Jones School of World Mission and Evangelism, Asbury Theological Seminary.

Stambaugh, John E. and David L. Balch
 1986 The New Testament in Its Social Environment. Philadelphia, PA: Westminster.

Talbert, Charles H.
 1974 Literary Patterns, Theological Themes, and the Genre of Luke-Acts. Missoula, MT: Scholars Press.

Tannehill, Robert C.
 1990 The Narrative Unity of Luke-Acts. vol. 2. Philadelphia and Minneapolis: Fortress Press.

Tickner, Arlene
 1998 "Colombia: Chronicle of a Crisis Foretold." *Current History*, February.

The Columbia Electronic Encyclopedia
 2005 "Buenos Aires." 6th ed. Copyright ©, Columbia University Press. Internet accessed on March 9, 2006. http://education.yahoo.com/reference/encyclopedia/entry?id=7434

The World Bank
 2006 "Global Monitoring Report." Internet accessed on August 7, 2006. http://web.worldbank.org/WBSITE/EXTERNAL/EXTDEC/EXTGLOBALMONITOR/EXTGLOBALMONITOR2006/0,,menuPK:2186472~pagePK:64218926~piPK:64218953~theSitePK:2186432,00.html

 2008 "Poverty Data: A Supplement to World Development Indicators 2008." Internet accessed on February 16, 2010. http://web.worldbank.org/WBSITE/EXTERNAL/DATASTATISTICS/0,,menuPK:232599~pagePK:64133170~piPK:64133498~theSitePK:239419,00.html

United Nations
 2001 Cities in a Globalizing World: Global Report on Human Settlements. London and sterling, VA: Earthscan Publications Ltd.

2005 "Report On the World Social Situation 2005: The Inequality Predicament." Internet accessed on March 30, 2006. http://www.un.org/esa/socdev/rwss/media%2005/cd-docs/FINAL% 20LAC%20Press%20Release.pdf

2008 "World Urbanization Prospects: The 2007 Revision Population Database." Internet accessed on February 17, 2010. http://esa.un.org/unup/index.asp

Wallerstein, Immanuel
    1979   The Capitalist World-Economy. Cambridge: Cambridge University Press.

Wilson, Stephen G.
    1983   Luke and the Law. Cambridge: Cambridge University Press.

World Christian Database
    2006   "Christianity in Latin America." Center of Study of Global Christianity Gordon-Conwell Theological Seminary. Internet accessed on March 1, 2006. http://worldchristiandatabase.org/wcd/esweb.asp?WCI=Results&Query=426.

Person Index

Aguila, Armando Basurdo 137-143
Aragon, Pablo Ignacio 98-101
Arenas Bolivar, Oswaldo 114-119
Arlandson, James Malcolm 62-63
Arsaine, Jorge Eduardo 98-104, 182

Balch, David L. 69
Barajas C. Wilson 114-119
Barrett, David B. 33-43
Barrios, Wilson C. 93-97
Baspineiro, Arturo Humberto 125-131, 177, 185
Blumer, Herbert 22
Boff, Leonardo 7, 56, 78
Bonino, Jose Miguez 7, 17, 26-27

Chomsky, Noan 7, 19-20, 32
Collins, Michael 25, 106
Correa, Manuel 158-163
Costas, Orlando E. 7, 17
Creswell, John W. 9-10, 14
Crockett, Larimore C. 8, 68
Crow, John A. 16, 28-33, 35, 37, 38, 41
Cruz, Victor Pedroza 108-113, 182

Daza, Fredys Samanca 86-90
Daza, Juan Bautista Gonzalez 144-149
Diamond, Jared M. 16
Douglas, Mary 7, 57-58, 72
Dumont, Louis 7, 60
Dunn, J. D. G. 70

Eilberg-Schwartz, Howard 60
Ellis, Joseph A. 37
Ember, Melvin 28-29, 40

Fahlbusch, Erwin 28, 30, 31, 33-43
Ferrer, Manuel 80-84
Fiorella, Bertha xv
Fox, Arturo A. 39
Frank, Andre Gunder 19

Galeano, Eduardo 7, 16-19
Gali, Jorge 126-132
Garcia Pinilla, Cesar Arturo xv, 114-119
Garcia, Aristobulo 144-149
Gilbert, Alan 20
González, Justo L. 8, 24
Green, Bill 13
Green, Joel B. xiv, xv, 8, 11, 13, 47, 49, 50, 52, 57, 63-66, 68-69, 71-72, 95, 174, 181
Guarillo, Jorge xv, 108-111, 113
Gugler, Josef 20
Gutierrez, Gustavo 7, 25, 38, 78
Gutierrez, Juan Angel 125-131

Herrera, Benjamin 80, 83-84, 179
Hoppe, Leslie J. 8, 57, 66-68, 74
Howell, Martha 10-11

Jedin, Hubert 34
John Paul II 82, 97, 106
Johnson, Luke T. 8, 71, 74, 76
Johnson, Todd M. 33, 35, 36
Jorguera, Gilberto 158-159, 161, 163, 166
Juliecer, Fernando 102-107

Klaiber, Jeffrey 31
Kurian, George T. 33, 35, 36
Latourette, Kenneth Scott 33
Lenski, G. E. 7, 62
Libânio, Joao Batista 26
Liñan, Florencio Romero 151-153, 156, 157
Loli, Marco Antonio 94, 96
Lopez, José Luis xv, 122-124
Lynch, John 30, 38

Mackay, John A. 7, 17, 23-24, 39
Magallanes, Hugo xv, 7, 189
Marshall, I. Howard 8, 50-52
Martinez, Noe 138-143
Martinez, Sergio Oliba 80, 82, 84-85
McGee, Gary B. 45
Milgrom, Jacom 59
Mitchell, Steven 165

Person Index   229

Miuler, Klaus 120-124
Moreno, Luis Alfredo 144-150

Newton, Rae R. 9
Nuñez, C. Emilio A. 7, 15, 23, 31

Obispo, Cutberto Ramirez 138-140
Ortiz Uribe, Daisy 1-2
O'Toole S.J., Robert F. 50

Pabón, Nelson Javier 86, 88, 90, 92, 93
Padilla, C. René xv, 5, 7, 18, 55, 76, 125
Palma, Marta 7, 15, 23
Palmer, D. James and Teresa 7, 29
Peña, Benjamin 137-140, 142, 143
Perez, Eli Gamas 107-109, 111-113
Perez, Luis Maria Carreño 86, 88-92
Pilgrim, Walter E. 73
Pohl, Christine D. 72
Powell, Mark Allen 50-52, 71, 74-75
Prada, José Manuel 120-124
Prevenir, Walter 10-11
Price, Matthew A. 25, 106
Prieto, Roberto 158-162, 183, 187
Puell, Roque Felix 120-123

Ramirez, Jose Antonio 80-85
Ramirez, Luis Alfonso 114-115, 117, 119
Ringe, Sharon H. 68
Robles, Mercelo 126, 128-133
Romero, Catalina 7, 21-23
Romero, Oscar 7, 25, 82, 106
Rudestam, Kjell Erik 9
Ruiz, Rony Sintia 150-156
Rynkiewich, Michael xv, 7, 59, 67

Sanders, J. A. 61, 65
Schmitt, Karl 25
Sendek, Elizabeth 13
Silva Becerro, Wilson 3
Sklair, Leslie 55
Sloan, Robert B. 66
Snyder, Howard A. xv, 7, 21, 67
Stambaugh, John E. 69

Talbert, Charles 50
Tannehill, Robert C. 52
Taylor, William D. 7, 15, 23, 31
Thorndike, Ricardo Wiesse 93-97, 105
Tickner, Arlene 7, 32, 46
Toxtle, Samuel Fernandez 108, 110-112

Ugarte, Oscar 151-154, 156, 157

Vargas, Jose Alberto Games 144-149
Velizaroff, Pedro Jorge 151-152, 154-157, 173
Vera Gomez, Luis Alberto xv, 1-4
Verdegal, Pablo 98-103, 182
Villavona, Herbert Monsalve 86-93
Vivian, Pablo 158, 161-162

Wallerstein, Immanuel 56
Wilson, Stephen G. 50

Scripture Index

OLD TESTAMENT

Genesis
1:9 59
1:5-10 58
8:14, 24 59
13:6 59
24:7 59
31:3 59
34:1, 21 59
45:18 59

Exodus
1:7 59
2:22 59
3:17 59
13:5 59
14:3 59
14:21 59
18:3 59
21:2-6 68
23: 10-11 68
23:9 59
33:3 59

Leviticus
11:1-8 58
11:9-12 58
11:13-23 58
11:46-47 58
12:1-8 61

13 61
13:1-43 61
13:45-46 61
14 61, 69
14:1-32 61
15 61
15:1-15 61
15:16-18 61
15:25-30 61
16 58
16:16 59
17 62
18:25 59
19:9-10 , 33-34 62
19:29 59
20 62
20:22-26 59
20:24 59
20:24b-25 59
21:16-24 61
21:18 72
23:22 62
25 178
25:2 59
25:2, 19 59
25: 19 59
25: 23 59, 67
25:42-55 67
26:4 59

35:33-34 59

Numbers
14:8 59
16:14 59

Deuteronomy
5:15 67
6 59
6:3 59
7:1-5 59
7:12-15 59
8:11a 129
10:18-19 62
11:9,17 59
14:21 59, 62
14:22-29 62
15 66, 178
15:1-18 68
15:15 67
21:23 59
22:5 140, 198
24:4 59
24:14-15 62
24:22 62
26:12-15 62
26:15 59
27:3 59
32:43 59

231

33:28 59

Joshua
4:18,22 59
5:6 59

Judges
3:11 59

Ruth
102, 210

1 Kings
17:8-27 68

2 Kings
5:1-19 68
18:32 59

2 Chronicles
7:14 59
36:21 59

Nehemiah
102, 210
9:11 59

Job
31:38 59

Psalms
137:4 59

Ecclesiastes
5:1-5 140

Isaiah
24:11 59
36:17 59
43:2 59
54 153, 207
56 62
58:6 66
58:9 65, 172
61:1-2 65, 66, 172

Jeremiah
3:1, 2, 9 59
4:20 59
11:5 59
12:4 59
32:22 59

Ezekiel
1:10 159-160, 211
14:13 59
39:1 59

Hosea
1:2 59
4:3 59

Joel
1:10 59
2:23, 28, 29 46

Jonah
1:13 59
2:10 59

Habakkuk
3:2 129, 211

Zechariah
12:12 59

NEW TESTAMENT

Matthew
5-7 110, 122, 198, 207
9:10,11 60
11:19 60
11:28 122, 207
25:36 101
28:19 122, 147, 203, 207

Mark
2:15, 16 60
12:30-31 129, 211

Luke
1:1-4 51
2:11 74
2:11,26 52
2: 14 75
3:12-13 69
3:10-14 71
3:15 52
3:21-22 51
4 84, 91, 96
4: 14-15 65
4:16-20 68

4:16-30 5, 6, 13, 45, 48, 51, 65, 68, 69, 71, 167, 168, 172, 184
4:16-36 64
4:18 64, 68, 176
4:18-19 4, 65, 74, 83, 91, 96, 101, 111, 117, 123, 129, 140, 147, 153, 154, 160, 172, 181, 187, 189, 196, 211
4:21-30 68-69
4:25-27 68, 69
4:41 52
5:17-26 51
5:27-32 5, 6, 13, 45, 48, 65, 69, 70, 71, 167, 168, 172
5:28 70
5:29 69
5:29-6:11 51
5:30 72, 60, 69
5:31-32 66
5:32 70
6:10 75
6:20 53, 64, 68
6:20-26 64
6:24-36 53
6:33 67
7:1-10 51
7:11-17 51
7:18-23 64
7:22 53, 64, 68
7:34 69
7:36 69
7:36-50 52, 66
7:48 75
8:40-47 53
8:48 75
9:51-19:28 51
9:20 52
10:1-12 51
10:29-37 53
11-15 72
11:37-42 72
11:40-41 73
11:41 72
11:42 67, 72
12:13-34 73
12:15 73
12:16-21 53

12:29-31 67
12:30-33 67
12:32-33 71
12:33 73
13:10-13 53
13:10-17 53
14:1 69
14:1-6 53
14:12-14, 15-24 64
14:13 54, 64
14:13, 21 68, 72
14:21 54, 64
15:1 60, 69
15:3-31 66
15:8-32 53
16:1-15 67
16:13 71
16:20, 21 64
16:20, 22 68
16:19-31 64
17:1-19 53
17:19 75
18:9-14 53
18:11 69
18:13 60
18:18-29 70, 172
18:18-30 73
18:22 71, 73
18:26 70
18:30 74
18:42 75
19:1-10 5, 6, 13, 49,
   51, 53, 63, 66, 65,
   69, 70, 71, 73, 167,
   168, 172
19:5 69, 75
19:7 69, 70
19:8 73
19:9 70, 71, 75
19:10 70
19:37 51
19:45-48 51
20:27-29
20:41 52
21:2 57
22:19 51
22:54 51
22:63-64 51
22:66-23:13 51
22:67 52

23:2,35,39 52
23:18 51
23:47 51
24:26,46 52
24:45-47 51

John
13 101, 211
17 161
17:21   96, 117, 181,
   203, 207

Acts
1 196
1:1-5 51
1:8 52, 110, 140, 148,
   198, 203
2 84, 111, 139, 140,
   182,198
2-15 52
2:1-13 51
2:14-40 51
2:31, 36, 38 52
2:42 74
2:42-44 101, 211
2:42-47 5, 6, 13, 45,
   49, 65, 73, 74, 75,
   84, 91, 96, 167, 168,
   180, 189
2:43-45 73, 74
2:44-45 67
2:46 73
3:1-10 51, 53
3:6, 18, 20 52
4 84, 111, 182
4:1-8:3 51
4:10 52
4:32 130
4:32-37 5, 6, 13, 45,
   49, 73, 74, 75, 67,
   167, 168, 180, 189
4:32, 34-35 73, 74
4:32-5:11 65, 73, 84,
   91
4:34 57, 74
5:12-16 53
5:42 52, 129, 211
6 179
8:5, 12 52
8:20 173

9:1-19 53
9:36-43 51
9:22, 34 52
10 53, 69
10:1-23 51
10:36,48 52 11:17 52
11 69
13:1-19:20 51
15:8-9 66
15:26 52
16:18 52
16:31 181, 207
17:3 52
18:5, 28 52
19:21-21:17 51
21:17-20 51
21:26 51
21:36 51
23:1-26:32 51
23:2 51
24:24 52
26:20 52
26:23 52
27:43 51
28:23-28 51
28:31 52

Romans
12:1-2 5

I Corinthians
1:10 140, 198
12 101, 211
12:28 165

Galatians
2:20 139

Ephesians
5:25-27 139

Philippians
2:1-11 101, 203, 211

Hebrews
13:8 147, 159, 203

Revelation
21:5-6 139

Subject Index

Argentina xii, xiii, 8-9, 15, 18, 22, 24, 28, 40-45, 79, 98-107, 125-134, 137, 147, 157-159, 161-164, 169-171, 173, 176-177, 180-181, 183, 185-187, 189, 190, 209, 211-212
Assemblies of God 39, 43, 144, 151-152

Baptist/*Iglesia Buatista* 9, 31, 35, 43, 114, 125-132, 177, 183, 185, 190
Bellavista Prison 2-4
Biblical Basis for their work 79, 83, 90, 96, 100, 110, 116, 122, 129, 139, 146-147, 153, 159, 179, 187, 192, 198, 203, 207, 211

Catholic, Roman 4-7, 9, 15-17, 23-28, 30-35, 37-40, 42, 44-45, 47, 56, 79-81, 83, 85-91, 93-95, 97-106, 113, 116, 123, 132, 134, 142, 148-149, 162-163, 165, 167-187, 190-191, 203, 212
Christian Missionary Alliance/*Alianza Cristiana y Misionera* 35, 39, 158-159, 161, 163, 166
Christology 17, 24, 45, 47, 78, 174
Church of the Nazarene/*Iglesia Nazarena* 107-109, 111-112
Colombia xii, xiii, 1-3, 8-9, 13, 15, 18-19, 22, 26, 28, 32-37, 43-45, 79, 86- 93, 97, 99, 104-105, 107, 114-122, 125, 128, 133-135, 137, 144-150, 153, 156-157, 159, 163, 165, 169-173, 176, 178-184, 189, 201, 203
Colonization 15-17, 19-21, 23, 28, 33, 37, 40, 44, 56, 142, 169-170, 174
Contextualization 26, 44, 119, 169, 174, 176-178
Creation care 168-169, 177-178, 191

Ecclesiology 4, 7, 47, 51, 53, 57, 69, 102, 124, 154, 157, 165, 168, 177, 184, 187, 212
Ecumenical 43, 86, 126, 128, 132-133, 162, 181, 183, 190, 212
Ecumenism 97, 103, 132, 134, 182-190, 218
Environment 43, 47, 57, 85, 128, 183-184, 212
Environmental (issues/plan/situation/realities) 5-6, 10, 13, 20, 28, 29-31, 36-38, 40, 43-45, 47, 68, 77, 83, 85, 90, 93, 97, 100, 104-105, 110, 116, 120, 122, 125, 128, 133-

134, 139, 141, 142, 146, 150, 153, 157, 159, 163-164, 167, 169-171, 177-178, 188, 191-192, 196
Environmental Involvement 3, 9-10, 79, 83, 90, 95, 100, 110, 116, 122, 128, 139, 146, 153, 159, 178, 198, 201, 206, 209
Episcopal 31
Evangelical 4, 13, 35, 39, 42-43, 56, 113, 124, 183, 199. *See also* Protestant.

Foursquare/*Cuadrangular* 1-3, 35, 144-149, 158-161, 165, 183, 187

Globalization 6, 13, 16, 20-21, 23, 44-45, 55, 169, 176, 191
Globalized 23, 112, 182

Holistic xi, 14, 66, 133

Incarnation/Incarnational 4, 6, 102, 125, 127, 130, 177
Independent Christian 35, 43, 108, 114, 120, 138, 140, 144, 151, 158, 183
Integral Mission xiv, 7, 12, 13, 28, 30, 131, 134, 154, 157, 165, 167-169, 177, 180, 184-187, 189, 191
Integral/Integrally/Integral ministry xii, 4-7, 12-13, 23, 25, 28, 47, 53, 83, 91-92, 96, 105-106, 111, 117-120, 124-125, 130, 132, 146, 148-149, 163-164, 169, 173, 174, 180, 186-188, 192, 198, 202-203, 205, 209, 210

Kingdom of God 43, 72, 75-76, 91-92, 104, 111-112, 117, 126, 128-132, 147, 152-153, 161, 163, 173, 184-186, 188, 190, 198, 203

Lukan/Luke-Acts xi, xii, 4-6, 8, 10-13, 45, 47-55, 57-59, 61, 63-78, 83- 84, 91, 96, 101, 111, 117, 123, 129, 140, 147, 153-154, 160, 167-169, 171-174, 176-178, 180, 184, 187-189, 191, 196, 198, 203, 207, 211
Lutheran 35, 43, 132
Lutheran, Free/*Libre Luterana* 121-124, 173, 176, 189

Mennonite 9, 176, 181-183
Mennonite Brother/*Hermanos Menonita* 121-125
Mennonite, Anabaptist Brother/*Anabautista Menonita* 108-109, 114
Mennonite, Alliance/*Alianza Menonita* 126
Methodist 9, 31, 39
Methodist Wesleyan 35
Methodist, Evangelical 43
Methodist, Free/*Metodista Libre* 108, 121, 189
Mexico xii, 8-9, 13, 15, 19, 22, 24, 28-32, 36, 40, 42-45, 55, 79-80, 82, 85-88, 93, 97, 99, 104-105, 107- 116, 120, 122, 125, 128, 133-134, 137-139, 141-144, 146, 148, 150, 152-153, 156-157, 159, 163, 166, 169-171, 178-179, 182-183, 185-186, 189, 197, 199
Micah Projects Inc. 152, 156, 166, 206
Missiology 4, 45, 51, 53, 57, 69, 102, 184, 187, 212

Peru xii, xiii, 8-9, 13, 15, 22, 24-25, 28, 37-40, 42-45, 55, 79, 93-94, 97-98, 100, 104-105, 107, 115, 120-125, 128, 130, 133-135, 137, 150-157, 159, 163, 169-173, 176-177, 179-183, 186, 189, 205, 207-208
Popular religiosity/religion 4, 17, 24, 105, 170, 186
Poverty 18, 21-22, 24, 26, 32, 36-38, 44-45, 54-55, 57, 67, 69, 75, 97, 109, 141-142, 163, 169, 171-176, 180

Subject Index   237

Poverty, Culture of 44, 171, 173
Presbyterian/*Presbiteriana* 9, 31, 35, 39, 42, 114, 117, 126, 132, 181, 183, 190
Protestant 4-7, 9, 13, 15, 23, 26-28, 31-32, 34-36, 39, 43, 45, 47, 53, 56, 103, 105, 107-117, 119-128, 131-135, 137-139, 141-147, 149-159, 161-165, 167-170, 172-177, 180-183, 185-187, 190, 192, 197-199, 201-205, 206-207. *See also* Evangelical.
Protestant, Mainline 9, 13, 36, 103, 105, 107-116, 118-123, 125-128, 131-134, 142, 159, 169, 172, 175, 177, 181-183, 185-187, 190, 197-199, 201-203, 205-212
Protestant, Pentecostal 9, 14, 31, 35-36, 39, 43, 45, 103, 113-115, 119-120, 125, 127, 134, 137-139, 140-145, 146-154, 156-166, 169-170, 172-173, 177-178, 181-183, 185-188, 190, 192, 197-199, 201-203, 205-212

Salvation 4, 13, 23, 26, 35-36, 47-50, 52-53, 64, 66, 68-72, 74-76, 78, 83, 96, 102, 112, 132, 141, 148, 153, 157, 160, 168- 169, 172-174, 181, 184-185, 187, 207, 211-212
Salvation Army 35
Social Involvement 82, 88, 90, 94, 99, 108, 111, 115, 118, 120, 122-123, 127, 131, 139, 146, 152, 157, 159, 164, 173, 177, 182, 185-186, 202, 207, 212
Syncretism/syncretistic religion 44, 174, 190

Theological Issues 5-10, 36, 67, 82-84, 86, 91, 96, 102, 112, 116, 118, 123, 130, 141, 148, 155, 161, 198, 202, 207, 210
Theology xi, xii, 4-7, 9-10, 12, 25, 30, 34, 45, 47, 49, 50-51, 53, 55, 57, 59, 61, 63, 65, 67, 69, 71, 73, 75, 77, 78-79, 81-85, 87, 89, 91-95, 97-99, 101, 103, 105, 107, 112, 114, 119, 121, 123-124, 131-135, 137, 139, 142, 151, 161-166, 167-169, 174-177, 180-181, 183-185, 187, 189, 197, 199, 201-203, 205, 207, 208-209, 211-212
Theology of prosperity 43, 112, 132, 155, 156, 162-165, 172-173, 175, 199, 212
Theology, Liberation 4, 13, 25, 30, 34, 78, 82, 92-93, 97-98, 119, 123, 133, 184, 203, 208, 212

Urban migration 32, 170
Urbanization 6, 13, 16, 20-21, 23, 28, 44, 169-170, 181, 191
Urbanized 20, 54

www.ingramcontent.com/pod-product-compliance
Lightning Source LLC
Chambersburg PA
CBHW020646300426
44112CB00007B/262